Empirical Ethics
in Psychiatry

International Perspectives in Philosophy and Psychiatry

Series editors: Bill (K.W.M.) Fulford, Katherine Morris, John Z Sadler and Giovanni Stanghellini

Forthcoming volumes in the series:

Empirical Ethics in Psychiatry

Edited by

Guy Widdershoven, John McMillan,
Tony Hope, & Lieke van der Scheer

OXFORD
UNIVERSITY PRESS

OXFORD
UNIVERSITY PRESS

Great Clarendon Street, Oxford OX2 6DP

Oxford University Press is a department of the University of Oxford.
It furthers the University's objective of excellence in research, scholarship,
and education by publishing worldwide in

Oxford New York

Auckland Cape Town Dar es Salaam Hong Kong Karachi
Kuala Lumpur Madrid Melbourne Mexico City Nairobi
New Delhi Shanghai Taipei Toronto

With offices in

Argentina Austria Brazil Chile Czech Republic France Greece
Guatemala Hungary Italy Japan Poland Portugal Singapore
South Korea Switzerland Thailand Turkey Ukraine Vietnam

Oxford is a registered trade mark of Oxford University Press
in the UK and in certain other countries

Published in the United States
by Oxford University Press Inc., New York

© Oxford University Press, 2008

The moral rights of the authors have been asserted

Database right Oxford University Press (maker)

First published 2008

British Library Cataloguing in Publication Data
Data available

Library of Congress Cataloging-in-Publication Data
Empirical ethics in psychiatry / edited by Guy Widdershoven . . . [et al.].
   p. ; cm.
   Includes bibliographical references.
   ISBN 978-0-19-929736-8 (alk. paper)
1. Psychiatric ethics. 2. Medicine, Empirical. I. Widdershoven, Guy, 1954-
   [DNLM: 1. Psychiatry—ethics. 2. Bioethical Issues. 3. Empirical Research. 4. Ethics,
Research. 5. Patient Rights—ethics. WM 62 E55 2008]
   RC455.2.E8E47 2008
   174.2'9689—dc22
                                                                    2007041185

Typeset by Cepha Imaging Private Ltd., Bangalore, India
Printed in Great Britain
on acid-free paper by
Ashford Colour Press Ltd, Gosport

ISBN 978-0-19-929736-8

10 9 8 7 6 5 4 3 2 1

Contents

Contributors

Gwen Adshead
Department of Forensic
Psychotherapy
Richard Dadd Centre
Broadmoor Hospital
Crowthorne, UK

Clive Baldwin
Bradford Dementia Group
School of Health Studies
Unity Building, UK

Bart van de Borne
Department of Health,
Ethics and Society, School for Public
Health and Primary Care (CAPHRI),
Faculty of Health, Medicine and Life
Sciences, Maastricht University,
The Netherlands

Pascal Borry
Centre for Biomedical Ethics
and Law,
Catholic University of Leuven,
Belgium

Christine Brown
Robert Baxter Research Fellow,
Department of Mental Health,
Exeter University, UK

Anthony Colombo
Postgraduate Course
Tutor in Criminology
Faculty of Health and Life
Sciences
University of Coventry, UK

Paul Curfs
Gouverneur Kremers Centre,
School for Public Health and
Primary Care (CAPHRI),
Faculty of Health,
Medicine and Life Sciences,
Maastricht University,
The Netherlands'

Kris Dierickx
Centre for Biomedical Ethics and
Law,
Catholic University of Leuven,
Belgium

Jonathon Glover
Centre of Medical Law and Ethics,
Kings College London, UK

Minke Goldsteen
Department of Health,
Ethics and Society, School for Public
Health and Primary Care (CAPHRI),
Faculty of Health,
Medicine and Life Sciences,
Maastricht University,
The Netherlands

Ine Gremmen
Nijmegen School of Management,
Radboud University Nijmegen,
The Netherlands

Tony Hope
The ETHOX Centre,
Department of Health and Primary
Care, University of Oxford, UK

Rob van Hooren
Department of Health,
Ethics and Society, School for Public
Health and Primary Care (CAPHRI),
Faculty of Health,
Medicine and Life Sciences,
Maastricht University,
The Netherlands

Julian C Hughes
Ash Court
POAS
North Tyneside General Hospital
Rake Lane
North Shields, UK

Marlieke De Jonge
University Medical Centre,
Groningen Health Sciences/Medical
Ethics, The Netherlands

John McMillan
Hull York Medical School, and
Philosophy Department,
University of Hull, UK

Jeannette Pols
Department of General Practice
Clinical Methods and Public Health
Amsterdam Medical
Centre/University of Amsterdam
The Netherlands

Louis Polstra
University Medical Centre,
Groningen Health Sciences/Medical
Ethics, The Netherlands

Lieke van der Scheer
Department of Health,
Ethics and Society, School for Public
Health and Primary Care (CAPHRI),
Faculty of Health,
Medicine and Life Sciences,
Maastricht University,
The Netherlands

Paul Schotsmans
Centre for Biomedical Ethics and
Law,
Catholic University of Leuven,
Belgium

Eva Skoe
Professor of Developmental
Psychology,
Centre for Research in Clinical
Psychology,
University of Oslo,
Norway

Jacinta Tan
The ETHOX Centre,
Department of Health and Primary
Care, University of Oxford, UK

Marian Verkerk
University Medical Centre
Groningen
Health Sciences/Medical Ethics
The Netherlands

Sander Welie
Department of Health,
Ethics and Society, School for Public
Health and Primary Care (CAPHRI),
Faculty of Health,
Medicine and Life Sciences,
Maastricht University,
The Netherlands

Guy Widdershoven
Department of Health,
Ethics and Society, School for Public
Health and Primary Care (CAPHRI),
Faculty of Health,
Medicine and Life Sciences,
Maastricht University,
The Netherlands

Chapter 1

Introduction

Guy Widdershoven, John McMillan,
Tony Hope, and Lieke van der Scheer

'[W]hen a man is faced with alternatives he chooses one at the expense of the others'. This sentence is spoken by Stephen Albert, shortly before he is murdered, in Borges' short story *The Garden of Forking Paths*. At many points in our lives we are faced with choices, and the choices we make take us down different paths, to further choices. From one starting point we could end up at very different places, depending on the series of choices that we make. This is the metaphor of the garden of forking paths. But the metaphor carries a further implication: that people, starting from different places, may come to share the same path, at least for a time.

In their seminal book *The Principles of Biomedical Ethics* Beauchamp and Childress propose a structure for the analysis of issues in medical ethics based on four principles. Each of the two authors has a fundamentally different view about the correct underlying ethical theory. One holds, primarily, a consequentialist view whilst the other is committed to a duty-based approach. And yet despite their different starting points they agree on the same four guiding principles in the analysis of practical dilemmas in medical ethics.

The four of us have for many years been working in the field of medical ethics. Our backgrounds and our philosophical commitments are different. But we found ourselves travelling companions along the same path: finding value in research in psychiatric ethics in which there is a significant empirical component. In both the Netherlands and the UK a number of researchers have been combining social science research with ethical analysis in examining ethical issues that arise in mental health practice. In recent years there has been a growing body of research in empirical medical ethics generally, and empirical psychiatric ethics specifically, and a growing interest in how empirical and philosophical methods can be combined. There are however few sources for examples of empirical psychiatric ethics gathered in one place. The purpose of this book is to be such a source and to demonstrate empirical psychiatric ethics through showcasing a number of specific examples.

The book is divided into two parts. In the first part there are discussions of the possibility of empirical ethics from a theoretical standpoint and an overview of the history of empirical medical ethics in general. The second, larger, part is made up of chapters, each of which discusses a specific research project in empirical psychiatric ethics. The chapter authors have been asked to reflect on their choice of methods: how and why they combine empirical and philosophical work, and how the two approaches relate to each other. The chapters in the second part thus have two purposes. The first is to present examples of empirical ethics in psychiatry; the second is to reflect on the way in which empirical research may support ethical analysis. The second goal relates back to the theoretical chapters in the first part of the book.

Although the field of empirical psychiatric ethics is growing it remains tentative and uncertain. Researchers are still discipline bound: philosophers find empirical research problematic, and social scientists find philosophical analysis daunting. Some theoreticians are sceptical that two such different methodologies can be effectively combined within a single research project. Funding organizations struggle with assessing applications. This book is not an attempt to review the field of empirical psychiatric ethics. It is an attempt to demonstrate sufficient examples in order to give confidence to those who are trying to work across the disciplines, and to give inspiration to others to do so.

*

The first part of this book introduces the topic of empirical ethics in psychiatry from a theoretical point of view. Chapters 2 and 3 defend the possibility of empirical ethics. The two chapters, however, are written from different theoretical standpoints. In the chapter by McMillan and Hope the principal philosophical stance is that of Anglo-American analytic philosophy. McMillan is a philosopher whose interest in the philosophy of mind and in ethics has led to an engagement with psychiatric practice. Hope is a psychiatrist by background who has had a major interest in medical ethics deriving principally from the medical perspective: that a component of medical decision-making involves ethical values and that it is important for health professionals to be trained in, and sensitive to, the ethical issues that arise from practice. The authors argue that even from the perspective of analytic philosophy, a perspective that emphasizes the differences between facts and values, there can be a coherent field of empirical ethics. They distinguish various ways in which empirical research and ethical analysis can inform one another. Their proposal is to restrict the term empirical ethics to research projects in which the gathering of empirical data and ethical analysis inform and influence each other in a cyclical way.

Widdershoven and Van der Scheer argue for empirical ethics from a different philosophical point of view. Widdershoven is a philosopher interested in continental philosophy, especially hermeneutics. Van der Scheer is a philosopher with a background in American pragmatism. Both hermeneutics and pragmatism focus on practical experience. People in practice have learned solutions through dealing with concrete problems in specific situations. They have practical knowledge and insight. This knowledge is valuable, but also bound to their perspective on the situation. The task of philosophy is to make explicit practical knowledge and help to develop it further by stimulating reflection on and exchange between various perspectives. In doing so, the philosopher not only registers what practitioners say, but investigates the validity of their views by raising questions, proposing interpretations, and suggesting possible changes of perspectives. In line with McMillan and Hope, this implies a cyclical process involving the gathering of empirical data on both practitioners' experiences and normative considerations on the one hand, and ethical analysis and deriving normative conclusions on the other hand. From a pragmatic hermeneutic point of view, this process implies a dialogue between practice and theory, in which practitioners and philosophers learn from each other, and jointly develop new ethical concepts and normative positions. Some theoretical and methodological consequences of this view are demonstrated with the help of a case example.

In Chapter 4, the final chapter of part I, Borry and colleagues describe the 'birth' of the empirical turn in bioethics. Given the interdisciplinary nature of bioethics, it is surprising that the integration of empirical methods has taken so long. The authors explain why bioethics has turned to empirical methods and why it has taken some time for this to occur. They show how empirical methods made it possible for bioethics to become more 'context sensitive', meaning that bioethics is less theory driven and more firmly grounded in practical issues. This, together with the influence of clinical ethics and evidence-based medicine, has helped to drive the development of empirical ethics. They offer three explanations for why it has taken so long for this to happen: the fact that social scientists often pose different research questions from philosophers; the priority that philosophy has had within bioethics; and meta-ethical worries about how empirical work can contribute to normative bioethics.

*

Each chapter in part II gives an example of research in empirical psychiatric ethics, and reflects upon the way in which empirical research and ethical analysis were combined in the project under consideration. The projects are based upon different empirical methodologies and exemplify diverse ways of performing normative analysis. They deal with various normative issues in several domains of psychiatry.

In Chapter 5, Pols presents an ethnography of 'good care', conducted in residential homes and long stay psychiatric wards. This research used participant observation techniques: she followed nurses and care assistants, observed their interactions with patients, and discussed these in interviews. Ideals of 'good care' were manifested in the everyday life of these institutions and the research process articulated them so that they became potential objects for reflection for all involved in the research process. 'Individualized care' is an ideal that emphasizes the importance of care and institutions being arranged so as to facilitate the independence of patients. 'Patient sociability' is an ideal focusing on interdependence and social relationships. This research conveys the creativity and imagination of those who successfully enact these ideals. It also shows how care ideals such as 'individualized care' and 'patient sociability' can conflict. This too enables us to critically reflect upon the reality of care ideals.

In Chapter 6, Colombo describes different models of mental disorder used by various participants in community-based multi-disciplinary teams. On the basis of a literature review, a case vignette was constructed with 12 questions, related to 12 dimensions, which could be used to distinguish six models of mental disorder. Compared with the method used by Pols, the method of Colombo is less open, and more theoretically structured. He found that psychiatrists, social workers, and patients use different models, leading to poor communication. Given that psychiatrists have more power, their model tends to become dominant. Discussions about treatment, for example, focus not on choices between medical and non-medical treatment, but on the required doses of medication. This shows that 'shared decision-making' is not as ideal as it seems, and can be criticized for being unethical. Colombo's chapter is an example of empirical research into models of mental disorders leading to, and supporting, an ethical evaluation of psychiatric practice.

Three chapters examine ethical issues that arise in the care of people with dementia. It is interesting to compare their methodologies. Goldsteen's research, presented in Chapter 7, starts with a specific theoretical framework – that of the philosopher Margaret Walker. According to this framework morality is situated in social practices and, in particular, around the question of who is responsible for what. The interviews (which were carried out with both family and professional carers) and the analyses were informed by this theoretical framework. Participants were asked specifically about their views on responsibility and the different roles that they thought family and professional carers should play. The analyses show that how carers define both themselves and each other affects their view of roles and responsibilities.

Baldwin, whose project is presented in Chapter 8, is also interested in exploring the 'moral world' of family carers of people with dementia. He adopted a modified grounded theory approach – starting, in other words, with a social science methodology rather than with a philosophical approach to morality. In order, however, to provide a focus on ethical issues the method was modified through using two interviews for each participant. The first interview involved asking in an open-ended way about the experience of caring for the family member with dementia. The second interview focused on what the research team identified from the first interview as ethical issues, and involved more questioning from the interviewer than the first interview. The identification of ethical issues involved both examining the transcripts of the interviews for content and picking out all uses of words that indicate ethical reasoning, such as ought and duty.

Hughes and Sabat's research, which is discussed in Chapter 9, also starts from social science methodology. Their material is a series of interviews with dementia patients. Each patient was interviewed weekly over a period of 4 months to 2 years. Three cases were analysed in order to shed light on philosophical problems concerning the relevance of advance directives in dementia. One such problem regards the question whether the person with dementia is the same person as the one who made the advance directives. Does she still hold the critical interests which were expressed in the advance directive? Is her now-self the same as her then-self? The authors show that conversations with persons with moderate to severe dementia indicate that they still value their former abilities and connect to them in their stories. Hughes and Sabat conclude that certain philosophical concepts (such as now-self and then-self) are abstract and create ethical problems. These problems can be solved by turning to practice. In practice, people do not distinguish between now-self and then-self; they consider themselves as the same person, although they also realize they are in some sense different. Being the same person is not dependant upon psychological recollections, but upon being able to perform meaningful actions in a social network. In a supportive environment, this ability tends to persist until very late stages of dementia.

Two studies examine the use of coercion and pressure in health care. In Chapter 10, Verkerk and colleagues present research on pressure in the care for chronic psychiatric patients. Utilizing Giddens' structuring theory as the theoretical model, they carried out a case history analysis which shows how the psychiatric health care system is structured by characteristics such as signification, standards, and power relations. They distinguish between two normative perspectives, that of treatment and that of counselling. The perspective of treatment is dominant, leading to a one-sided practice of coercion. On the basis of this sociological analysis, the authors argue, like Colombo in Chapter 6, that current psychiatric practice is one-sided. They argue for the need for improvement of the power balance between the perspective of treatment and that of counselling. On a theoretical level, they underline the relevance of ethics of care for analysing and justifying the use of pressure.

The research of Van Hooren and colleagues, discussed in Chapter 11, also focuses on coercion, especially in the care of people with a mental disability. They examined the conflict between, on the one hand, providing good care for people with Prader–Willi syndrome, and on the other hand, respecting their autonomy. Prader–Willi syndrome is a condition that can lead to problematic obesity. Good care might involve restricting food intake which requires a certain amount of coercion. The starting point for this research was the examination of care practices through qualitative interviews with carers. The results led the researchers to see similarities between how carers talked about the dilemmas they faced and the four models of the patient–physician relationship proposed by Emanuel and Emanuel. This motivated the researchers to design a quantitative study based on these four models which complemented the qualitative study. One result from these studies was that although carers sought ways to create the context for fostering autonomy nevertheless both professional and family carers' 'bottom line' was to choose to intervene to protect health. The authors also discuss the relationships between the qualitative and the quantitative studies.

A final range of studies touch upon issues related to the law. In Chapter 12, Gremmen examines 'Ulysses arrangements' in the care of people with relapsing psychosis. Such people will often resist treatment when in relapse: just when treatment is most needed. The traditional legal approach to this problem is to allow enforced treatment at a point when the person is severely ill and has become a danger to himself/herself or his/her environment. As long as danger is not imminent, it is not permitted to overrule the person's refusal of treatment. The legal system in the Netherlands is developing to enhance respect for the autonomy of patients who lack capacity. Ulysses arrangements have been proposed, as part of this development. They are a type of advance decision-making. Under an Ulysses arrangement a patient, when in remission and with capacity, agrees voluntarily to have his refusal of treatment, when in relapse, overridden. The Ulysses arrangement provides reasons for overriding treatment refusal on the grounds of respecting the patient's autonomy, rather than relying on a principle of beneficence. Such arrangements are designed to be used at a point relatively early in relapse – at a time when carers would be reluctant to override refusal of treatment had they not had the prior agreement of the patient to do so. Ulysses arrangements are a proposed solution to a practical problem based on ethical analysis. The aim of Gremmen's research was to examine the likely consequences of adopting Ulysses arrangements as a legally valid approach. One finding was that planning for enforced treatment through setting up a Ulysses arrangement would probably reduce the need for coercion. This is because it would lead to an altered relationship between patient and carers that would stimulate carers to negotiate with the patient and lead the patient to accept treatment at an earlier stage in relapse. Thus, the legal possibility to enforce treatment earlier would not necessarily lead to more coercion. The research also showed that the Ulysses arrangements would not solve the ethical dilemmas for carers. It would shift the focus away from a clash between autonomy and beneficence to one between coercion and care; and it would increase the salience for carers of the issue of trust.

The starting point for Tan and Hope's work, presented in Chapter 13, was their clinical experience with patients with anorexia nervosa. This experience suggested that the current legal and ethical approaches to capacity do not cope well with this condition. The standard approach to capacity focuses on the intellectual ability to understand key facts, think through the issues, and come to a decision. Many people with anorexia have capacity according to this standard analysis, and yet there are reasons to be concerned about this result. Interviews with people with anorexia and their families were carried out. The findings showed that the decision to refuse treatment was influenced by many factors that are not included in current concepts of capacity. In particular there were a wide variety of values related to the anorexia that played a part in the decision, not only the value given to pursuing thinness, but also various views about the danger of dying, and ideas about personal identity. This research provides data for further ethical and conceptual analysis, and challenges current ethical and legal concepts of capacity.

In Chapter 14, Adshead and colleagues discuss the study of moral reasoning in forensic psychiatric patients. They argue that the emphasis should not only be on knowledge of moral principles, but also on personal commitment to them. Forensic psychiatric patients may be able to reason cognitively, but they may lack moral identity and personal identification with certain values. This appears from a narrative analysis of transcripts of these patients' comments to vignettes presenting moral dilemmas. The dilemmas which Adshead and colleagues use are not related to general rights and duties, but to responsibilities in personal relationships. In many respondents, the analysis shows lack of engagement and coherence. This empirical result has ethical and legal relevance. A forensic psychiatric patient has committed one or more criminal acts. For the judge, the question is whether the patient is responsible for breaking the rules. The authors argue that the answer to this question is related to the issue of moral identity. If the person does not identify with the values underlying the rules, one may doubt whether breaking the rules can be seen as an expression of autonomy. Thus, empirical insight into moral reasoning and moral identity is relevant to the issue of responsibility.

In Chapter 15, Welie argues that empirical research has a significant role to play in legal analysis. The starting point for Welie's research was to examine, using both observations and interviews, how health professionals assessed the decision-making capacity of elderly patients in a geriatric care setting. The idea had been to see to what extent the legal criteria for capacity were used by health professionals. The preliminary data showed, however, that health professionals rarely assess capacity. In the light of these results the research question was adapted and changed to the following two questions: (*a*) do health care professionals discuss their patients' decision-making capacity; and (*b*) if not, why not? The results suggested that patient capacity was neither widely assessed nor considered. Welie argues that this calls for legal arrangements in which the emphasis is not on criteria for capacity, but on the presupposition of capacity in health care practice.

*

Medical ethics has always been regarded as an interdisciplinary enterprise. Yet, for a long time empirical research has not played a significant role in this domain. Over the past few years, however, empirical studies have become more and more accepted. This book presents examples in the area of psychiatric ethics, and reflects upon the relationship between empirical research and ethical analysis in these studies. Using the metaphor of the garden of the forking paths again, one might say that in the garden of medical ethics, the pathways of philosophy and social science, after having been apart for decades, have moved towards one another, providing interesting intersections and mergers. Walking on the path of philosophical analysis, one may meet fellow travellers coming from an empirical science direction, providing new perspectives on the way forward. Following the path of empirical science, one may come across philosophical pathways, inviting the traveller to explore new directions. In the garden of medical ethics, pathways are never straight and simple; they tend to be complex and curvy. The purpose of this book is not to pave a highway for empirical psychiatric ethics, with one lane for empirical research and one for philosophical analysis, but to show how empirical and philosophical roads can touch one another and can get connected, inviting and stimulating the traveller to go ahead into new and challenging territory.

Chapter 2

The possibility of empirical psychiatric ethics

John McMillan and Tony Hope

2.1. Introduction

Over 20 years ago Raanan Gillon wrote *Philosophical Medical Ethics* (Gillon 1985). The title was chosen to contradict the idea, then prevalent amongst clinicians, that ethics was simply a matter of common sense and experience. Gillon emphasized the importance of a proper philosophical approach to the increasingly complex and sophisticated field of medical ethics. There are now available a large number of excellent books that demonstrate the value and richness of bringing philosophical analysis to bear on matters of medical ethics. *Philosophical Medical Ethics* has come of age. Its younger sibling is *empirical medical ethics*: the close combination of philosophical analyses and empirical studies in research on issues in medical ethics. Empirical medical ethics, both as a concept and as a practice, is still in its infancy (see Borry *et al.*, Chapter 4 in this volume). For some, the very idea of empirical ethics is incoherent. We believe, however, not only that it is coherent but also that it constitutes an important approach to research in medical ethics in general, and in psychiatric ethics in particular.

The aim of this book is to demonstrate the practice of empirical psychiatric ethics through specific examples. The aim of this chapter is to defend the very idea of an empirical ethics and to try and do that from within the tradition of analytic philosophy: a tradition that might at first sight seem to be particularly antagonistic to combining empirical methods (that deal with facts) with ethical analyses (that deal with values).

2.2. The philosopher interested in psychiatry

For those philosophers who are interested in psychiatry and know that it is an area that contains an array of difficult ethical problems, it is sometimes difficult to move beyond the obvious issues (such as criminal responsibility and mental disorder) or indeed to gain new insights into those issues. The immersion within the day-to-day life of psychiatric practice will enable philosophers to engage with issues relevant and important to health care professionals and service users, and will help ensure that the philosophical analyses are properly informed by the realities of the experiences of both those with mental disorders and the people who try to help them.

Karl Jaspers famously emphasized the importance for psychiatrists of empathy with, and understanding of, the subjective elements of the patient's experience (Jaspers 1997 [1913]). Jaspers believed that understanding the meaningful connections between psychic events is essential for the effectiveness and progress of psychiatry. In an analogous way, we believe that engaging with the ethical issues that are features of clinical practice is likewise important for the progress and relevance of psychiatric ethics. Ethicists interested in psychiatry need a method for gaining insight into the practical ethical problems faced by those working and being treated within mental health.

A particularly interesting issue for psychiatry is the relationship between socio-historical forces and clinical life. Ground-breaking historical work was done by Michel Foucault in *Madness and Civilisation* (Foucault 1961) and *The Birth of the Clinic* (Foucault 1973) on the ways in which broad socio-historical changes can impact upon the dynamics of the psychiatrist–patient interaction. While Foucault makes his argument with historical accounts it is less obvious how an ethicist who wishes to engage with the realities of contemporary clinical experience should proceed.

One option is to turn to literature that depicts the patient's experience of psychiatry. There are numerous novels such as Kevin Kesey's *One Flew Over the Cuckoo's Nest* (Kesey 1973) and Janet Frame's *Owls do Cry* (Frame 1985) that give phenomenologically rich accounts of clinical psychiatry. Many of these classic works are from the 1960s and 70s when there was a very different ethos in psychiatry and in society more generally. In general, the anti-psychiatry literature of this period tended to develop Foucauldian analyses of power and knowledge. There is also a wealth of more recent literature such as Lauren Slater's *Prozac Diary* (Slater 1998). Phenomenologically rich accounts of psychiatry can be used for philosophical and ethical analysis. A fine example of this is the way that Louis Sass uses Dr Schreber's first person account of his 'nervous condition' to unpack some of Wittgenstein's remarks about solipsism (Sass 1995). In addition to patient experiences, the perspectives of both professional and family carers are also relevant to the philosopher.

While literature can be useful, the empirically minded ethicist needs to engage with the reality of clinical life in a more direct way – and should be interested in her own judgements and reactions to events. First person accounts do provide invaluable insights but they are always written from another agent's perspective and often with a particular end in mind. An alternative to using literature is to adapt methods developed in the social sciences. A number of the chapters in this book exemplify this kind of motivation and approach. Jeanette Pols, for example, in a study of professional carers, gives an insight into the changes in the 'care ideals' that have occurred in more recent times and how these structure and influence psychiatric wards in subtle ways (see Chapter 5 in this volume). One of the major aims of this book is to show how empirical ethics can help ethicists engage with the realities of mental health.

2.3. The health professional interested in philosophy

Medicine, nursing, and other health professions are, to a significant extent, learned as an apprenticeship. This is a powerful and valuable way of learning but it has a central weakness: that the neophyte health professional learns what to do by seeing and practicing how it is done. This leads to two related problems: first, it is conservative – students learn that *this* is what to do rather than critically evaluating or reassessing what should be done. Second it tends to hide the values and ethical issues that underpin practice with the result that they are not subjected to any questioning or analysis. The student learns to recognize what to do in specific situations. How to behave becomes a fact. The apprentice is not encouraged to ask, is it right that we do this, or what are the reasons why we do that?

Evidence-based medicine arose in part as a reaction to this apprenticeship learning. Evidence-based medicine emphasizes that we must have good reasons for preferring this way to that way. It is not the authority of doctors, for example, however experienced, that justifies a particular intervention, but the evidence for that intervention. Similarly medical ethics challenges the value base: it is not the fact that experienced doctors do this that tells us it is ethically right but the reasons that are given for acting in that particular way.

The very vocabulary of medical decisions helps keep ethical issues concealed. Consider the phrase 'not clinically indicated' said perhaps about a major operation for an elderly patient. The phrase justifies not offering the patient the operation and it sounds reassuringly scientific and authoritative. But what values lie hidden? Perhaps those used to assess the best interests of the patient: the operation might risk a high chance that the patient will die as a result. But if the operation is 'not clinically indicated' for that reason we need to know the patient's values. Perhaps for the particular patient the risk of death is worth taking given the potential for benefit and the patient's condition without an operation. But 'not clinically indicated' might hide quite different values. Resources might be stretched. The operation is expensive. Many younger and fitter patients may benefit more from this limited resource.

To carry out this operation on this patient may not be a good use of resources but it is difficult for professionals to admit this even to themselves. 'Not clinically indicated' keeps hidden these uncomfortable considerations.

Thus health professionals may fail to see that their decisions have important and contestable value judgements hidden behind the guise of clinical judgement. This is the converse of the problem faced by the philosopher. The philosopher who engages in medical ethics may fail to realize that there are some key empirical issues that bear in an important way on the questions that are being analysed. Several chapters in this book give examples of this kind. The health professional, on the other hand, fails to see that there are some important value judgements lying behind the clinical decisions – judgements that need to be critically analysed.

2.4. **Issues not methodologies**

We have come to believe that the idea of empirical psychiatric ethics (or empirical medical ethics, more broadly) is both an important and a coherent approach to research. We ourselves were educated in different disciplines from each other: philosophy in one case, and psychiatry and neuroscience, in the other. We share however the same broad intellectual approach: that of Anglo-American analytic philosophy. From the perspective of this approach the very idea of empirical ethics might seem intrinsically contradictory. Of all the major philosophical approaches Anglo-American philosophy may at first sight be the least indulgent to combining in a single research enterprise such diametrically opposed methodologies as the collection and analysis of empirical data with the normative analysis of ethical arguments.

Before we examine the case against an empirical ethics we will mention a distinction between *issues* and *methodologies*. In the setting of research it is our view that it is issues that are primary. Methodologies are tools to be used to shed light on issues – to answer questions that are interesting or important. Thus, when we are examining a particular research issue or question we should use whatever methodologies are most suitable to the research aims. It is limiting to restrict one's field of interest by a methodology: to say, for example, that one is interested only in the scientific questions; or conversely that one is interested only in the philosophical issues. In other words, methods follow aims, not the other way about. What makes intellectual enquiry important and ultimately interesting is that there is a question or issue that it is important to explore. And many questions of any complexity require a range of methodologies. In the practice of health care the question continually arises: what should be done in this situation? And often, in answering this question, both empirical and philosophical (including ethical) issues are relevant.

2.5. **The arguments against the possibility of empirical ethics**

We have argued that the philosopher interested in psychiatry, or indeed any health care practice, would do well to engage with the empirical reality of that practice. Conversely the health professional faces ethical issues for which the skills of ethical analysis might be valuable. We have suggested that research in medical ethics will start with aims, or issues, and that to pursue these aims may require a combination of empirical and philosophical (often ethical) methods. But, by itself, this does not justify a concept of empirical medical ethics. Perhaps there are two quite separate methodologies each of which may contribute to some research questions. We will now examine the reasons against the possibility of empirical ethics.

2.5.1. **Is/ought and the naturalistic fallacy**

Promoting the use of empirical methods in ethics might appear to fall foul of the is/ought problem and the naturalistic fallacy. The two problems are distinct so we will discuss them briefly in turn.

In book three of the *Treatise of Human Nature* (Hume, 1978 [1740], pp. 469–70) David Hume comments upon the tendency of his contemporaries to proceed from statements of fact to statements about what ought to be the case. There is a significant debate in philosophy about exactly what Hume intended in this passage but the general lesson for ethics is that there is a logical problem in deriving normative or moral conclusions from matters of fact (Pigden 1989).

The naturalistic fallacy originates in G.E. Moore's *Principia Ethica* (Moore 1966 [1903]). Essentially the complaint is that moral philosophers should not attempt to define properties such as right or good in terms of 'natural' properties such as 'pleasure' or 'happiness'. Moore singles out John Stuart Mill as a philosopher who commits this fallacy. Moore accused Mill of attempting to show that 'good' is really just the same thing as 'happiness'. Happiness is, according to Moore, a 'natural' thing while good is non-natural or not analysable in terms of other facts in the world.

Perhaps the most important difference between these two philosophical problems is that Hume is making a point about validity while Moore is pointing out that there is something normative about moral terms that can't be captured purely in terms of matters of fact. Nonetheless, they both have at the core the insight that there is something essentially normative about moral prescriptions that can't be captured by exclusively factual description. These philosophical worries might be taken to present a major challenge to the concept of an empirical ethic. This is a key issue for us, given that the title of this book unabashedly uses the terms 'empirical ethics', and that many people might argue that the normativity of ethics rules out the possibility of its being done in a factual or empirical way.

In less abstract terms the case against empirical ethics can be put as follows: Ethics is concerned with the *ought* – with what we *ought* to do. No amount of empirical information (which is concerned with the *is*) will add up to an ought. Empirical work will not be ethics and so empirical medical ethics is a contradiction in terms. Whatever we find out about what *is* the case, we are left with questions about what we *ought* to do. All the focus groups in the world, all the social science results about what people think, supply us, in the end, only with facts – what is the case – and fail to provide a reason for what we ought to do.

This argument might reasonably be countered by saying that it shows only that empirical medical ethics cannot consist *only* of empirical work. So further argument is needed, argument that recognizes that in carrying out research in medical ethics we often need to combine empirical work with ethical analysis. Such further argument is that although both facts and values are relevant to ethical decision-making these two aspects can be readily separated. Research about facts is science, research about values is ethics. There is no reason to conceive of a discipline of *empirical medical ethics*: let us keep the conceptual distinction between the two types of research methodology.

These philosophical arguments against the possibility of empirical medical ethics can be strengthened by a social science perspective. Those with expertise in the social sciences might object to the tendency of ethicists to enter into qualitative research with specific moral questions or other theoretical commitments. This kind of approach might be thought to compromise the integrity of the qualitative work that results. Whereas philosophical ethics uses traditional philosophical methods of argument for pursuing robustly defended moral claims, sociology tends to use broader social observations about the motives and function of society. In short, the principal reason why research into ethics is different from the social sciences is because it uses different methods of critical analysis that are primarily philosophical. Thus the critical analyses of the data in ethics and in the social sciences are quite different from, and at odds with, each other. Again the conclusion is that the empirical work and the ethical work are separate and should not be combined under a single misleading concept of empirical medical ethics.

2.6. **The arguments in favour of empirical medical ethics**

We believe that there are a number of reasons why these objections to empirical ethics fail.

First, there is what we call the 'obvious moral premise' response. It is important to bear in mind that Hume is making a point about moral reasoning. He is saying (at least on the most common interpretation) that it is logically invalid to proceed from a description of some state of affairs to a moral conclusion. This does not rule out the possibility that a moral premise can be added so that a chain of moral reason is logically valid. The emphasis in an empirical study may be on the description of a morally relevant phenomenon and the ethicist writing up this study may want to draw normative conclusions from it. It does not follow, however, that the ethicist is guilty of fallacious reasoning, even if she does not explicitly use moral premises in her reasoning. Suppose an ethicist describes the way in which a group of psychiatrists and patients have radically different understandings of a particular diagnosis with the result that some significant degree of mistrust results. An ethicist might draw the conclusion that something *ought* to be done to improve the communication in this context, without explicitly defending a moral premise. However the moral premise in this kind of case seems fairly unproblematic, it would be something like 'when there is a risk of interdependent people mistrusting each other because of communication and there is a straightforward way of helping to overcome this distrust then something should be done'. Given the ungainliness of this premise and its obviousness it seems reasonable to suppress it, and not explicitly argue for it, when interpreting this study.

A second possibility is that for some studies it might be appropriate not to reach a moral conclusion. Some empirical ethicists do not draw any moral claims from their work but these studies should be considered 'empirical ethics' nonetheless. This is because there are some areas of inquiry that are highly pertinent to normative inquiry in virtue of their content. For example a qualitative study that investigated what patients, enrolled in a clinical trial, understood about the nature of the trial should perhaps count as empirical ethics even if the researcher does not draw any moral conclusions. Information of this kind is so obviously relevant to ethics that its content alone is sufficient for considering it ethics. We return to the question of whether studies of this kind should be regarded as examples of 'empirical ethics' below.

A third, more radical, response is to say that empirical ethics engages directly with moral norms. If studies can produce normative observations they will avoid committing the Humean fallacy because the study will not omit moral premises. It also avoids the naturalistic fallacy because it does not attempt to describe moral properties as factual ones. It is important to bear in mind that Moore himself thought that we could only be aware of moral properties by directly intuiting them in the actions of others. An ethicist who places himself in a clinical context seems, on Moorean grounds, ideally situated to study moral norms. In fact, for a Moorean, the empirical ethicist is better situated to inquire into moral norms than the philosopher sitting at her desk.

2.7. **Various ways in which ethics and empirical work can be combined in medical ethics**

For the reasons given above we do not believe that there are fundamental theoretical objections to the concept of empirical medical ethics. But the question remains as to whether the concept of empirical medical ethics is useful.

At root the question is whether there are research aims and issues that require a methodology that combines empirical work with ethical analysis so closely that separating the two components into different pieces or research is problematically atomistic. We believe that there is such research and that the close intertwining of empirical work and ethical analysis is necessary in order to address some significant research questions. In order to argue for this position it is helpful we believe to distinguish different types of research that combine empirical and ethical components. We will outline six types of research.

1. Empirical work with a 'suppressed' normative premise

   Consider the question: what drugs should doctors give a patient following a heart attack? This is a normative question about what we ought to do. A current issue, let us suppose, is whether a promising new drug (drug A) should be given. A large randomized controlled trial of drug A is carried out. Drug A is found to decrease mortality and morbidity following heart attack to a greater extent than alternatives. We conclude that we *ought* to offer drug A to relevant patients.

   We come to this conclusion as a result of our normative beliefs (that doctors should, normally, maximize healthy life) and the empirical facts about what the effect of drug A is. We combine facts and values, in a way that is quite compatible with Hume, using the 'suppressed' normative premise that it is right to maximize healthy life. No one, however, would argue that the conducting of large randomized trials of this type is engaging in empirical medical *ethics*: although a normative conclusion is reached, there is no ethical analysis or research.

2. The survey of ethical beliefs

   Consider a study of people's views about active euthanasia. Such a study might make a contribution to the development of policy. For example were most medical practitioners in a country to favour the practice of active euthanasia then the legalization of that practice might be much more straightforward than if most medical practitioners were against the practice.

The views of groups of people who have particular types of experience – health professionals working in palliative care, for example – would certainly be of significance in an ethical debate about active euthanasia. But of course a head count of people's beliefs is not itself ethics because it does not engage with ethical argument. Such 'head counts' of ethical views might however be valuable not only in identifying the level of support for different views, it may also be a starting point for exploring reasons for one ethical view or another. Thus, for example, if palliative care doctors are for the most part against active euthanasia and (let us suppose for the sake of exposition) general practitioners are generally in favour of euthanasia, the question arises as to why this difference. Is it for example based on experiences of different types of situation or on differing expertise or what? The survey of ethical views can be an important preliminary to ethical analysis. It might quite reasonably be funded as part of a programme in medical ethics. But it should not in our view be called empirical medical ethics because it lacks normative analysis.

There are, however, many types of study that involve a closer connection between the normative and both qualitative and quantitative empirical work.

3. When ethical analysis identifies key empirical questions

Philosophical argument often depends on key empirical facts. One reason, for example, why doctors should keep patient information confidential is in order to foster patient trust and ensure that people seek appropriate medical help. And yet the effect of specific breaches of confidentiality on trust and behaviour is an empirical issue.

An initial ethical analysis, for example an analysis of what justifies a doctor breaching confidentiality, helps identify which empirical facts may be important. An empirical study might then be designed to collect the data identified as of crucial ethical importance. The results of the empirical study may then be fed back into the ethical analysis in order to come to a view about when it is right and when it is wrong to breach confidentiality. Ethical analysis and empirical studies inform each other and together contribute to the research aim and the final analysis.

4. Assessing ethical interventions

Medical ethics is increasingly developing what are, effectively, interventions: advance directives, consent procedures, ethics committees (research or clinical). The methodology for assessing the effectiveness of interventions is now well established in the medical sciences. The use, in the field of medical ethics, of a methodology now standard in medical science is a significant development. Ethical analysis contributes to the development of the 'ethical intervention' and empirical assessment of the intervention can lead back to a reconsideration of the ethical issues.

5. Ethical theories can lead directly to empirical work

Some ethical theories lead directly to empirical work. An outstanding example is QALY theory. Three quite different types of empirical study follow from this theory. The first is the establishing of what quality adjustment should be made for different states of health. The second, which is becoming quite standard in analyses of health care interventions, is the cost per QALY. A third type of study would examine what resource allocation (or rationing) decisions have actually been made by some body responsible for a health care budget. This could be followed by examining the extent to which such decisions are consistent with a QALY approach. Almost certainly they will not be entirely consistent. The question then arises as to whether, in those cases where the decisions are not consistent with QALYs, this is anomalous; or whether there are important values which are reflected in these decisions which are not captured by the QALY approach.

In all the examples above sceptics of empirical medical ethics might argue that although empirical work and ethical analysis can interact, and both might be necessary to address a particular research question, they are still separate and separable components: there is no need to combine the two into a single concept of empirical ethics. This view is more difficult to sustain for our sixth example.

6. Empirical studies can directly engage with ethical concepts

In the second section of this book there are many examples of this sixth category. The empirical research involved is primarily qualitative. In this category ethical analysis and qualitative data are closely entwined. Consider the study of capacity and decision-making in anorexia nervosa for example described in Chapter 13 by Tan and Hope. Knowledge from clinical practice of patients with anorexia led to the realization that current legal and ethical analyses of decision-making capacity were problematic in this setting. These current analyses led to the identification of the issues and beliefs that an empirical study of capacity in people with anorexia should address. The empirical results shed doubt on the adequacy of the current analyses. This, in turn, is leading to further ethical and conceptual analysis.

In carrying out qualitative work of this kind the data collection itself can engage with the ethical thinking of the participants. In the survey of views on euthanasia discussed above it was assumed that the empirical study collected the data in a rather straightforward way: participants were asked what their views about active euthanasia were. But a qualitative study can itself explore why participants hold the views they do; and even challenge, with counter-arguments, the reasons that participants give. Such engagement between researcher and participant stretches conventional social science methods and raises interesting issues about research methodology. It also represents a very close connection indeed between ethical analysis and empirical methods. Some of the studies described in this book use methods that involve some normative discussion between researcher and participant. Widdershoven and Van der Scheer's concept of 'pragmatic hermeneutics' (see Chapter 3 in this volume) binds the empirical and the normative in a particularly tight way. For them and a number of the other contributors to this book, the research process can articulate and produce situated moral norms. Research of this kind comes close to the Moorean ideal becoming directly aware of normativity *in situ*.

2.8. **Towards defining empirical medical ethics**

The above discussion suggests that there is no clear defining feature of a project in empirical medical ethics, as opposed to a project that combines both ethical analysis and empirical work. A project that uses only empirical methods, but that uses those to address an ethical issue (the survey example 2 above) might be called a project in empirical medical ethics. We suggest however that the term empirical ethics is better reserved for a closer interaction between ethics and empirical work. There is a spectrum in terms of the closeness in connection. We suggest that for an enterprise to be called empirical medical ethics it must include ethical (normative) analysis. And to be *empirical* it must involve the *systematic* collection of data. Furthermore, the interaction should perhaps be more than linear. That is if the only relationship were that either empirical work provided the material for ethical analysis, or that ethical analysis provided the subject for an empirical survey, then the empirical and ethical components would so easily be separable that the endeavour would not merit the name *empirical ethics*. But many studies are better represented by a cyclical model, in which ethical analysis and empirical data collection inform each other in an interactive cycle.

This 'cyclical' interaction, seems to us to justify the term 'empirical ethics'. At the extreme the interaction between the normative and the empirical is so close and continuous that the idea of a cycle gives way to a blend. In this way, empirical ethics becomes a recognizable interdisciplinary field. It involves a cycle, at the macro- or micro-levels, in which ethical analysis leads to empirical

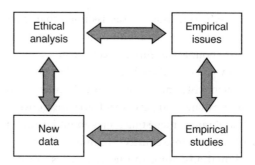

work that demands more ethical and conceptual analysis and, perhaps, continuing round the cycle. The concept of empirical ethics that we propose here is a version of Borry's third approach (see Chapter 4): 'normative interpretation of empirical ethics'.

2.9. Conclusions

We have argued that the increased use of empirical methods by ethicists interested in psychiatry, and an interest in using ethical analysis in research by scientists and clinicians, are important new developments. Encouraging the fit between what is written about psychiatric ethics in an academic context and the actual ethical problems and issues for those working in psychiatry, service users and their families is an appropriate way for this area to develop and empirical ethics is a promising way to help achieve this aim.

We believe that the philosophical worries about incorporating empirical work into ethical analysis are not insurmountable. Both Humean worries about moving from the descriptive to the normative and the naturalistic fallacy are not as problematic for empirical ethics as might at first be thought.

We have discussed various ways in which empirical work and ethical analyses can be combined in order to address research issues. In some of these examples we believe that the two approaches to research remain sufficiently separated for it to be reasonable to claim that rather than talking of empirical ethics we can talk of a research project that has separate empirical and ethical components. But at the other end of the spectrum there are research projects that involve such an intimate and mutually interactive relationship between the empirical work and the ethical analyses that it is more reasonable to talk of a research method that is *empirical medical ethics*.

Bioethics is an intellectual enterprise where academics from various disciplines debate moral questions. Acquiring and developing methodologies from the contributing disciplines is integral to the future development of bioethics as an area. An important challenge to interdisciplinary inquiry is the temptation to defend the boundaries and methodologies of one's discipline of origin. Using qualitative methodologies for empirical psychiatric ethics is a useful and legitimate way to develop psychiatric ethics.

Empirical medical ethics is in one sense trivially a multidisciplinary field. In order to develop it will need partnerships between researchers with differing disciplinary backgrounds and research skills. But this might be only a phase. What start out as multidisciplinary fields can develop into single fields. Clinical trials started as a development involving mathematicians, scientists, and clinicians. Now there is a generation of academics with integrated trial skills. Chemical engineering is a well-established university degree – separate from and more mathematically informed than chemistry. In future generations of young researchers may well master the skills of, say, social science and ethics so completely that combining the skills is effortless and indeed experienced as using a single research method. Discipline boundaries and research methods are fluid: what is now experienced as an uncomfortable marriage of opposites may come to be seen as an integrated unity.

In this chapter we have argued in favour of the concept of empirical psychiatric ethics. The purpose of Section 2 of this book is to demonstrate its practice.

References

Foucault M (1961). *Madness and civilisation*. Tavistock, London.

Foucault M (1973). *The birth of the clinic*. Tavistock, London.

Frame J (1985). *Owls do cry*. Women's Press Limited, London.

Gillon R (1985). *Philosophical medical ethics*. John Wiley, Chichester.

Hedgecoe A (2004). Critical bioethics: beyond the social science critique of applied ethics. *Bioethics*, **18**(2) 120-43.

Hedgecoe A (2007). Medical sociology and the redundancy of empirical ethics. In E Ashcroft, A Dawson, H Draper and J McMillan, eds. *The principles of health care ethics* (2nd edn.), pp. 167–75, John Wiley, London.

Hume D (1978) [1740]. In LA Selby-Bigge and PH Nidditch, eds. *A treatise concerning human nature*, pp. 469-70. Clarendon, Oxford.

Jaspers K (1997) [1913]. In Trans J Hoenig and Marian Hamilton, eds. *General psychopathology* Vol 1. Johns Hopkins University Press, Baltimore.

Kesey K (1973). *One flew over the Cuckoo's nest*. Picador, London.

McMillan J (2007). Mental illness and compulsory treatment. In E Ashcroft, A Dawson, H Draper and J McMillan, eds. *The principles of health care ethics* (2nd edn.), pp. 443–8, John Wiley, London.

Moore GE (1966) [1903]. *Principia ethica*. Cambridge University Press, Cambridge.

Pigden C (1989). Logic and the autonomy of ethics. *Australasian Journal of Philosophy*, **67**, 127-51.

Sass L (1995). *The paradoxes of delusion: Wittgenstein, Schreber and the Schizophrenic mind.* Cornell University Press, New York.

Sayre-McCord G (1988). *Essays on moral realism.* Cornell University Press, New York.

Slater L (1998). *Prozac diary.* Hamish Hamilton, London.

Chapter 3

Theory and methodology of empirical ethics: a pragmatic hermeneutic perspective

Guy Widdershoven and Lieke van der Scheer

3.1. Introduction

Empirical science and ethics are traditionally viewed as distinct disciplines. Empirical science deals with facts; ethics deals with norms and values. Empirical science is descriptive; ethics is prescriptive. Yet, if ethics wants to say things about the real world, it has to take into account facts. Medical ethics has been developed in close interaction with medical practice. Its problems come from practice, and solutions for these problems are found through interaction between ethicists and physicians.

Whereas interaction between ethicists and physicians has always been important in medical ethics, the notion of empirical ethics is more recent. Combining empirical research and philosophical analysis has become more accepted in twentieth century philosophy, such as ordinary language philosophy, phenomenology, and philosophy of science. In medicine, the plea for evidence-based practice has become prominent, implying the need for empirical research in all medical disciplines. These developments have influenced the rise of empirical ethics in the area of medicine (see Borry *et al.*, Chapter 4 in this volume).

Although empirical ethics has gained considerable attention over the past years, traditional doubts about merging facts and values have not vanished. It is not clear for everyone that empirical research and ethics can be combined in a productive way, without committing the naturalistic fallacy (see McMillan and Hope, Chapter 2 in this volume). Systematic reflection upon the theoretical and methodological issues involved in combining empirical research and ethics is scarce. Facts evidently matter for ethics, but how can the results of empirical research be integrated into ethical reasoning? How can normative conclusions be based upon empirical studies?

In this chapter, we will attempt to find an answer to these questions. We will first explain what it means to see practice as a source of ethics. Next, we sketch our theoretical perspective, combining two philosophical approaches: pragmatism and hermeneutics. In line with the view that practice is important for understanding and developing theory, we will present an example of an empirical ethical project in psychiatry, making use of a pragmatic hermeneutic approach. Reflecting upon this example, we will discuss the role of method in empirical ethics. We will argue, along with Gadamer, that truth is more fundamental than method. Furthermore, we explain the role of general rules and principles. Referring to Aristotle's notion of practical wisdom (*phronèsis*), we will argue that understanding general rules requires knowledge of their application to concrete situations. Finally, we will discuss the way in which our approach combines facts and norms. We will show that the normative outcome of the project is related to the process of negotiation about the claims of the participants.

3.2. **Practice as a source of ethics**

The growing attention to empirical research in ethics can be regarded as a result of the practical turn in ethics in the last half of the twentieth century. From a highly academic philosophical enterprise, ethics changed into a discipline aimed to help solve real-life ethical problems. This is very clear in medicine, where ethicists have played an important role in debates about, for example, end-of-life decisions.

In the discussion of empirical ethics in medicine, two positions regarding the role of empirical data can be distinguished. The first position says that empirical research can help to establish which issues are relevant for practice (Brody 1993). Which problems do practitioners experience? These problems are the proper object for normative analysis. Moreover, empirical research can help to apply the results of normative analysis to practice. Characteristic of this first position is the view that normative analysis itself is not influenced by empirical elements.

The second position states that practice not only helps in determining the relevant moral problems, but also that it is itself, a source of ethics. The way in which practitioners think and act is morally relevant, because they have moral experience. Their judgements and actions contain moral insights, which have to be acknowledged in moral reflection. The view that practitioners have moral knowledge is put forward by, for instance, Beauchamp and Childress (1994). They regard moral principles, such as beneficence and non-maleficence, as expressions of perspectives operating in medical practice. In philosophical ethics, this view is endorsed by Rawls (1971). He states that the way in which experienced persons, such as judges, deal with moral issues is relevant for ethics. Moral judgements of experienced practitioners can be used as input into the process of reflective equilibrium, characteristic for ethical reasoning.

The view that moral practice is a source for philosophical ethics is akin to the view that scientific practice is relevant to the philosophy of science. This view goes back to the work of Kuhn (1970). Kuhn criticized Popper's theory of science, by pointing out that scientists do not follow the rules laid down in Popper's methodology. They do not try to falsify theories, but they take their theoretical framework for granted, and use it for solving puzzles. Rather than trying to refute a theory, they extend and refine it. Kuhn used the results of empirical research into the practice of science for building up a new philosophy of science, introducing notions like normal science, paradigm, and puzzle solving. Popper was not convinced by these empirical arguments. He argued that the facts Kuhn had discovered were not a problem for the logic of falsificationism, but that they showed that scientists were wrong. Other philosophers of science, such as Lakatos, stated that the facts could be used to reflect upon and adjust the current logic of scientific research. This implies an interaction between research into facts about scientific development and the analysis of the logic of science.

If practice is seen as a source for ethics, the experience, insight, and arguments of practitioners form the point of departure for philosophical ethics. In the case of health care ethics, practitioners include not only physicians and nurses, but also other people with experience, such as patients and family. The aim of ethical reflection is to make practical experience explicit, to examine it, and to give it a place in ethical analysis. The idea is that ethicists can learn from practice which moral views and arguments are relevant in specific situations. Practitioners may teach ethicists how to reason better and how to improve normative analysis. Ethicists, in turn, may help practitioners to make implicit knowledge explicit, investigate its validity and develop it further.

3.3. **Pragmatic hermeneutics**

The background of our approach to empirical ethics is a combination of pragmatism and hermeneutics, which we call pragmatic hermeneutics. In line with Dewey's pragmatism, we take the position that the meaning of concepts lies in their practical consequences (Van der Scheer 1999). Following Gadamer's philosophical hermeneutics, we think that meaning is related to historical tradition (Gadamer 1960). Pragmatic hermeneutics stresses the importance of practical processes of meaning-making, related to concrete problems. It is critical of all attempts to frame the problem in terms of strictly defined principles and to solve it through abstract procedures. Ethical problems in health care are always complex and concrete (Leder 1994). One should investigate what the situation means for those who are practically involved in it. How do they define the issue? What solutions do they envisage? What problems do they encounter? Pragmatic hermeneutics is sceptical about general and a-historic interpretations. In trying to make sense of a situation, one should be aware of its intricacy and of its historical and contextual background.

Pragmatic hermeneutics emphasizes that moral knowledge is not theoretical, but embedded in action. This view is in line with Aristotle's practical philosophy. For Aristotle, ethics is based upon practical experience. One needs experience in moral life in order to understand moral issues and to decide what should be done. According to Aristotle, morality is the basis of ethics. The distinction between morality and ethics may be compared to the distinction between *logica utens* and *logica docens* (or for that matter to the distinction between the grammar people use in their ordinary conversations and the grammar they learn in school). *Logica utens* is the logic which human beings intuitively or instinctively apply. If we had to wait for children to understand the formal intricacies of the principle of contradiction before allowing them to act on this principle, we probably would wait a long time. Similarly, Aristotle did not invent logic, but he was the first in the western world to codify the rules people apply when communicating with each other. And this first code has in the course of time been reflected upon, refined, and improved so as to become a tool in all sorts of human applications. In other words, practice precedes science, especially in the prescriptive sciences.

For Aristotle, moral action is socially embedded. People learn morality through education and habituating the behaviour of others. In moral practice, people learn from one another how to distinguish the morally relevant aspects of a situation. Likewise, an ethicist can learn from practitioners what is relevant to moral decision-making. According to Gadamer (1960), this learning process is dialogical. We do not learn by taking things over mechanically, but by investigating the validity of the other's point of view. Dialogical understanding means that one tries to see the point the other makes. It means being open to what the other has to say, being prepared to accept it as relevant and valid for oneself (Gadamer 1960; Widdershoven 2005). To quote Gadamer: 'Openness to the other, then, involves recognizing that I myself must accept something against me, even though no one else would bring this up' (1960, p. 343). According to Gadamer, dialogue results in a fusion of horizons. The point of view of the participants merge, and change into a new, common perspective. This perspective is fundamentally different from the two perspectives that were there at the start, like bronze is different from copper and tin.

3.4. **An example: the quality of coercion and compulsion in psychiatry**

From a pragmatic hermeneutic perspective, practice is the basis of theory. This maxim can also be applied to empirical ethics. Empirical ethics should not primarily be understood as a set of theoretical principles; what is at stake in empirical ethics should be understood from practice. To help explain our view on empirical ethics, we will outline an empirical ethics project that illustrates the theoretical and methodological aspects of a pragmatic hermeneutic approach.

The project concerns the development of guidelines for the quality of coercion and compulsion in psychiatry (Berghmans *et al.* 2001). Coercion and compulsion are problematic elements in psychiatric care. They attempt to subject a patient to something or incite the patient to commit or to forego some action. When coercion is applied, alternatives of action are excluded for the patient; he/she can do nothing but undergo what is imposed (for instance, medicine administered against his or her will, or the application of seclusion). In the case of compulsion, the patient's freedom of choice is not limited in an absolute sense. Nevertheless, it is to a greater or lower extent restricted, for instance, by presenting an unattractive option. ('If you don't take this medicine, you can't go home for the weekend.', 'If you don't take moments of rest, we'll have to put you in seclusion.').

The purpose of the project was to engender a dialogue about the application of coercion and compulsion in a number of Dutch mental health institutions, in order to collect material for improving the quality of care. Practical experience was taken as the starting point for the research. The research methods included in-depth interviews and focus groups on an institutional level and on a national level. The focus groups were mixed (psychiatrists, nurses, patients, family).

By analysing the material from the interviews and the focus groups, the researchers were able to establish practical problems about coercion and compulsion, and to develop guidelines for action, which were called quality criteria. These criteria were again discussed within the focus groups, and changed where necessary. The quality criteria included the following:

- be aware of contradictory obligations in handling situations of coercion
- create room for emotions, reflect upon them and discuss them
- pay attention to the process character of coercion: anticipate and evaluate incidents
- pay attention to communication: be attentive and open towards the patient
- reflect upon goals and means

All the groups taking part in the process of development supported the quality criteria: psychiatrists, nurses, patients, and family. This was unique, since in public debates on coercion these parties tend to take different positions. The agreement was largely due to the fact that people listened to each other's experiences around coercion and compulsion, and came to understand uncertainties and worries. Moreover, the continuous discussion on and reworking of the documents enabled the participants to influence the process and secured their commitment.

After the drafting of the document, the next phase of the project started. In 12 institutions, implementation activities were set up. These were different for each institution, based upon local context and expertise. Staff from the institutions coordinated the activities, while the ethicists focussed on giving feedback and organizing meetings between the local organizers to exchange experiences and learn from one another. Ethicists and local staff wrote down their experiences in a book, describing both the tensions in the project and the positive outcomes (best practices) (Abma *et al.* 2005). After this phase, a nationwide process of implementation was set up, engendered by the national organization of mental health institutions.

3.5. **Truth and method**

Reflecting on the project, we can say that it was successful because it started from concrete problems about coercion and compulsion. The project was able to develop new ways of dealing with these problems by engendering a process of listening to participants in practice. What issues are crucial for them? What solutions do they propose? This process of listening requires openness. One should be prepared to see the perspective of the other as relevant to oneself. According to Gadamer (1960), openness is the essence of hermeneutic understanding. One should be open to the claim to truth encountered in the perspective of the other. According to Gadamer, truth is more important than method. 'Hermeneutic consciousness culminates not in methodological sureness of itself, but in the same readiness for experience that distinguishes the experienced man from the man captivated in dogma' (p. 344). The pragmatic hermeneutic approach of the project aimed at bringing about truth by fostering openness, both on the side of the ethicists and on the side of the various parties involved in the practice of coercion and compulsion.

The focus on hermeneutic truth does not mean that method played no role in the project: during the project, several methods were used. Interviews were held, based upon an interview guide; focus groups were organized around specific topics (coming from the analysis of the interviews); documents were drafted relating the outcome of interviews and focus groups to ethical theories;

guidelines were discussed with parties in order to get their feedback. These steps were carefully planned, based upon literature on qualitative research methods. Methodically, the project combined social scientific elements (interviews, content analysis, focus groups) and philosophical elements (comparing results from content analysis with concepts from ethical theories). The project was supervised by a steering committee, including scientists, ethicists, and directors of mental health institutions. In the steering group, the planning of the project was discussed and adjusted, if necessary. All these steps can be regarded as part of the method of the project. They were laid out beforehand in the project plan, and changes were documented.

Although methodological elements clearly were necessary to attain conclusions, the results of the project did not simply follow from the application of methodological steps. For each of the elements in the research process, the conclusions were significant because they said something about the intricate process of dealing with coercion. Whether or not the results were significant was not determined by method, but by recognition of the parties involved. Of course, the process of reaching recognition was organized in a carefully planned manner, but planning does not produce recognition; recognition requires a process of agreement on the issue under consideration. The limitations of method became clearly visible at moments when one or more of the parties involved did not agree with the interpretation proposed by the researchers. In such cases, the natural response is to back up one's interpretation by referring to the methodological steps on which it was based. Yet, it proved to be more useful to listen to the reasons for disagreement, and try to be open to them. Agreement on interpretations cannot be enforced by method, it requires a dialogue between the parties involved.

We may conclude that the various steps in the project, although methodologically planned, were only successful if they resulted in mutual agreement. This was also the case for the project as a whole. The meetings in which the quality criteria were discussed, were not just instances of formal approval. They were experienced as events in which new ways of dealing with the problem were acknowledged and jointly embraced. They motivated all parties to try and change their practice into a more humane way of dealing with coercion and compulsion. From a hermeneutic perspective, the meetings were a shared experience of truth, which was not the result of the methodical steps taken, although the latter were certainly helpful in bringing about the dialogue.

3.6. **Phronèsis**

Reflecting further on the project, we can conclude that it did not aim at generating universal imperatives. The criteria, which were developed, are formulated in general terms, but they can only be understood if one takes the context into consideration. The criteria that emerged are related to the context, namely psychiatric care practice. They are tailored to concrete problems, questions, and opportunities for coping with coercion and compulsion. The discussion in the focus groups often focused on the question whether a certain generally formulated criterion was actually fitted to the specific situation, and if so, how it should be applied.

An example is the discussion, which took place in a focus group, about the criterion 'pay attention to communication'. It was agreed that communication includes telling the patient what is going to happen. Yet, psychiatric nurses questioned whether this would make sense when the patient was in a state of excitation during a coercive intervention. They said that in such conditions, patients do not understand what is being said to them; therefore it is not useful to explain the action being performed, or to give reasons for it. In answer to this, a patient in the focus group remarked that indeed in a crisis he was not able to actually listen to what was being said to him; but he was aware that he was being talked to, and this made him feel like he was being treated as a human being. If the staff did not say anything, he felt treated like a thing. This response was an eye-opener for the nurses. Explaining the situation and giving reasons for the intervention may not be effective in the sense of giving information, but it may be helpful in making the patient feel being treated as a person. Thus, talking to the patient is required, even if one cannot expect that the person hears what is being said.

The example shows that general rules and guidelines can only function in the right way if the participants in a practice know how to apply them. This requires experience with the situation. Someone who lacks the experience of a psychiatric nurse might think that 'paying attention to communication' means telling what is going to happen, whether or not the situation is one of crisis. On the basis of their experience, psychiatric nurses questioned the general applicability of the rule. They did this because they rightly doubted whether the patient would understand what is being said. Yet, this does not justify the conclusion that explaining the situation is meaningless in a crisis. The patient's story made the nurses see that communication is useful, even if one cannot expect the patient to understand the information. The rule is therefore applicable, albeit in a specific sense. The point of the rule in this specific situation is not to make sure that the patient has sufficient information, but that he feels treated as a human being. Through the discussion, the experience of the nurses was enlarged. They came to know better how to apply the rule in the specific context.

From a pragmatic hermeneutic perspective, ethics should not only aim at finding general rules and principles, which can serve as a solid base for moral action, but also help people to know how to act in a specific situation. According to Aristotle, moral action requires *phronèsis* (practical wisdom): the insight or understanding born from and guiding experience and the capacity of, respectively, acting, judging, and living accordingly. This action cannot be deduced from rules, but requires insight into how they are to be applied. Ethics can only help people in acting morally, if it provides people with insight in the appropriate application of rules. The discussion in the focus group about 'paying attention to communication' is a good example. It resulted in a joint learning process about the interpretation of the rule. By discussing it, the participants learned how to apply the quality criterion in a crisis situation.

According to Aristotle, a person with *phronèsis* is able to understand how general principles apply to the specific situation. In the process of applying the principle to the situation, the principle itself is understood in a new and better way. This is also what happens when a judge applies a law to a specific case. In applying the law to the specific case, he makes the normative content of the law more visible (Gadamer 1960, p. 309). This can also be seen in the phenomenon of jurisprudence: through the history of the application of the law, its meaning becomes more clear. The general principle behind the law is made concrete in its applications.

According to Aristotle, *phronèsis* is both relevant for moral life and for ethical theory. Without practical wisdom one cannot live well; practical wisdom is also required for understanding the general principles of moral life, since these cannot be understood if one does not know how they are to be applied in concrete cases. Empirical ethics underlines the importance of *phronèsis*. It is based upon *phronèsis*, since it makes use of the practical insight of participants in a practice. It requires *phronèsis*, since the participants in the research process have to be able to see the relevance of each other's claims and arguments. Finally, it furthers *phronèsis*, since it stimulates participants to exchange experiences and to learn from one another.

3.7. Combining empirical and normative aspects

Reflection on the example, finally, shows that it resulted in drawing normative conclusions from empirical research. The project made use of facts (factual experiences, views, and claims of participants), and the outcome was normative: the quality criteria state that caregivers in psychiatry should perform certain actions (reflect upon emotions, anticipate, evaluate, communicate, etc.). How was the project able to bridge the gap between 'is' and 'ought'? An explanation for this 'magic' result is, that the facts which were used, themselves had a normative character. The participants did not just report what the situation meant to them; their stories implied normative claims as to what should be done.

Drawing conclusions from such normative claims does not lead to a naturalistic fallacy. If it can be established that one or more of the normative claims, which are factually made by participants in a practice, are valid, the guidelines, which follow from these claims, are ethically justifiable (see also McMillan and Hope, Chapter 2 in this volume).

The question then is, how the research process during the project can establish the validity of the claims put forward by the persons involved. Our pragmatic hermeneutic approach is based upon the assumption that participants in a practice in general have sound views, because they are experienced. This idea is in line with Aristotle's view that experienced persons have practical knowledge about what is good and bad in the concrete situation. Furthermore, we do not assume that the views of practitioners are perfect; they are open for improvement. This is not in contradiction with the assumption that practitioners always already have practical insight. On the contrary, practical insight includes awareness of limitations, and thus of the need for improvement. Moreover, practical insight is required for improvement, because the participants should be able to judge whether certain alternative views are better than the view they endorse at the moment.

From a pragmatic hermeneutic perspective, the process of improvement is essentially dialogical. People learn from one another by exchanging views on the situation, negotiating validity claims, and coming to an agreement about what is the best way to solve concrete problems. We thus presuppose that exchanging claims in a dialogue is a guarantee for coming to valid conclusions. Of course this validity is again not perfect. The agreement reached will be valid only for a specific situation and a specific time. As the norms and guidelines, which are agreed upon, are applied, one may get results that are not acceptable for everybody. New claims will be put forward, and negotiation will start again. This process can, if agreement is reached, result in new and better norms.

The dialogical nature of normative learning is based upon the presupposition that the perspectives of the participants in a practice are limited. Each person has a specific view of the situation. This view is in general useful. It has been developed in a process of experience. Yet, it can also turn out to be problematic. This results in the experience of breakdown. The view one endorsed is no longer valid. Moments of breakdown are possible instances for learning. Breakdown typically occurs when one is confronted with the views of others. This will result in a process of reflection on one's own views. The process of reflection is not something that happens inside the head of the person, it is a process of negotiation between people investigating each other's views and responding to each other's claims.

The pragmatic hermeneutic approach resembles the method of reflective equilibrium, developed by Rawls for developing and justifying ethical theories (Rawls 1971). According to Rawls, ethical theories get validity by a process of balancing various considerations through reflection and argumentation. In this process, well-considered judgements are tested against more general notions and principles. Rawls' method not only applies to developing moral theories, but can also be used to solve moral problems. An example of this is the way in which a judge comes to a verdict by balancing relevant moral (and non-moral) considerations with legal principles and rules. For Rawls, reflective equilibrium is essentially a process of individual argumentation, starting from one's initial moral judgements and integrating them with more general principles and theories. This process can lead to revision or discarding of one or more of the initial moral judgements or the theoretical principles. The end result is a balanced whole of judgements and principles, or a state of reflective equilibrium. Rawls' model has been presented as a method for empirical ethics (Van Delden and Van Thiel 1998; Van Delden 2002). This adaptation of the model says that the ethicist can find well-considered judgements in practice (through empirical research), and then use them as input for the balancing process. The balancing itself, however, remains an act of the individual ethicist. The pragmatic hermeneutic approach takes one further step. It says that practice can not only serve as a source of well-considered judgements, but can also play a crucial role in the process of finding out which judgements are tenable. The argumentative process, which Rawls sees as the work of the ethicist, can be found in practice, where participants negotiate about the validity of their normative claims. The task of the ethicist is to stimulate the dialogue between practitioners, and ensure that a balanced solution is reached, by giving equal opportunity to all participants, and by securing critical examination of proposals in practice.

What then is the role of the ethicist in the pragmatic hermeneutic approach? The major activity of the ethicist is to stimulate the practical process of exchanging views, claims, and arguments. The ethicist helps the participants to formulate their views and claims, and to respond to those of others. The emphasis is on supporting the process of making explicit and exchanging experiences. Yet, in doing so, the ethicist herself becomes part of the process. In making claims explicit, the ethicist doesn't simply listen to what the parties say, she will also question claims in the light of her own knowledge of the situation and in anticipation of possible objections by other parties. The ethicist will also make links between concrete claims and theoretical views which might make the claim more general. The ethicist becomes part of the dialogue by trying to understand the perspectives of practitioners from her own experience, which integrates prior research and theories relevant for the practice under consideration. The position of the ethicist in the process is not different from that of other stakeholders, because the ethicist has experience, which implies practical knowledge, but also, because of its limitations, the need to be open to the experiences of others.

3.8. Conclusion

Empirical ethics combines social science and philosophy. From a pragmatic hermeneutic perspective, this combination is more than a juxtaposition of the two disciplines. It transcends the traditional division of labour between social science and philosophy. Social science should not only establish facts about views in society and social relationships, but should also further the development of these views and relationships by helping the participants to make explicit claims and negotiate about them in dialogue (Abma and Widdershoven 2005). The researcher is not dissociated, but actively involved in the social process of finding normative solutions to practical problems. Philosophy should not be confined to individual reflection and argumentation, but should find new and better solutions for practical problems in interaction with practitioners. The ethicist does not formulate rules for practice, but develops these rules together with participants in a practice. This implies an integration of empirical research and ethics (Van der Scheer and Widdershoven 2004).

From a pragmatic hermeneutic perspective, empirical ethics implies helping practitioners to formulate their experience and further it by dialogue with others. This is a process of finding truth, which requires method, but cannot be produced by method alone. It is based upon practical moral knowledge (*phronèsis*), and helps to develop it further. It combines empirical and normative elements, by supporting practitioners in making explicit claims and negotiating about them, in order to reach a common agreement about what should be done, and to develop shared guidelines for future action. The process of balancing views and merging perspectives ensures that the factual solutions have moral validity. This validity is general, in that it is based upon agreement of all parties concerned, and aims to guide all future action. Yet it is also concrete, in that it is related to a specific practice, and is in need of application to new practical problems.

References

Abma TA and Widdershoven GAM (2005). Sharing stories. Narrative and dialogue in responsive nursing evaluation. *Evaluation and the Health Professions*, **28**, 90-109.

Abma T, Widdershoven G and Lendemeijer B (eds.) (2005). *Dwang en drang in de psychiatrie. Kwaliteit van vrijheidsbeperkende interventies.* Lemma, Utrecht.

Beauchamp TL and Childress JF (1994). *Principles of biomedical ethics.* Oxford University Press, Oxford.

Berghmans R, Elfahmi D, Goldsteen M and Widdershoven G (2001). *Kwaliteit van dwang en drang in de psychiatrie. Eindrapport.* GGZ Nederland,Universiteit Maastricht, Utrecht/Maastricht.

Brody B (1993). Assessing empirical research in bioethics. *Theoretical Medicine,* **14**, 211–19.

Delden JJM van (2002). Moral intuitions as a source for empirical ethics. *Politeia,* **18**(67), 20–4.

Gadamer H-G (1960). *Wahrheit und methode.* J.C.B. Mohr, Tübingen.

Kuhn TS (1970). *The structure of scientific revolutions.* Chicago University Press, Chicago.

Leder D (1994). Toward a hermeneutical bioethics. In E Dubose, R Hamel and L O'Connell, eds. *A matter of principles?* Trinity Press International, Valley Forge.

Rawls J (1971). *A theory of justice.* Harvard University Press, Cambridge, MA.

Van Delden JJM Van and Van Thiel GJMW (1998). Reflective equilibrium as a normative empirical model in bioethics. In W van der Burg and T van Willigenburg, eds. *Reflective equilibrium* pp. 251–9. Kluwer.

Van der Scheer L (1999). *Ongeregelde moraal. Dewey's ervaringsbegrip als basis voor een nieuwe gezondheidsethiek.* Valkhof Pers, Nijmegen.

Van der Scheer L and Widdershoven G (2004). Integrated empirical ethics. Loss of normativity? *Medicine, Health Care and Philosophy,* **7**, 71-9.

Widdershoven G (2005). Interpretation and dialogue in hermeneutic ethics. In R Ashcroft, A Lucassen, M Parker, M Verkerk and G Widdershoven, eds. *Case analysis in clinical ethics,* pp. 57–76. University Press, Cambridge.

Chapter 4

The origin and emergence of empirical ethics

Pascal Borry, Paul Schotsmans, and Kris Dierickx

Research for this article has been made possible by a grant from the Fund for Scientific Research – Flanders (Belgium).

4.1. Introduction

Psychiatry is a medical sub-discipline with its own task (the care of mentally ill patients), its own practice, its own research questions, and its own ethical challenges. Psychiatric ethics covers different domains, from ethical questions concerning research into mental illnesses, to the professional ethics required in the fields of psychiatric practice and psychiatric care, and the range of moral problems arising in the mental health care setting and organization (Radden 2002). Psychiatric ethics, however, is not fundamentally different from medical ethics. It is in fact medical ethics, shaped and conditioned by the different purposes of psychiatric practice, research, and organization. By its grounding in medical ethics, psychiatric ethics has always been about how ethical principles such as autonomy, beneficence, and confidentiality can guide psychiatric practice and research. A philosophical and moral challenge, for example, has been to determine the extent to which psychiatric patients possess the capabilities necessary for being an autonomous agent or for being able to give informed consent. In addition to these philosophical issues, in the last two decades various topics in psychiatric ethics have been studied in an empirical way, for example informed consent in the context of mental illness (Stanley *et al.* 1987; Roberts 1998; Sugarman 1999).

In the field of medical and bioethics, the interest for, and the number of publications (Borry *et al.* 2006a) with an empirical design has recently increased. Renowned bioethicists (Callahan 1980; Thomasma 1985) made appeals for ethicists to work together with social scientists, being convinced that their research findings could improve ethical decision-making. These appeals did not fall on deaf ears; various authors in the past decade have indicated that a novel form of scholarship in bioethics (Brody 1990) or a 'new form of ethics paper', has appeared (Arnold and Forrow 1993) and that ethicists' interest in empirical data continues to grow (Molewijk 2004). By 'a new form of ethics paper' we mean literature that is categorized as sociological (Fox and De Vries 1998), empirical (Singer *et al.* 1990), or experimental (Thomasma 1985), but which also focuses on bioethical themes. This alternative bioethical literature has methodological roots in the social sciences and uses methods such as case studies, surveys, experiments, interviews, and participatory observation. The common objective is the gathering of qualitative and quantitative data about ethical issues. We consider the empirical field developed here to be an interdisciplinary one that benefits not only from the work of sociologists and social psychologists, but also from researchers in medicine and public health, epidemiologists, health economists, physicians, and ethicists.

In the first part of this chapter a number of hypotheses will be advanced as to why the relationship between ethics and the empirical sciences has improved. These hypotheses involve an analysis of how a theory-driven bioethics that did not sufficiently take practical reality into account has been criticized, how clinical ethics increased the awareness of empirical research in bioethics, and how the paradigm of evidence-based approaches is taken up in the vocabulary of bioethics.

The second part of this chapter will focus on three reasons which could explain why medical ethics and bioethics did not take the empirical sciences seriously or incorporate empirical data into their normative concepts and judgements. The three reasons are: dialogues between disciplines run the added risk of communication problems and opposing objectives; the social sciences have historically been absent partners since the genesis of medical ethics and bioethics as a discipline; and the meta-ethical distinction between 'is' and 'ought' has created a 'natural' border between ethics and the social sciences (Borry *et al.* 2005).

4.2. **The concept of empirical ethics**

The term 'empirical ethics' is not really new. Philosophers and ethicists had already used the term 'empirical ethics' from the 1930s through until the 1950s (Vivas 1939; Ritchie 1940; Feibleman 1955). Even though the concept of 'empirical ethics' in that period was not clearly defined, it is plain that the term was used against the background of the distinction between empirical and non-empirical philosophy (Schuster 1957), that has been made by Kant amongst others.[1] Kant referred to empirical philosophy as moral anthropology, practical anthropology, applied moral philosophy, and sometimes simply anthropology, but the important point is that it dealt with the empirical study of human nature rather than with pure (non-empirical) principles.

In the 1970s, psychiatrist Clarence Blomquist described the goal of empirical ethics as 'to look around and see how people actually solve ethical problems and make ethical decisions, how they learn ethical norms, and what arguments, if any, they use for or against ethical opinions' (Blomquist 1975). For her, empirical ethics should not study what people ought to do, but how they reason and act. She considered empirical ethics to be a non-normative perspective, focusing on the empirical study of moral practice and attitudes. Empirical medical ethics should not aim at the formulation of norms and recommendations for human conduct, but at the elaboration and realization of empirical studies.

The recent emergence of the concept of empirical ethics aims at enhancing the dialogue between ethics and empirical research. In this sense, empirical ethics is a broad category, grasping different interpretations of combining or trying to integrate ethics and empirical research. Although there are various ways of combining empirical research and ethical reflection (and of doing empirical ethics), they all have some basic assumptions in common: firstly, empirical ethics states that the study of people's actual moral beliefs, intuitions, behaviour and reasoning yields information that is meaningful for ethics and should be the starting point of ethics; secondly, empirical ethics acknowledges that the methodology of the social sciences (with quantitative and qualitative methods such as case studies, surveys, experiments, interviews, and participatory observation) is a way (and probably the best way) to map this reality; thirdly, empirical ethics states that the crucial distinction between descriptive and prescriptive aspects should be more flexible. Empirical ethics denies the structural incompatibility of empirical and normative approaches, and believes in their fundamental complementarity; fourthly, empirical ethics is a heuristic term which argues for an integration of empirical methodology or empirical research evidence in the process of ethical reflection. In its overarching meaning, empirical ethics is not a methodology for doing ethics, but a basic methodological attitude to use the findings from empirical research in

---

1 'All philosophy is either knowledge from pure reason, or knowledge obtained by reason from empirical principles. The first is called pure, the second empirical philosophy' (Kritik der reinen Vernunft (Critique of Pure Reason) A 840/B868). Louden (2000) calls this second form of knowledge empirical (or impure) ethics.

ethical reflection and decision-making; finally, empirical ethics cannot be considered to be an anti-theorist approach, in which the context and only the context would dictate what is morally good or evil, because then it would cease to be a rational reflection and it would cease to be ethics.

Is empirical ethics a new approach? On one hand it is arguably not because the concept is not completely new; empirical research on bioethical issues (Fox 1989) and combinations of ethical and empirical research (Edel 1955) has been around for many years. On the other hand, for the first time many more empirical studies focusing on bioethical issues are being published. This new empirical work is being done by researchers in medicine and public health, epidemiologists, health economists, physicians, and even ethicists in addition to sociologists or anthropologists. For the first time theologians, philosophers, health care scientists, social scientists, and medical scientists are being challenged in an interdisciplinary debate to clarify the value for ethical reflection that they attribute to empirical evidence.

4.3. **Why has empirical ethics emerged?**

In the second part of this chapter we will offer some explanations for why 'empirical ethics' as a normative approach has recently emerged. Three possible explanations will be discussed: firstly, dissatisfaction with current medical ethics led to stimulated attempts to incorporate empirical research; secondly, clinical ethicists became engaged in empirical research due to their strong integration in the medical setting; thirdly, the rise of the evidence-based paradigm had an influence on the practice of ethics.

4.3.1. **Context-sensitivity**

In spite of the interdisciplinary nature of bioethics and medical ethics, the field remained rather reluctant about collaborating with the social sciences. Medical ethics and bioethics were primarily philosophical enquiries (with the aim of logical reasoning, conceptual clarity, coherence, and rational justification). This philosophical stance has led to medical ethics being criticized for being too abstract, too general, too speculative, and too dogmatic, as well as far removed from clinical reality, insensitive to the peculiarities of specific situations, and unable to adequately consider the nature of diseases and the clinical contexts in which clinicians and patients were confronted with ethical problems (Ten Have and Lelie 1998). They explain why some voices in medical ethics and bioethics (Callahan 1980; Thomasma 1985) pleaded for stronger collaboration with the social sciences and for stronger involvement with the social, cultural, and cross-cultural aspects of morality; with the opinions, interests and beliefs of patients, families, physicians, nurses, and others involved in caregiving; and with national and international policy. In line with approaches such as hermeneutics, casuistry, narrative ethics, and care ethics, empirical ethics attempts to answer this plea by locating ethical reflection in a social and historical context, influenced by cultural values and enriched by personal narratives.

These criticisms originated from a concept of ethics, anchored in the fields of theology and philosophy and tailored to the methods, categories, and concepts used in these fields. Medical ethics developed normative ethical theories to determine which general moral norms should guide and evaluate moral conduct. Medical ethics developed as a field of application of applied ethics. Its methods consisted of applying theoretical principles to the practice of health care – 'first principles, then practice' (Ten Have and Lelie 1998). This was a translation of basic principles and rules into practice tools, thus making them available for everyday judgements and decisions. The concept of applied ethics was based on a top-down rationalistic and deductive model, and was used for all kinds of ethical problems (i.e. suicide, abortion, animal rights, nuclear arms, euthanasia, etc.). By applying ethical theories and principles, professional ethicists could proffer practical recommendations and prescriptions on ethical problems supplied mainly by non-ethicists (Ten Have 1994). In response to the critiques of the foundationalist approach in applied ethics, and as part of the attempt to operationalize its basic principles, the focus of bioethics drifted away from a purely theory-driven approach towards moral theory that is more grounded in practical reality. Dissatisfaction with the one-sided interpretation of applied ethics provided a strong argument for integrating social and cultural contexts with ethical clarification and decision-making. These trends stimulated the incorporation of empirical research in bioethics. Some authors presumed that the use of empirical research in ethics could help translate more general and abstract principles into concrete and specific action-driven directives and guidelines that are both morally justified and workable in practice (Birnbacher 1999). Attention to context can make ethics more feasible and practicable in particular cases (Musschenga 2003). Empirical studies could rectify bioethical short-sightedness and provide better, more workable solutions for moral dilemmas (Fox and De Vries 1998). The call for empirical research should make ethicists better able to take into account actual experiences, meanings, and moral decisions of caregivers and care-receivers in their ethical frameworks. The focus on empirical knowledge supports Hoffmaster's statement that moral decision-making has more to do with 'muddling through' problems than with rational problem-solving (Hoffmaster 1992).

4.3.2. **Clinical ethics**

The stimulus to increase empirical research on bioethical issues came not from psychologists, anthropologists, or sociologists, but from clinical ethicists in particular. In response to the previously described inadequacies of applied ethics, clinical ethics developed as a 'bedside' form of ethics that takes the reality of the clinician–patient encounter as its starting point. Clinical ethics evolved into a distinct field, with an emphasis on the ethical problems that arise in caring for patients and an aversion to the deductive model of ethical analysis. It focuses on elaborating a method of ethical evaluation that is particularly well-suited to individual clinical cases (Siegler 1978, 1982). Clinical ethics also finds methodological support in the renewal of interest in casuistry (Jonsen and Toulmin 1988; Jonsen 1991). Clinical ethics is mainly practised by clinicians (such as physicians, nurses, social workers, etc.), and differs in that respect from applied ethics, which is most often practised by non-clinicians. Due to their solid medical knowledge, those clinicians with knowledge of an ethical vocabulary and methodology are considered by many to function better in a clinical setting than non-clinicians, who often are regarded skeptically by clinicians. It is not surprising that clinical ethicists became engaged in empirical research to measure the frequency of ethical problems, the practical impact of ethical policies, and the way in which ethical decisions are made. In a taxonomy of clinical ethics research, Singer *et al.* (1990) distinguish, according to methodology, four types of empirical approaches to research in ethics: social sciences, decision analysis, clinical epidemiology, and health services research. In their desire to bring ethics closer to the realities of clinical practise, clinical ethicists have followed the path of ethnographic and sociological research. As an illustration we can refer to the multidisciplinary Empirical Ethics Group in the Department of Psychiatry at the New University of New Mexico in the United States, which was created in 1996 through the collaboration of Teddy D. Warner, Janet Brody, Brian Roberts, and Laura Roberts (Roberts *et al.* 2000, 2002, 2003). The Empirical Ethics Group holds the conviction that ethics inquiry 'entails both elegant theoretical work and inelegant everyday, experience-bound, practical work. It requires both richly informed conceptual analysis and real world empirical hypothesis-testing' (Roberts 2001). Their aim is not to disregard ethical theory but to build and enrich it through empirical enquiry. Their approach seeks to test the mettle of ideas and yet also give them substance and sustenance. They set as the ultimate goal of their work 'to enhance the life experiences and to improve the care of people who suffer from serious mental and physical illnesses'. Their team's research and educational efforts are, in essence, psychiatric clinical ethics and are informed by the team's shared expertise in clinical medicine, psychiatry, philosophical bioethics, psychology, public health, sociology, and social scientific methodology.

4.3.3. **Evidence-based approaches**

The emergence of evidence-based approaches in health care was typified by the systematic introduction of scientific proof in health-related interventions. This movement relies on the conviction that health care practises will improve by means of decision-making based on a careful appraisal of the best available evidence (Gray 1997). Evidence-based medicine (EBM) is a clinical method that aims to base medical decision-making for individual patients on 'the conscientious, explicit, and judicious use of current best evidence' (Sackett *et al.* 1996). According to EBM, medical decision-making must be based on 'the integration of best research evidence with clinical expertise and patient values' (Sackett *et al.* 2003). Through the systematic use of scientific evidence in clinical decision-making, practitioners of EBM hope to deliver better, more responsible care (Sackett *et al.* 1996). Those who defend EBM assert that patients do not always receive the best available care because of professional habits, ignorance, uncertainty, or financial motives. More diagnostic explorations and therapeutic interventions are executed and more drugs prescribed than is strictly necessary. According to EBM, health care could be adjusted and made more uniform by utilizing the latest scientific evidence. Since the movement's manifesto in 1992 (Evidence-Based Medicine Working Group 1992), EBM has gained more name, recognition and is now used in combinations such as evidence-based practice, nursing, public health, health care, decision–making, and even ethics. Jon Tyson (Tyson 1995; Major-Kincade *et al.* 2001; Tyson and Stoll 2003) coined the term evidence-based ethics in order to argue for the integration of evidence-based medicine in ethical decision-making. Tyson believes that evidence-based ethics – ethical decision-making based on the conscientious, explicit, and judicious use of current best medical evidence in making decisions about the care of individual patients – will promote better informed and better justified ethical decision-making. This method proceeds from two powerful assumptions. One is that ethical decision-making must necessarily be based on the use of the latest and best available medical research findings. The second assumption is that the use of these research findings will lead automatically to better ethical decision-making, because it will be better informed and better justified (Borry *et al.* 2005a). That our culture is imbued with the evidence-based doctrine emerges, amongst other ways, from the growing requirement to connect an empirical component to bioethical research in order to obtain research grants (Magnus 2002).

4.4. Why did 'empirical ethics' not rise earlier?

It still remains to explain why 'empirical ethics' is a relatively recent phenomenon and did not originate earlier. We suggest that there are three reasons for this. First, there is a pragmatic reason in that an interdisciplinary dialogue runs the risk of communication problems and divergent objectives. Second, there is a historical reason in that the social sciences were not involved in bioethics from its beginning. Third, there is a meta-ethical worry in that it was not obvious how to integrate empirical research into ethical reflection without committing the 'naturalistic fallacy'.

4.4.1. Pragmatic reason

Bioethics began as an interdisciplinary field with methodological and epistemological input from many different disciplines, including law, philosophy, theology, medicine, biology, and the social sciences. This interdisciplinarity supports the notion that input from different fields can expedite and improve the analysis and solution of particular problems. However, interdisciplinarity does not always guarantee better results and also has drawbacks (Birnbacher 1999). The biggest difficulty that interdisciplinarity carries, is the gap that can exist between the conversing disciplines. This gap can cause miscommunication which may involve, for example, speaking past one another, cognitive and conceptual dissonance, different cultures and styles, a lack of structural background and a lack of knowledge to judge or criticize the research results of another discipline. The interdisciplinary gap also can result in opposing objectives that limit the conversing disciplines in their interaction.

Normative ethics and most empirical approaches start from different research questions. While the first is interested in conceptual clarification and normative justification, the second is focused on empirical description, reconstruction, and analysis (Schmidt 1999). These divergent research questions make bioethics a prescriptive discipline whose task is moral evaluation, and empirical sciences a descriptive discipline that stresses the cultural setting (De Vries and Subedi 1998). The empirical sciences study bioethics for their own scientific agenda and are not necessarily interested in helping bioethics make better decisions. Most sociologists do not want to solve ethical problems or evaluate whether ethical problems are solved properly or improperly. They are interested in how ethical problems arise, how they are structured, and how they are managed. By contrast, bioethics aims at clarity and analysing the principles that should guide decision-making (Bosk 1999). If bioethics improves because of sociological input, this is mostly an 'unintended and unavoidable outcome': De Vries and Subedi speak in this context about a 'sociological version of the bioethical idea of double effect' (De Vries and Subedi 1998).

Therefore, it is not surprising that it has taken so long for empirical work to become integrated with bioethics.

4.4.2. Historical reasons

The domain of bioethics has developed into an autonomous research field over the last four decades. Medical ethics and bioethics evolved as a field after originally being grafted onto theology and philosophy: initially this left little room for the social sciences. The specific intellectual and cultural background that formed the substratum for the emergence of bioethics was dominated by the phantom of the atomic experience. After the atomic bombing of Hiroshima and Nagasaki, a tradition of ambivalence towards scientific progress was born: scientific research did not necessarily lead to a better world, but could lead to death and murder. Tina Stevens (2001) is correct in her interpretation that historians of medical ethics and bioethics tend to underestimate the formative nature of the post-atomic culture of the 1950s. However, the ambivalent stance towards techno-scientific advances would not lead to a dominant posture of antagonism towards medicine and science. It would instead place ethical reflection in the footsteps of the post-war 'responsible science movement', which called for greater thoughtfulness about the regulation of atomic power (Stevens 2001). Nevertheless, ethics in the field of medicine could only emerge thanks to a combination of this cultural background and some catalysing events of the 1960s and 1970s.

The first development was the exponential proliferation of technological innovations in biotechnology, molecular biochemistry, and pharmacology, which challenged traditional medical knowledge and practise. More precisely, medical innovations such as dialysis and kidney transplant, artificial respiration, resuscitation techniques, and prenatal diagnosis invited profound reflection (Gracia 2001). Second, the debates on equal access to health services and equitable distribution of limited economic resources also required ethical reflection. Third, social changes led to an emancipatory movement for the patient. Previously, decisions at the bedside were almost exclusively the concern of the individual physician; the authority of the physician and the traditional paternalistic relationship were now put under review. The physician encountered a new kind of patient, one who wanted to be heard and involved in medical decisions (Rothman 1991). Finally, the lack of a common interpretative framework of moral guidelines for daily action, which Jean-François Lyotard calls the 'post-modern condition' (Lyotard 1979), strengthened the importance of ethical reflection (Engelhardt 1986). The coexistence of opposing moral opinions and the presence of an intrinsically pluralistic moral context called for ethical reflection. These events explain why ethical reflection received increasing attention and why medical ethics and bioethics as a discipline could start, even if it has a tradition going back to Hippocrates. Initially, people from many different disciplines, such as medicine, law, theology, biological sciences, social sciences, philosophy, humanities, etc. entered the dialogue. However, in a process of professionalization and institutionalization, the ethical discussions quickly became anchored in the fields of theology and philosophy. How dominant the discipline of theology has been for ethics in terms of presence and levelling the ethical debates, yet how modest its influence in elaborating the conceptual framework of medical ethics! Mainstream medical ethics and bioethics evolved towards becoming a philosophical undertaking with the aim of finding solutions for moral problems in an impartial, unprejudiced, and non-culturally biased way. Ethical practice now involved a consideration of advantages and disadvantages in the search to justify one particular ethical option. The objective of this type of argumentation was not an absolute and definitive answer for moral problems, but rather a coherent and rational way of problem-solving. Mainstream medical ethics and bioethics focused on the application of ethical principles to concrete moral questions – mostly ethical dilemmas in terms of micro-relations (i.e. doctor–patient interaction) or macro-relations (i.e. allocation of resources) (Wolpe 2000). Other disciplines such as law, medicine, and biology latched onto the bioethical field. A number of medical sociologists and anthropologists also had an interest in the bioethical debates. Their presence, however, was minimal, and certainly not wished for by most ethicists. Sociological studies were depicted as irrelevant for medical ethics and bioethics because the ethicists feared being influenced too strongly by historical and sociological contextualization, which could bog them down in cultural and ethical relativism. The hegemony of the philosophical tradition in bioethics since the inception of the discipline has led to the present situation, in which the social sciences are considered epiphenomenonal and peripheral to dominant bioethical thought. A fundamental meta-ethical reason stands at the base of this fear.

4.4.3. **A meta-ethical reason**

The fundamental reason that bioethics keeps empirical approaches outside its borders has to do with the usually strict distinction between descriptive and normative ethics. Descriptive ethics is the field in which empirical data about moral issues are gathered. It is the domain 'par excellence' of sociology, anthropology, psychology, and epidemiology, and it aims at describing peoples' temporal values, rules, preferences, norms, and actions. These disciplines describe how reality is constructed – they describe what 'is'. However, they can never tell how people ought to behave, or what kinds of decisions are morally acceptable. According to most authors, this fundamental distinction stems from a small paragraph in David Hume's *Treatise of Human Nature* (1740), and is traditionally called the naturalistic fallacy. It is a logical mistake to infer a necessary conclusion from premises that are contingent in their modality, or to assign contingency to a conclusion that is inferred from premises that are necessary in their modality. The naturalistic fallacy consequently stresses that it is invalid reasoning to draw an ought-conclusion from premises that entirely consists of is-statements – one can never extrapolate an 'ought' from an 'is'. For this reason, ethicists became convinced that the results of social science research could never be useful for ethical reflection.

4.5. **Conclusion**

The relationship between empirical and normative approaches to bioethics has been an uneasy one, which has been depicted as 'contentious and adversarial' (Campbell 2003). Empirical approaches in bioethics were mostly unwelcome in the field due to interdisciplinary boundaries; the historical context in which bioethics emerged and the meta-ethical distinction between 'is' and 'ought'. Empirical ethics is a new trend in ethical research with the goal of bringing empirical and normative approaches closer to each other and of connecting the empirical with the normative. Empirical ethics is a heuristic concept that aims to increase the attention for empirical research in bioethics. It wants ethicists to participate in empirical research and/or to develop a sensibility to empirical research. As empirical research has been in the past in most cases for ethicists an issue *non grata*, empirical ethics has the merit of introducing the discussion about the relevance of empirical research to bioethics and of stressing that facts are more than facts alone and can induce normativity (Borry *et al.* 2004). As narrative ethics, care ethics, and virtue ethics plead for the value of narratives, care, and virtue, empirical ethics wants to stress the importance of empirical contributions in the field of bioethics. The recent emergence of the concept of empirical ethics is not a coincidence, but is linked to increasing attention for empirical contributions in bioethics, due to the request for more context-sensitivity, the development of clinical ethics and of evidence-based approaches.

The concept empirical ethics carries, however, a controversial connotation. While the concept in reality wants to look for ways to bridge the empirical and the normative, the concept in itself can lead to an interpretation in which the predicate (empirical) dictates the noun (ethics). In this interpretation ethics would only be a puppet on a string, controlled and moved as a consequence of empirical research findings. Ethics would lose all reflexivity and would cease to be ethics. Even if most of the researchers using the concept empirical ethics would deny that they are defending a position in which empirical research findings alone could dictate what ought to be done, empirical ethics carries the risk of a faulty interpretation of the concept. Some authors have used other terms to formulate the same idea. On the one hand authors used terms such as 'ethics-related empirical research' (Miller 2002), 'empirical methods in bioethics' (Ashcroft 2003) or 'empirical research to bioethics' (Bennett and Cribb 2003) when talking about empirical studies in the field of medical ethics and bioethics. On the other hand authors used descriptions such as 'the relevance of empirical research to bioethics' (Bennett and Cribb 2003), 'the contribution of empirical research to bioethics' (Haimes 2002), and 'the normative-empirical dialogue' (Singer 2000) when talking about the normative implications of empirical studies. Using this terminology would probably re-focus the discussion on the relation between empirical and normative approaches in bioethics, and less on the concept and definition of empirical ethics, which is subordinate to the first issue.

References

Arnold R and Forrow L (1993). Empirical research in medical ethics: an introduction. *Theoretical Medicine*, **14**, 195-6.

Ashcroft RE (2003). Constructing empirical bioethics: Foucauldian reflections on the empirical turn in bioethics research. *Health Care Analysis*, **11**(1), 3-13.

Bennett R and Cribb A (2003). The relevance of empirical research to bioethics: reviewing the debate. In M Häyry and T Takala, eds. *Scratching the surface of bioethics*, pp. 9-18. Rodopi, Amsterdam.

Birnbacher D (1999). Ethics and social science: which kind of co-operation. *Ethical Theory and Moral Practice*, **2**(4), 319-36.

Blomquist C (1975). The teaching of medical ethics in Sweden. *Journal of Medical Ethics*, **1**, 96-8.

Borry P, Schotsmans P and Dierickx K (2004). What is the contribution of empirical research in bioethics? An ethical analysis. *Medicine, Health Care, and Philosophy*, **7**(1), 41-53.

Borry P, Schotsmans P and Dierickx K (2005). The birth of the empirical turn in bioethics. *Bioethics*, **19**(1), 49-71.

Borry P, Schotsmans P and Dierickx K (2006a). Empirical research in bioethical journals. A quantitative analysis. *Journal of Medical Ethics*. **32**(4), 240–5.

Borry P, Schotsmans P and Dierickx K (2006b). Evidence-based medicine and its role in ethical decision-making. *Journal of Evaluation in Clinical Practice*. **12**(3), 306–11.

Bosk C (1999). Professional ethicist available: logical, secular, friendly. *Daedalus*, **128**(4), 47-68.

Brody BA (1990). Quality of scholarship in bioethics. *The Journal of Medicine and Philosophy*, **15**(2), 161-78.

Callahan D (1980). Shattuck lecture – contemporary biomedical ethics. *The New England Journal of Medicine*, **302**, 1228-32.

Campbell C (2003). Ethics in the twilight zone. *Hastings Cent. Rep.*, **33**(2), 44-6.

De Vries R and Subedi J (eds.) (1998). *Preface to bioethics and society. Constructing the ethical enterprise.* Prentice Hall, New Jersey.

Engelhardt HT Jr. (1986) *The foundation of bioethics.* Oxford University Press, New York.

Evidence-Based Medicine Working Group (1992). Evidence-based medicine. A new approach to teaching the practice of medicine. *Journal of American Medical Association*, **268**(17), 2420-5.

Feibleman JK (1955). Introduction to an objective, empirical ethics. *Ethics: An International Journal of Social, Political, and Legal Philosophy*, **65**, 102-15.

Fox RC and De Vries R (1998). Afterword: The sociology of bioethics. In R De Vries and J Subedi, eds. *Bioethics and society: constructing the ethical enterprise*, 1st edn., pp. 270-6. Prentice Hall, New Jersey.

Gracia D (2001). History of medical ethics. In H Ten Have and B Gordijn, eds. *Bioethics in a European perspective*, pp. 17-50. Kluwer Academic Publishers, Dordrecht.

Gray JAM (1997). *Evidence-based health care: how to make health policy and management decisions.* Churchill Livingstone, New York.

Haimes E (2002). What can the social sciences contribute to the study of ethics? Theoretical, empirical and substantive considerations. *Bioethics*, **16**(2), 89-113.

Hoffmaster B (1992). Can ethnography save the life of medical ethics? *Social Science and Medicine*, **35**(12), 1421-31.

Jonsen AR (1991). Casuistry as methodology in clinical ethics. *Theoretical Medicine*, **12**(4), 295-307.

Jonsen AR and Toulmin SE (1988). *The abuse of casuistry: a history of moral reasoning.* University of California Press, Berkeley.

Louden RB (2000). *Kant's impure ethics: from rational beings to human beings.* Oxford University Press, New York.

Lyotard J-F (1979). *La condition postmoderne: rapport sur le savoir.* Editions de Minuit, Paris.

Magnus D (2002). Careers in bioethics. *Penn Bioethics*, **10**(1), 6-7.

Major-Kincade TL, Tyson JE and Kennedy KA (2001).Training pediatric house staff in evidence-based ethics: an exploratory controlled trial. *Journal of Perinatology*, **21**(3), 161-6.

Miller FG (2002). Ethical significance of ethics-related empirical research. *Journal of National Cancer Institute*, **94**(24), 1821-22.

Molewijk AC (2004). Integrated empirical ethics: in search for clarifying identities, *Medicine, Health Care, and Philosophy*, **7**(1), 85-7.

Musschenga AW (2003). Empirical ethics: context-sensitivity or contextuality. In *International Conference, Ethics and Public Policy*, Utrecht, pp. 17-40. NWO, The Hague.

Radden J (2002). Psychiatric ethics. *Bioethics*, **16**(5), 397-411.

Ritchie BF (1940). A framework for an empirical ethics. *Philosophical Science*, **7**(4), 476-91.

Roberts LW (1998). The ethical basis of psychiatric research: conceptual issues and empirical findings. *Comprehensive Psychiatry*, **39**, 99-110.

Roberts LW (2001). Introducing the empirical ethics group. *Footsteps*, **1**, 1-13.

Roberts LW, Warner TD and Brody JL (2000). Perspectives of patients with schizophrenia and psychiatrists regarding ethically important aspects of research participation. *The American Journal of Psychiatry*, **157**(1), 67-74.

Roberts LW, Warner TD, Brody JL, Roberts B, Lauriello J and Lyketsos C (2002). Patient and psychiatrist ratings of hypothetical schizophrenia research protocols: assessments of harm potential and factors influencing participation decisions. *The American Journal of Psychiatry*, **159**(4), 573-84.

Roberts LW, Geppert C, Connor R, Nguyen, K and Warner TD (2003). An invitation for medical educators to focus on ethical and policy issues in research and scholarly practice. *Academy of Medicine*, **76**(9), 876-85.

Rothman DJ (1991). *Strangers at the bedside*. Basic Books, New York.

Sackett DL, Rosenberg WMC, Gray JAM, Haynes RB and Richardson WS (1996). Evidence based medicine: what it is and what it isn't. *BMJ*, **312**(7023), 71-2.

Sackett DL, Straus SE, Richardson WS, Rosenberg W and Haynes B (2003). *Evidence-based medicine: how to practice and teach EBM*. Churchill Livingstone, Edinburgh.

Schmidt V (1999). Introduction: across the disciplinary borders. *Ethical Theory and Moral Practice*, **2**(4), 315-8.

Schuster C (1957). C.I. Lewis and emotive theories of values, or, should, empirical ethics declare bankrupcy. *Journal of Philosophy*, **54**(7), 169-80.

Siegler M (1978). A legacy of Osler. Teaching clinical ethics at the bedside. *Journal of American Medical Association*, **239**, 951-9.

Siegler M (1982). Decision-making strategy for clinical-ethical problems in medicine. *Archives of Internal Medicine*, **142**(12), 2178-9.

Singer MS (2000). Ethical and fair work behaviour: a normative-empirical dialogue concerning ethics and justice. *Journal of Business Ethics*, **28**, 187-209.

Singer P, Pellegrino E and Siegler M (1990). Research in clinical ethics. *The Journal of Clinical Ethics*, **2**, 95-9.

Stanley B, Sieber JE and Melton GB (1987). Empirical studies of ethical issues in research. *American Psychologist*, **42**, 735-41.

Stevens MLT (2001). *Bioethics in America. Origins and cultural politics*. The Johns Hopkins University Press, Baltimore.

Sugarman J (1999). Empirical research on informed consent: an annotated bibliography. Hastings Centre Report No. 1.

Ten Have H (1994). The hyperreality of clinical ethics: a unitary theory and hermeneutics. *Theoretical Medicine*, **2**(15), 113-1.

Ten Have H and Lelie A (1998). Medical ethics research between theory and practice. *Theoretical Medicine and Bioethics*, **19**(3), 263-76.

Thomasma DC (1985). Empirical methodology in medical ethics. *Journal of the American Geriatrics Society*, **33**(5), 313-4.

Tyson J (1995). Evidence-based ethics and the care of premature infants. *Future Child*, **5**(1), 197-213.

Tyson JE and Stoll BJ (2003). Evidence-based ethics and the care and outcome of extremely premature infants. *Clinical Perinatology*, **30**(2), 363-87.

Vivas E (1939). Force in empirical ethics. Ethics: *An International Journal of Social, Political, and Legal Philosophy*, **49**, 85-92.

Wolpe PR (2000). From bedside to boardroom: sociological shifts and bioethics. *HEC Forum*, **12**(3), 191-201.

Chapter 5

Which empirical research, whose ethics? Articulating ideals in long-term mental health care

Jeannette Pols

5.1. Introduction

> I ask Lisa, a psychiatric nurse, if she notices any differences between before and after rehabilitation was introduced on the long-stay ward. She says she does. She says care used to be oriented towards managing the patients as a group. 'Now an individualised approach is central. Much more attention is given to the patients' self-organisation and their own responsibility'.

This fieldnote shows one of the most influential ideals in present long-term mental health care: the ideal of individualized care. Individualized care is regarded as a way of improving care and is contrasted with older forms of care that did not help patients to develop and be cared for according to their own preferences and possibilities. In this chapter I will study the ideal of individualization in order to demonstrate a specific form of empirical ethics: a theoretically informed ethnography of good care.[1] What characterizes this style of empirical ethics?

First, the object of research is 'good care'. However, what constitutes 'good' care is not defined beforehand, but is studied in an ethnographic way. The characteristics of good care in my study were explored by observing how nurses and patients in their daily life and work try to shape good care. I analysed everyday caring situations and discussed these with the participants. Key questions that emerged were: how can actual care-practices be perceived as 'good' practices, or as attempts to practise good care? What ideals of good care are thus at stake?

....

[1] Creswell (1998) describes ethnography as: 'a description and interpretation of a culture or social group or system. Ethnography involves prolonged observation of the group, typically through participant observation, in which the researcher is immersed in the day-to-day lives of the people or through one-on-one interviews with members of the group.'

Analysing the nature of good care was done in a specific way: instead of attending to culture or talk about good care, I specifically attended to 'practices' of good care. Good care was analysed as it was shaped in daily activities, events, and routines. Together, people and artefacts were observed as doing different forms of good care. This is called the performance or enactment of ideals (Mol 1998, 2002).

A result of such an analysis is that forms of good care are made explicit. Thus, ideals that are taken for granted can become topics for discussion, for instance by analysing what type of practices come into being by enacting specific ideals. I questioned whether a certain ideal is dominant, are other ideals pushed to one side as a result? And is this what we actually want? This is an important characteristic of this style of empirical ethics: it 'articulates' ideals and their related practices that were tacit, taken for granted, pushed away, or 'forgotten' (Haraway 1991, 1992). In this process, words are given to implicit ways of framing good care. As I will show later, the ideal that runs the risk of being pushed to one side by the dominant ideal of individualization is the ideal of patient sociability.

By articulating ideals that are embedded in care-practices, this style of empirical ethics aims not to describe practice and neither does it aim to judge it. It does aim to interfere in the practices studied by opening up implicit notions of good care for (self) reflection. Thus, this style of empirical ethics does not restrict itself to describing what others think is good, neither does it impose its own norms in the form of prescriptions. Harbers (2005) calls the resulting interference the 're-scription' of practice. It questions norms and ideals by articulating them as they are hidden in activities and routines to provide participants with fresh ways to look at their practice.

In order to present this style of empirical ethics I will not talk about it, but demonstrate it by analysing the enactments of the ideal of individualization.[2] Fieldwork for this study was done in four long-stay wards in two psychiatric hospitals, and five residential homes for the elderly that started housing patients who left the long-stay ward.[3] In the psychiatric hospitals, individualization inspired the development of a method of caring called rehabilitation,

[2] The idea that concepts get their meaning by the way they are used is developed by Wittgenstein (1953). Explicitly involving materiality and practice shows the influence of Foucault (1971).

[3] See Pols et al. (1998; 2001) for the original reports. In the psychiatric hospitals 40 days of participant observation took place, 19 members of staff were interviewed and 8 patients. In the residential homes, 60 days of participant observation took place, 14 residents and 39 members of staff were interviewed.

adapting it for the patients who did not make it out of the hospital. For the psychiatric nurses in the residential homes individualization of care is thought of as one of the benefits of this new care setting, as opposed to the long-stay wards of the psychiatric hospitals where they came from. I will discuss more backgrounds later, but will start by developing the concept of enactment. What does it mean to study enactments and how can the ideal of individualization be seen as enacted in daily care?

5.2. Enactments of individualization

Out of the different ways in which individualization is enacted, I will outline two ways. In the first way of 'doing individualization', the nurses help patients to develop their individual skills. In the second, the nurses create space for individual preferences.

For the first way to individualize care the nurses formulate the aim to make individual patients more independent from their caregivers by helping patients to develop their individual skills. The idea behind the individual skills training is that people lost skills in the hospital environment, because they never had to practise them. Thus, they became passive and hospitalized, and this process should be reversed.

> Psychiatric nurse: An extreme example is from another ward where I worked, also with long-term mentally ill elderly persons. For years and years sugar and milk was mixed with the coffee in the coffeepot by the nurses, and then served. And we said at a certain moment: 'We want these people to do this themselves again, and how can they learn this'. We put the coffeepot and the empty cups on the table: nothing happened. Nobody moved a finger, because it was always done for them. And, well, eventually they would pour the coffee, but the relations between sugar, milk, and coffee appeared to be far from clear. They would put in the milk, and when they wanted to pour the coffee, they saw that the cup was already full. [laughs]

By letting people practise these little routines themselves, the idea is that they will learn these skills again and keep them intact. Eventually, this may lead to patients becoming independent from their caregivers, even allowing them to move out of the hospital. But even if moving is not an option, practising individual skills makes the patients as independent as possible. Being able to do things for yourself allows a person to organize the day according to individual preferences. The nurses only take over tasks people are not able to do, but leave as much activity as possible to the patients.

Part of the attractiveness of individual skills training for the nurses is that psychiatric symptoms in themselves are not seen as disruptive for individual skills. Rehabilitation by training individual skills allows for individual progress, even when 'cure' is not an option.

So ideals are enacted in seemingly trivial routines such as making coffee. But there is another way of enacting individualization. Instead of becoming skilled, in this second way of enacting individualization more importance is attached to being enabled to live according to individual preferences. A way to give space to individual preferences is to flexibly organize breakfast, so that whoever wants to can sleep in. Sleeping rooms were kept open during day-time, enabling individual patients to use them as private rooms.

> Psychiatric nurse: Take Harold. He also has the right to withdraw to his room. But he smokes like a chimney, so we were worried he would set the sheets on fire. How to solve this problem? He now has loads of little boxes around, filled with sand so he can put out his ciggies. And we bought a fireproof bedspread, so he can lie on the bed and smoke without setting it alight. His door has to be locked in the night [because he wanders], but you try to make it as pleasant as possible for him. A nice little night-light, because he likes the light on, but the big white light is too bright. He is extremely fond of classical music, so he has loads of CD's and a player. We put pictures from his family album on the wall. We try to offer people a home, as far as possible.

The nurses try to find out what a person's interests and hobbies are and look for clues via family members if patients cannot put things forward themselves. Psychiatric symptoms are not seen as affecting the possibility of having individual preferences. Again, a vocabulary for rehabilitation and nursing is developed that does not depart from symptoms, but from positive possibilities. It allows the nurses to give 'good care', even though this type of caring does not lead to cure.

These two short outlines show a sensitivity to everyday activities, such as ways of organizing coffee, the decoration, layout and use of private rooms, and the material objects that are used to bring about good care. This shows a theoretical inspiration from Actor Network Studies of science, technology, and society (Latour 1987; Law 1994; Berg 1997; Hendriks 1998; Willems 1998, 2001; Moser 2000; Winance 2001, 2002). The practical matters can be connected to activities of the nurses, and to their stories about what they are doing. By relating these elements, nurses and patients can be seen to enact, or as trying to enact good care in their daily activities.

But something else is enacted too. With the help of these practical arrangements, specific forms of subjectivity for the patients are enacted. For the skills training, it is important that patients are active and do things to become independent, or as independent as possible. Whether they want to learn skills is of less relevance. Deciding what one wants comes after the skills training. When individual preferences are at stake, however, deciding or wishing comes first. It is deemed important for the patients to decide things for themselves, or recognize themselves in objects and arrangements around them. It is not important to be active, but to find one's individuality reflected in the ways one's life is organized.

Thus, the nurses and patients enact two types of subject positions, one in which independence is a central concern and another in which identity is a keyword. The role of the nurses differs likewise. Instead of assisting the doctors with treating patients, the nurses become trainers of skilled individuals, or rather facilitators of individuals living their personally preferred lives.

This analysis of individualization as it is enacted can make visible that an ideal may inspire different practices, even if the overall ideal is said to be the same. Attending to activities and practicalities makes it possible to articulate different forms of *tacit ethics* that travel by the same name, and the different ways of enacting patients as subjects in good care.

5.3. **Conflicting ideals**

One ideal may inspire different practices of enacting this ideal. These matters become urgent when an ideal encounters other ideals that are in conflict with it. How can such a conflict be analysed? Again, the ideal of individualization is the example. Here, the conflicting and marginalized ideal turns out to be the ideal of sociability amongst patients.

> Geriatric assistant: Yes, taking care of people was always the first thing here, with a lot of attention for the residents. To play on the needs they have. It wasn't a therapeutic happening here, really. That is still a strong motivation in this team [of geriatric assistants]: life has to be enjoyable [gezellig]. Not forgetting their freedom, of course. But you look at what people want. The afternoons with a video, or to get everyone together for a drink are always a success. Sometimes it is extra special. With a bite to eat, and then 'all together'. And then people really start telling stories. Yes, this 'being together', this feeling that has always been most appealing.

Specifically in care for the elderly, so-called 'group care' (groepsopvang) was thought to bring pleasure as well as a healing and safe environment for people suffering from dementia or other psychiatric problems. Geriatric assistants still put forward this ideal for positive patient sociability. However, psychiatric nurses who are new professionals in the residential homes argue for individualization and contest the ideal of patient sociability as unprofessional and 'group oriented' (Atkinson 1998). Individualization and patient sociability seem to be in conflict with one another: but in what ways exactly? To answer this question I will look again at the enactments of individualization described earlier.

Take the skills training: that the training of individual skills leads to conflicts with notions of sociability can be demonstrated by the practice of learning to make coffee. In the residential home everybody has their own coffeemaker in their private apartments. The idea is that if everybody learns to make coffee, nobody is dependent on staff to get it.

> Elsa [geriatric assistant] talks about the little refrigerators the residents have in their apartment: nobody uses them! That's a mere electricity bill, she complains. She says the same counts for the individual coffeemakers. Nobody uses them, the residents come out to the common room for coffee. But Jolene [psychiatric nurse] is hopeful: when new people arrive [who are not hospitalised] this will work out better, and people can make coffee when they feel like it.

Being able to make coffee in your own apartment allows for individualization of coffee-routines. Making coffee is thus seen as an individual skill that is needed to organize one's life in ways one prefers. Not using this skill is perceived as an effect of hospitalization and a lack of ability to use individual opportunities.

However, on another residential home ward residents do make coffee. They do not do this in their private apartments, but in the common room.

> Kim has put the cups on the table, together with the milk and the sugar. She has also made the coffee. She does not seem to be very stable on her feet. But she manages, even though it takes her about half an hour to organise the morning coffee.

On this ward, Kim usually organizes the morning coffee. Other residents take turns in preparing the afternoon tea and coffee. Making coffee is not seen as an individual skill to be practised, but as a means to bring about the social event of having coffee together. People who like making coffee over other little domestic duties, take up the work.

When making coffee is approached as an individual skill and activity, the individual and the social can be in conflict. Individual activities are valued as meaningful, whereas social activities are perceived as marking an established routine and lack of individual abilities, and therefore choice. The problem to be solved was defined as 'depending on staff', but the value of social events was not even considered: 'old routines, this will change when new patients arrive'. That having coffee together might be an activity residents actually enjoy, is made invisible by a perspective on individual skills; following preferences comes after the training of skills, otherwise there can be no choice.

There is another way that skills training is in tension with patient sociability. When individual skills are stressed, everybody has to practise them. For each patient, the highest possible level of independence and activity is aimed for. Because individual activity is important, helping each other can be valued negatively.

> Meeting to inform residents about changes in care on the ward. The co-ordinator talks about sharing responsibilities for the domestic work. Mrs Crow is asked to stop setting the tables for the meals, as she always does. Mrs Crow does not understand this: shouldn't the tables be set? And wasn't that what she was doing? The co-ordinator explains that others may want to do this as well, and that this would be good for them,

if only to get some exercise for the hands. Mrs Crow looks puzzled. Mr Blanche inter-feres. He says people can do sports if they want to exercise. He points to the two oldest women on the ward, 102 and 97 years old. "Look at these old ladies," he says, "Should they do the work? Isn't this an economic thing, that we have to work because the house cuts down on staff?"

Neither Mrs Crow nor Mr Blanche connects setting the table with individual skills or responsibility. They rather see links between work and setting tables. Setting the table is a necessity, and has to be done before one is able to have a meal. Who does it is of minor importance, as long as the person volunteers and is not too old to work. For developing individual skills, however, it does indeed matter who is active, because everybody should be trained to keep fit, to become active and independent. It is a difference in ideals and pragmatics between patients and staff. Individualizing care by developing individual skills is in ten-sion with more instrumental visions and social values the patients hold dear.

In this analysis, seemingly prosaic activities such as making coffee or doing domestic work are described. What makes these activities of ethical interest is that the ways of practising these daily routines, the ideals that inspire them and the subjects enacted, are in conflict. In the situation described, the patients put forward alternative, competing forms of subjectivity. Instead of enacting themselves as skilled individuals, they put forward social and prag-matic forms of subjectivity. These alternative forms of subjectivity point to different ideals of good care, such as taking care of older persons by doing work for them, or helping others. These ideals are hard to interpret for nurses who practise individual skills training. The different practises incorporate dif-ferent ideals of what is a good life and what is good care. Articulating these brings these tensions to the fore.

5.4. **Subjects as results**

Analysing good care as conflicting ideals and practises has implications for the analysis of who or what the 'ethical subject' is. Who can be the 'ethical sub-ject' in practical situations?[4] To demonstrate this, I will use an example of a conflict between giving space to individual preferences and patient sociability. The example here is the puzzling wish of patients not to leave the hospital when chances are provided to move to a better situation.

----

4 Note the difference between the 'ethical subject', who is a person that is ascribed responsi-bility for what is good, and the actor, which is active in producing a form of good care. The ethical subject is not necessarily active, and the actor can also be non-human, such as the coffee makers. One can be an ethical subject without being an actor and vice versa.

Interviewer: And the patients, did they want to move from the psychiatric hospital to
the residential home?
Psychiatric nurse: No, they didn't. A survey was done to ask them, and none of
them wanted to go. No, really, one wanted to go, because this village has a Hema [pop-
ular discount warehouse]. But the people who did the survey were against the move.
And now nobody wants to go back.

The nurses were happy they could suggest the move to a residential home. The
residential homes provide private apartments in a non-stigmatizing living
environment, service for the elderly, and are located nearer to community
services, family and friends. The patients, however, made it clear they did not
want to move. This opinion is not limited to the patients referred to in the
interview. During the years of research in psychiatric hospitals and residential
homes, I have heard many patients expressing their attachment to even the
most worn out buildings on partly abandoned hospital terrains. One 60-year-old
patient who did make the move from the hospital to a modern building on the
other side of the street, positioned his chair in front of the window, so he
could sit and stare at the old hospital building where he had spent his days
since his 18th birthday.

The refusal of patients to move and their attachment to the hospital baffled
well-meaning reformers in mental health care, and is not always taken seriously. The patients seem to refuse an obvious improvement of their situation.
Their reluctance to move is, again, interpreted as a sign of hospitalization,
a lack of ideas, or fears for what opportunities await them elsewhere.
Hospitalization here is not so much the effect of 'not being able' or missing the
skills to act differently, but of not making an individual decision to act differently. Staying in the hospital is not seen as the consequence of individual
choice and is not different from the old situation. After their move they will
see this, and be happy they have left the hospital.

An analysis of practises in which notions of good care are embedded can,
however, articulate how the patients value the hospital environment, or are
attached to their routines or to one another. The patients can be seen to
organize their routines together and stick to them. If patients would leave the
hospital individually, they would probably lose more contacts than they would
ever be able to re-establish. Thus, the patients can be seen as putting forward
an ideal of sociability in their activities. In this explanation, the refusal to
move can be interpreted in a way that takes the patients seriously and does not
describe them as irrational or as unable to make decisions that are in their best
interest. The explanation of hospitalization runs the risk of dismissing social
preferences too quickly, because social values are not considered and are
explained away as unfree, because they are not individual, and are not choices
because they are not different compared to what people are used to.

In these examples, the shaping of the ethical subject, or person pursuing what is good, differs according to the situation one observes. To be a subject who decides for him/herself in his/her best interest, proposes a different form of subjectivity from the one in which social interests are valued. In this analysis, the characteristics of the ethical subject are not defined beforehand but are analysed as the outcome of ways in which ideals are put to practice. It is not questioned that people pursue what is good in their practices, but the specific forms this goodness takes, and hence the characteristics the ethical subject has, are analysed as the result of these practices rather than preceding them. In this way, this form of empirical ethics does not put forward a substantial (e.g. Kantian) ethical theory that grounds ethics in human faculties such as reason or on principles such as justice or autonomy. It rather analyses what an ethical subject is as the result of the different ways of ethically framing situations in practice (Gallagher *et al.* 1998). In our example, enhancing autonomy appears not to work as such when people do not perceive themselves as autonomous individuals. Ironically, this contradicts the aim to which individualization was put forward in the first place: to make the patients heard and emancipate them. The different forms of subjectivity and their related notions of good care are analysed as effects rather than intentions, thus allowing for a critical appreciation of the desirability of these effects.

5.5. History of ideals: connecting heterogeneous elements

So far, I have shown that this way of analysing good care looks for relations between ideals, activities, practical events, and things. Different ideals are enacted in different repertoires of activities, incorporating different ideals of good care. Who or what the ethical subject is, is analysed as the outcome of these specific practices and ideals, rather than preceding them, and the same person may take different subject-positions in different situations.

Now I want to turn to the question what makes care 'good care' for the persons practising it? What is this 'good' and what is it made of? Why do participants think one form of good care is better than another? Again I take the ideals of individualization and patient sociability as examples. I will look more closely at the historical and practical context in which individualization became popular. To what problem is individualization supposed to be the solution? What was changed and what remained the same? The analysis serves to draw out that what is thought of as 'good' does not only relate to ethical questions, but also to historical developments, ways in which hospitals are built and ways in which the problems of patients are defined.

5.5.1. **Counter-position of individualization**

The nurses in my study articulated a clear counter-position of individualization: the 'hospital regime' or 'group regime'. In the images of the old hospital regimes invoked in the interviews, patients lived under strict and general rules that organized the day for them. The institution dictated at what time everybody should get out of bed, when breakfast ended, and therapies started. Showering was group-wise on fixed days and was supervised by the nurses. In this horrific institution there was no privacy. Sleeping rooms were shared and closed to the patients during the day.

Individualization of care was a solution to what came to be called the 'regime of the group', but with the regime, patient sociability also came under attack. The hospital in itself became suspicious; nobody had chosen to live there, nobody chose the persons they were forced to live with, or the number of persons to live with.

> I have been a psychiatric nurse for fifteen years now. And in the early days the approach was much more directive and it was more common to force patients to do things. I have worked on a ward where everybody had to be up at eight and, as a good nurse, you took care that this happened. And now you would discuss it with individual patients. "What do you want to do with your day? You do not want to get up at eight, but you do want to be at vocational therapy at nine. It is impossible to do both. How can we solve this, do you have a suggestion how you can get yourself out of bed? Or do you want to go to therapy later?" This way you discuss things, while the standard used to be: therapy starts at nine, so we make sure everyone is there.

Instead of subordinating the individual to the institution, caregivers now help the patients to develop their individually preferred routines. Working from this individual approach, patients are stimulated to find a better place to live, outside the hospital, outside of large groups. And if institutional care is the only alternative, care can be organized in ways that leave the patients as much individual space as possible.

So the nurses present individualization as the answer to a grim situation in urgent need of an alternative. 'Everything has to change', were the revolutionary terms used. Psychiatric nurses were supposed to 'turn 180 degrees' in order to change 'thinking for the patients' into 'thinking with each individual patient'. But with this image of the group regime, the other patients are perceived as irrelevant to or hindering the individual. This is an unintended consequence of the ideal of individualization. How could this link be made?

A first explanation for why this led to patient sociability being negatively valued can be found in the image of the group regime. Instead of the group regime being a way of thinking about social relations between patients, in the way the nurses describe it, it appears to be a way of not thinking about the social. How patients should relate to large numbers of other patients was not relevant for the regimes, but merely provoked questions for the nurses of how to maintain order, reducing relations between patients to the orderly coexistence of 'inmates'. Their being together on the ward was not considered to be in any way beneficial or of therapeutic value, or even pleasurable, but was a practical way of organizing medical treatment. Both in the hospital regime and in notions of individualization, the value of patient sociability is discredited. Historically speaking, this negative evaluation of patient sociability stems from a situation where sociability was not valued in the first place.

5.5.2. **Supporting positions for individualization**

The counter-position of the group regime pointed out the forced living together of patients as a major problem. On the other hand, thinking in terms of individuals appears to be not so new. The nurses and doctors were already used to thinking about individual cases, in terms of patients with individual diagnoses and treatment. This form of individualization came, historically speaking, before the skills and preferences and was directed towards 'cure' (Boschma 2003), hence, treatment in hospitals came into being. [5] Nursing care and medical reasoning share the common value of improvement of individual patients. The aim of dismissing patients from the hospital is shared in both rationalities, either in the form of functioning better by developing individual competence or wishes, or by the treatment of symptoms. So if individualization was presented as a revolutionary turn against hospital regimes, it is certainly not a revolution from medical, and thus, individualized ways of thinking and acting.

So with the framing of a counter-position, a specific solution is favoured over another. At the same time, there were elements established in practice that supported some ways of thinking (in terms of individuals and individual progress) over others. So instead of the change from forced sociability to individualization, the analysis shows this process can be better understood as an elaboration and strengthening of notions of individuality that were already there. The 'revolution' (almost) did away with ideals of patient sociability in psychiatric nursing, but the history shows continuity concerning assumed revolutionary notions of individualization. And while neither way of reasoning incorporates positive ideals of patient sociability, when they are combined patient sociability becomes hard to imagine at all.

What I want to draw out with these examples is that what is good care is not only connected to questions or principles that we can intuitively label as

---

[5] Before these reforms in the 1920s patients were primarily perceived and taken care of as mad, but most of all *poor* people. See De Goei (2001).

'ethical'. The framing of the hospital regime links the way hospitals are built and organized (good at one time, bad in later times), routines of the nurses and perceptions of what is the matter. The diagnosis or description of the old situation provides important clues for framing the right 'treatment'.

On the other hand, the underlying rationality for organizing hospital care on large wards, a medical rationality, was (and is) not perceived as problematic.[6] That this medical rationality incorporates notions of individuality provides fertile grounds for the new ideals in care. However, individual treatment is not perceived as an ethical notion, but as a way of framing good psychiatric knowledge and treatment. 'Knowing patients' in a medical way, however, brings with it specific forms of good care, i.e. improving individuals and repairing functioning by treatment. This connects perfectly well with the new solutions in nursing care. So the practically interpreted and historically evolved definitions of good care, can be seen to link specific ways of knowing the object of care, and acting accordingly. This ethnographic analysis of good care articulates the relations between facts, values, routines, activities, and buildings. How good care is defined cannot be separated from practical matters or ways of defining what is the problem. Rather, their interrelations show that different repertoires of doing good are also different repertoires of knowing psychiatry, and of building and arranging hospitals (Harbers *et al.* 2002). Good care is made by connecting heterogeneous elements and should be studied accordingly. Articulating how the ideal of patient sociability in the historical and conceptual development of ideals of individualization is almost accidentally marginalized, opens up possibilities for a rehabilitation of this ideal.

5.6. **Coexistence of conflicting ideals**

This empirical ethical analysis studies what is 'good care' as the complex relations of diverse and heterogeneous elements. Because of their interdependencies, revolutionary turns in care are not taken at their advocates' word, but can be seen to incorporate change as well as continuity. These (dis)continuities may or may not be transparent to the participants. But how can ideals in care be in conflict, and still be practised together? Discerning different repertoires or embedded theories of good care does not mean that nurses and others

---

[6] Rehabilitation is often perceived as *complementary* to treatment, not an alternative to it (Anthony *et al.* 1990). Recently, this separation is challenged. The active client movement in mental health care develops a vocabulary of 'recovery' (see Deegan 1993; Boevink *et al.* 2002).

always consistently act according to one of these repertoires. There are overlaps and shared values, as with the medical and other individualization repertoires. And it is also possible to change repertoires from the inside. This happened for instance when the geriatric assistants incorporated skills training in their care practise for the reason that 'this makes the patients feel better' (instead of doing this to improve individual functioning) (Pols 2000). And the ideal of patient sociability has a hard time, but it can still be traced. So if an ideal is still there, how can it be practised next to caring repertoires that seem to be in conflict with them?

Let's look again at the ideal of patient sociability. In some places even psychiatric nurses perceive a lack of possibilities for positive interactions as a problem. A first example is a ward where the meals were delivered on individual trays. The trays were put on the tables where everyone gathered to eat. Sure, you can choose what to eat and you can start with the dessert, have the soup as a main dish and skip the potatoes altogether. But these individual variations were consumed in silence. The team reorganized the meal by serving it in dishes.

> We have an eating-project here. People do not get individual meals on trays, but have to dish up the food, because the meal is served in dishes for each table. And what you see happen is that contacts between the residents develop, also in between meals. Because, well, you have to pass a person a dish, or ask for the salt. And they clear up the table together. And you can see that, apart from the meals, they get along more with each other. The thing is: now people notice each other, and become interested in their environment. They suddenly see that the neighbour wears a nice dress. And they never noticed that before, let alone that they would say something about it. But it happens here.

The new material infrastructure allowed for interactions that cheered up the meal. This enabled a more meaningful way of having a meal together and influenced social contacts on the ward. In this scenario, the others are not only thought of as restrictive to the individual, but can become of value too.

Another example is a ward where the residents did the housekeeping together. To organize domestic work, the nurses made a schedule, so everybody could read who is on for what task. Instead of this being a new institutional regime and restriction of individual freedom many individual variations could be spotted. One man chose to organize all his duties one after the other for 2 weeks and after that he had a week off. Three women did specific tasks they appreciated; one makes the coffee, the other lays the table and the third clears away the dishes from the dishwasher. Others traded their jobs amongst each other for cigarettes or money. The conflicting ideals seem to be reconciled. Or are they?

Psychiatric nurse: It [the group regime] is hard to influence. But the other side is that you notice that the dynamics of the group is what keeps it together. Then you can think: I want to go around that for the sake of the individual, but this stirs up so much in the group that I should maybe leave it alone. They can really fight, swear at each other, but after ten minutes they can arrange things together again 'Ok, fight's over, we have to go on'. That is really amazing and really valuable.

This nurses' positive labelling of living in groups is still contrasted with 'the sake of the individual'. But it is there and the nurse accepts it as a different, alternative 'good', even though this will not mean she gives up on her own ideals of individualizing care. So this analysis shows that care is made up from different, sometimes conflicting repertoires and ideals of good care. Revolutions do not seem to make ideals disappear, but insert new (or re-insert not so new) ideals in practice. These ideals are interpreted in relation to embedded notions of good care that already exist in practice. The older ideals do not – or not completely – disappear, but can still be put to practice, even if they do not match.

In this case, the residents educated the nurse. They were not a sad and passive hospitalized group, but found a way of living together that allowed for conflicts and cooperation. Part of the reason why they could is that they have lived together for a long time. They have learned how to develop a supporting sociability. And this may be a good thing. The loneliness and depressions of people living amongst others in care institutes are well documented. The problem of the group regimes and hospitalization practises could be that it is hard to live amongst others with whom one shares nothing but their mere presence.

Thus a diverse array of coexisting ethics in practise can be articulated.[7] It can be explored how ideals of good care take shape within daily practice, with nurses and patients as 'practising ethicists', people who orient their practise to and incorporate different notions of doing good in their activities. These notions of doing good are formed, as I argued above, by connecting heterogeneous elements, such as knowing what is the matter, organizing daily practice and objects that are used. Therefore, empirical research and ethics go together in this ethnography of good care. Ethics, morality and ideals do not (only) come from the outside, but are abundant inside everyday care-practice, in activities, objects, and concepts that intend to bring about good care. Articulating these forms of everyday morality, questions their self-evidence.

---

[7] For different ways in which conflicting realities can exist together see: Mol (2002), Boltanski and Thévenot (1991), Law (1994), and Pols (2003).

5.7. **Conclusions: interventions**

To what kind of contributions might this style of doing empirical ethics lead? What kind of ethical interventions can it make? In opposition to a position where empirical research and ethics are kept separate and the ethicist adds the ethical reflection to the empirical study, this ethnography of good care creates a different relation to the field. Instead of judging care-practices, by classifying acts as good or bad, or providing guidelines and rules practice should adhere to, ethics and morality that are enacted in daily care-practice, implicit or explicit, are articulated. Thus, not only big ethical issues, such as euthanasia or involuntary treatment can be reflected upon, but also day-to-day dilemma's can be articulated as effects of specific ways of framing good care.

I see the articulation of these different and complex ways in which good care gets its shape as the first intervention of this style of doing empirical ethics. Articulating different practices of good care makes it possible to reflect upon their differences. To realize that there is not just one form of good care but that there are different, conflicting forms that each have good and bad effects by enacting different kinds of subjects and embedded theories, invites participants to critical (self-) reflection.

The second intervention takes the form of a proposal. Showing the alternative workings of the ideal of patient sociability next to its marginalization by ideals of individualization is also a suggestion for the rehabilitation of this ideal. This ethical intervention does not take the form of a prescription or rule formulated by the ethicist who is outside of practise ('You must attend to patient sociability'). It is a suggestion by demonstration of possibilities of this ideal. Participants in the field may be moved or seduced to work with its positive potentials, and become cautious considering the workings and the blind spots of individualization ideals.

In this way the ethnographer of good care does not merely describe how others do good, but neither does she/he 'know best' and present external guidelines for practice, other than insisting on stimulating reflexivity in practice.[8] This style of empirical ethics speaks to professionals and patients as striving for the good in their practice. What these goods are may be contested, but they are there and they are taken seriously.

Finally, I think this type of empirical ethics also speaks to ethics as an academic discipline. It points to the workings of ideals, not only to their theoretical

---

[8] Practically, this self-reflexivity can be organized on different levels, as team-meetings, meetings between different professions, patients and family-members, over different organizations and so on. See for instance Delnoij and Van Dalen (2003) and Manschot and Van Dartel (2003).

characteristics. By studying ideals of good care ethnographically, it can be articulated what types of psychiatric practises and ethical subjects they bring into being. These effects are hard to predict by theorizing, as they are the result of the interaction and connections of ideals, specific types of knowledge, routines, problems to be solved, characteristics of, and positions taken by participants. The effects of ideals can only be learned by studying these interactions in practice.

Bibliography

Anthony W, Cohen M and Farkas M (1990). *Psychiatric rehabilitation*, Boston University Press, Boston.

Atkinson D (1998). Living in residential care. In A Brechin, J Walmsley, J Katz and S Pace, eds. *Care matters: concepts, practice and research in health and social care*, pp. 13-26. Sage Publications, London.

Berg M (1997). *Rationalizing medical work*. MIT Press, Cambridge, MA.

Boevink W, Van Beuzekom J, Gaal E *et al*. (2002). *Samen werken aan herstel: van ervaringen delen naar kennis overdragen* ('Working together for recovery: from swapping experiences towards sharing knowledge'). Trimbos-instituut, Utrecht.

Boltanski L and Thévenot L (1991). *Des justifications: les économies de la grandeur* ('On justification: economies of grandeur'). Editions Gallimard, Paris.

Boschma G (2003). *The rise of mental health nursing: a history of psychiatric care in Dutch asylums. 1890–1920*. Amsterdam University Press, Amsterdam.

Creswell JW (1998). *Qualitative inquiry and research design: choosing among five traditions*. Sage Publications, London.

Deegan PE (1993). Recovering our sense of value after being labeled 'mentally ill'. *Journal of Psychosocial Nursing*, **31**, 7-11.

De Goei L (2001). *De psychohygiënisten. Psychiatrie, cultuurkritiek en de beweging voor geestelijke volksgezondheid in Nederland, 1924-1970*. (Psychohygienists. Psychiatry, culture critique and the movement for mental health care in the Netherlands, 1924-1970). Sun, Nijmegen.

Delnoij J and Van Dalen W (2003). *Het socratisch gesprek* ('The Socratic conversation'). Uitgeverij Damon, Budel.

Foucault M (1971). *L'ordre du discourse*. Gallimard, Paris.

Gallagher EB, Schlomann P, Sloan RS *et al*. (1998). To enrich bioethics, add one part social to one part clinical. In R De Vries and J Subedi, eds. *Bioethics and society: constructing the ethical enterprise*. Prentice Hall, Upper Saddle River, NJ.

Haraway DH (1991). Situated knowledges. The science question in feminism and the privilege of partial perspective. In H Haraway, ed. *Simians, cyborgs and women: the re-invention of nature*, pp. 183-201. Routledge, New York.

Haraway DH (1992). The promises of monsters. A regenerative politics for inappropriate/d others. In L Grossberg, C Nelson and PA Treichler, eds. *Cultural studies*, pp. 295-337. Routledge, New York.

Harbers H (2005). Introduction. In H Harbers, ed. *Inside the politics ofTechnology. Agency and normativity in the co-production of technology and society*. Amsterdam University Press, Amsterdam.

Harbers H, Mol A and Stollmeyer A (2002). Food matters; Arguments for an ethnography of daily care. *Theory, Culture & Society*, **19**, 207-26.

Hendriks R (1998). Egg timers, human values and the care of autistic youths. *Science, Technology and Human Values*, **23**, 399-424.

Latour B (1987). *Science in action: how to follow scientists and engineers through society*. Harvard University Press, Cambridge, MA.

Law J (1994). *Organising modernity*. Blackwell Publishers, Oxford.

Manschot H and Van Dartel H, eds. (2003). In gesprek over goede zorg. Overlegmethoden voor ethiek in de praktijk. Boom, Amsterdam.

Mol A (1998). Missing links, making links. The performance of some Atheroscleroses. In M Berg and A Mol, eds. *Differences in medicine: unraveling practices, techniques and bodies*, pp. 144-65.. Duke University Press, Durham, London.

Mol A (2002). *The body multiple. An ontology of medical practice*. Duke University Press, Durham.

Moser I (2000). Against normalisation: subverting norms of ability and disability. *Science as Culture*, **9**, 201-40.

Pols AJ (2000). *Drie manieren om het goede te doen: ouderenpsychiatrie in het verzorgingshui*. ('Three ways of doing good: psychiatry for the elderly in residential homes'). In J Graste and D Bauduin, eds. *Waardenvol werk: ethiek in de geestelijke gezondheidszorg*, pp 212-29. Van Gorcum, Assen.

Pols J (2003). Enforcing patient rights or improving care? The interference of two modes of doing good in mental health care. *Sociology of Health and Illness*, **25**, 320-47.

Pols AJ, Depla M and De Lange J (1998). *Gewoon oud en chronisch: mogelijkheden en beperkingen in de zorg voor ouderen met een psychiatrische achtergrond in het verzorgingshuis*. ('Simply old and chronic: opportunities and restrictions in care for elderly with a psychiatric background in residential homes). Trimbos-instituut, Utrecht.

Pols AJ, Michon H, Depla M and Kroon H (2001). *Rehabilitatie als praktijk. Een etnografisch onderzoek in twee psychiatrische ziekenhuizen*. [Rehabilitation as practice. An ethnography in two mental hospitals.] Trimbos-instituut, Utrecht.

Tronto J (1993). *Moral boundaries: a political argument for an ethic of care*. Routledge, New York.

Willems D (1998). Inhaling drugs and making worlds: the proliferation of lungs and asthmas. In A Mol and M Berg eds. *Differences in medicine: unravelling practices, techniques and bodies*, pp. 105-18. Duke University Press, Durham, NC.

Willems D (2001). Dokters en patiënten in kleine medische technologie. ('Doctors and patients in small medical technology'). In A Mol and M Berg, eds. *Ingebouwde normen: edische technieken doorgelicht* ('Norms incorporated: medical techniques scrutinized'), pp. 61-70. Van der Wees uitgeverij, Utrecht.

Winance M (2001). *Thèse et prothèse: le processus d'habilitation comme fabrication de la personne*. L'Association Française contre les myopathies face au handicap, Department of Socio-Economie de l'Innovation, ENSMP, CSI., Paris.

Winance M (2002). The making of the person through the process of 'habilitation'. The French muscular dystrophy association against disabilities. Paper presented at the conference of the European Association for the Study of Science and Technology, York.

Wittgenstein L (1953). *Philosophical investigations/ Philosophische Untersuchungen*. Blackwell Publishers, Oxford.

Chapter 6

Models of mental disorder: how philosophy and the social sciences can illuminate psychiatric ethics

Anthony Colombo

6.1. Introduction

The principle aim of this chapter is to discuss the development and implications for psychiatric ethics of a new empirical research initiative that combines linguistic analytic philosophy and social science methodologies.

More specifically, this chapter demonstrates how a particular empirical study, designed to evaluate the influence of implicit models of mental disorder on shared decision-making within community-based multi-disciplinary teams, used philosophic and social scientific ideas in order to: clarify the distinction between explicit and implicit models and their role in conceptualizing the definitional problem of mental disorder; develop an intuitively powerful models-grid heuristic in order to represent an 'ideal type' formation of the territory covered by the term mental disorder; design an empirical approach which recognizes and values the contribution of all participants by generating a 'level playing field' between patients and practitioners; elucidate the range of implicit model patterns used by the study's multi-agency groups in order to define the high-level concept 'mental disorder'; and facilitate the transition of research into practice by using the empirical data on models in order to draw out some ethical implications of current approaches to shared decision-making. Each of these issues will be critically considered throughout this paper with strong emphasis placed on discussing the research findings and their potential implications for psychiatric ethics.

6.2. Rationale

It is now well established that the most efficient and effective way to organize and deliver mental health services is through multi-disciplinary teams (MDTs)

(Colombo 1997; Department of Health 1999a; Colombo *et al.* 2003). An equally significant development centres on the need to appreciate the autonomy of patients and informal carers, and the distinctive contribution these groups can make to the decision-making process within MDTs (Becker and Silburn 1999; Bracken and Thomas 1999).

However, despite both political and professional acknowledgement of the importance of these requirements, official enquiry findings and research evidence continue to show that shared clinical decision-making between different practitioners within MDTs, and between practitioners, patients, and informal carers remains generally poor (Department of Health 1999b; Dunn 1999) and, on occasion, so inadequate as to seriously compromise public safety and the welfare of patients (Clunis Report 1994; Rogers and Pilgrim 1996).

Several factors may help explain problems of communication during multidisciplinary encounters: limited resources, professional rivalry, lack of training, personality differences, and excessive bureaucracy (Sainsbury Centre for Mental Health 1998). Though another proposition, which has been drawn out from practice-based anecdotal evidence together with theoretical and empirical work in analytic philosophy and the social sciences (Fulford 1995; Colombo 1997), suggests that people with different backgrounds and experiences hold very different models of mental disorder.

To elaborate on this point: Unlike physical medicine, where it is assumed (due to the presence of physical signs that can be scientifically validated) that doctors understand something about physical illness/disorder, psychiatrists do not know what they mean explicitly by mental illness/disorder (which are frequently diagnosed through value-based as well as evidence-based criteria about a person's mental state). According to Wittgenstein (1958) this is because the conceptualizations we use in order to structure and make sense of the world are generally organized hierarchically. For example, 'chair', as a low-level concept is easier to define than 'furniture', which in turn is easier to define than 'functional object' (Fulford *et al.*, forthcoming, Chapter 5). Thus, Wittgenstein (1958) argues that attempts to define high-level concepts such as 'mental disorder' (which empirically are not well delineated) produce what amount to 'delusions of language'. The delusion centres on the fact that when we try to define high-level concepts we tend to implicitly latch on to one facet of what is really a very complex set of meanings and then accept that part for the whole, generating a limited and distorted interpretation (Austin 1956/57 p. 23). Conversely, this distortion has resulted on the one hand in mutually competing claims about the power of medical, psychological, social, or political models to explain mental disorder and on the other practitioner's explicit support for a broad catch-all, yet vague, definition increasingly referred to as the 'biopsychosocial' model. This clearly suggests that the meanings of high-level concepts are to a greater or lesser extent hidden as a result of a divide between explicit definitions and implicit use. Moreover, it is this explicit/implicit divide that is crucial to the linguistic analytic claim that the meanings attributed to high-level concepts are implicit in, and so can be revealed through a greater understanding of, the way they are used in everyday practice.

If this linguistic analytical insight is correct, then it can be argued that an understanding of how such concepts are used during the course of responding to and dealing with mental disorders is likely to present a clearer guide to meaning than explicit definitions or textbook responses. Furthermore, on the basis of this premise, and research findings from empirical work carried out on social learning theory (Bandura 1986) it can also be argued that we learn the meaning of concepts, partly by being handed down explicit definitions, but largely through shared use within a social/situational context (Wittgenstein 1958). Different professional groups, patients, and carers, therefore, through their training and lived experiences, have different developmental histories. Hence, we should expect that they would hold different implicit models of mental disorder.

At this point we are in a position to refine our earlier proposition to state that: failures of collaborative community mental health care may be due, in part, to unrecognized differences between different agencies, patients, and informal carers in terms of their respective implicit models of mental disorder, which when used in clinical practice, may play an important role within the decision-making process through generating conflicting assumptions and misunderstandings between multi-agency groups. To paraphrase Austin (1956/57): It is only when things go wrong and we run into difficulties concerning the use of a high-level concept that we are prompted to break through the 'blinding veil' and address issues around the true complexity of meaning.

Moreover, the use of these implicit models of mental disorder during the course of making clinical decisions are likely to have significant ethical implications for the treatment, management, and care of patients. For example, to rely solely on a medical model interpretation of mental disorder will result in the patient being given a label such as 'schizophrenia' which can have a significant impact on that person's self-identity and how others perceive him/her (Goffman 1961, 1963). The medically based treatment offered to patients may result in side-effects and if the patient refuses treatment this raises civil rights issues as to whether or not it should be compulsorily administered.

From this observation – that concept use is meaning – Austin believed that rather than simply searching introspectively for meaning, or seeking explicit definitions, we should go out into the field and observe the ways in which concepts are actually used in practice; we should become engaged in philosophical fieldwork.

The empirical 'models of mental disorder' study discussed in this chapter is an attempt to take up Austin's idea of philosophical field work through forging a natural partnership between the methodological strengths of the social sciences, which are able to supply techniques for empirical observation with known or measurable psychometric properties, and the conceptual clarity provided by linguistic analysis, which can help shape and define the content and empirical design of the study. Precisely how this partnership between linguistic analytic philosophy and the social sciences operates in order to bring about the methodological and empirical structure of this research project on models of mental disorder is discussed in the following section of this chapter.

6.3. Methods

6.3.1. Developing the models-grid

In order to empirically test the proposition 'that there exists a difference between practitioners, patients and informal carers in terms of their implicit models of mental disorder', we needed to develop an empirical research design which operationalized each group's implicit use of models.

As a starting point, we again referred back to the work of Wittgenstein and his point about delusions of definition: that we are drawn towards a small aspect of conceptual meaning and accept that particular facet as explicitly defining the whole, thus generating a series of incomplete and detached approaches to the problem of mental disorder. However, instead of treating the diverse range of definitions explicitly presented in the literature as mutually exclusive fragments of information, they were interpreted more constructively for the purposes of the study so that each fragmented approach could be understood as illustrating different parts of a complex whole.

Thus, an important early step in the partnership between linguistic analysis and empirical research involved carrying out a meta-analysis of attempts to define the high-level concept 'mental disorder'. The purpose being to identify, characterize, and aggregate the diversity of meaning about mental disorder.

From reviews of the theoretical literature (Siegler and Osmond 1966; Colombo 1997; Fulford 1998; Colombo et al. 2003), six explicit or formal models of mental disorder may be systematically identified – the medical (organic), social (stresses), cognitive-behavioural, psychotherapeutic, family interactions, and conspiratorial (see Table 6.1, Row 1) – each of which may be classified and meaningfully differentiated from one another on the basis of 12 key dimensions (see Table 6.1, Column 2). These dimensions internally define for each particular model: What is the nature of mental disorder (diagnosis/definition, interpretation of behaviour, labels, aetiology)? What should be done about it (treatment, function of psychiatric hospital, facilities in community, prognosis)? And how should the people involved – society, practitioners, patients, and informal carers – behave towards each other (rights/duties of the patient and rights/duties of society)? A summary definition of these 12 dimensions across the six models of mental disorder is presented in the component-cells of Table 6.1. The overall structure of Table 6.1 is referred to as a models-grid and the information presented within the component-cells of the grid can be understood as representing an 'ideal type' formation (Giddens 1975): a taxonomy of the explicit theoretical content of a phenomenon – in this case mental disorder – which, although present in reality is rarely, if ever, found in this form.

The social scientific notion of constructing 'ideal types' is also particularly significant within the current context because they provide the foundations of an empirical research design that will make it possible to carry out 'philosophical fieldwork' on the implicit use of models of mental disorder. According to the sociologist Max Weber the primary purpose of constructing an 'ideal type' is to help 'social scientists attempt to delineate, through empirical examination, the most important respects in relation to the concerns he has set himself' (Giddens 1975).

Thus, in the current study, the concern was to obtain empirical data that would make it possible to delineate implicit models of mental disorder. As a prerequisite, an 'ideal type' of the phenomenon 'mental disorder' was established, through a conceptual meta-analysis of previous literature, and the explicit theoretical content of the review organized/presented within a models-grid. Ultimately, this explicit information was used to operationalize the study's empirical design and facilitate the analysis of research findings by providing a baseline against which implicit professional, patient, and informal carer perspectives may be identified and compared.

6.3.2. Designing the measuring instrument

Employing the information contained in the models-grid as a baseline against which to evaluate the implicit use of models of mental disorder across a range of multi-agency groups is fraught with a range of philosophical and empirical difficulties. Firstly, if implicit use rather than explicit definition is a more

Table 6.1 Summary definitions of the nature of the six key models of mental disorder

Questions addressed	Models/elements	Medical (organic)	Social (stresses)	Cognitive-behavioural	Psychotherapeutic	Family interactions	Conspiratorial
What is the nature of mental disorder?	Diagnosis/definition	Physical health – illness continuum	Health/low stress – illness/high - stress continuum	Normal–abnormal continuum	Continuum of emotional distress/difficulties	Whole family is sick, not just patient	Mental illness is a myth. A continuum of deviance?
	Interpretation of behaviour	Symptoms of illness are a rough guide to severity	Symptoms may indicate degrees of stress	Taken at face value, seen as acceptable-not-acceptable	Decode/interpret symbolically to give it meaning	Look at behaviour of all family members	Result of way person is expected to behave by others
	Labels	Based on a patient's collection of symptoms	Person is seen as a victim of social social forces and not as ill	Not important. Should focus on actual problem behaviour	Discussions about labels hide the individual	Externalize an illness which is inherent in the family itself	Create the mental mental illness Cause stigma, etc.
	Aetiology	Physiochemical changes in the brain. Genetic factors	Social and economic stress, cultural conflict, marginal status, etc	Inappropriate . learning, poor coping skills, etc.	Unusual/traumatic early experience	Patient acts in response to family pressures	Mental illness is not something that is socially defined
What should be done about it	Treatment	Medical and surgucal procedures, drugs, etc.	Social change change to reduce stress stress	Increase patient's patient's rresponsibility for own behaviour	Long-term one-to-one therapy	Family therapy/help therapy/help and support	None. Aim to empower people

Function of psychiatric hospital	To facilitate the care, treatment and cure of	A place of respite for those unable to cope	To provide training, OT CBT [n7]	To maximize contact with psychotherapist	Not important. important Whole family needs help	Controls those at risk to themselves or others
Facilities in community	Work towards developing a seamless services between hospital and community care	To provide flexible/short-stay homes for respite/time out	To provide day hospitals offering training/therapy	To provide short-stay homes that provide therapy/counselling	Family training and support centres	Not relevant to the description this model
Prognosis	Many symptoms can be controlled	Good if changes made at the social level	Partly depends on severity of learning problems problems	Depends on level of ego strength. Therapy may be long term	Good if services available for carers	Not relevant. Nothing considered to be be wrong
How should the people involved behave towards each other — Rights of the patient	To the sick role, given sympathy, not blamed for problem, etc.	To receive help and support as a victim of a stressful society	To leave hospital when behaviour acceptable	To be spared moral judgment for what is said or done	To expect whole family to see themselves as needing support	To privacy, personal freedom, a; same civil rights as anyone
Duties of the patient	To cooperate and take medication. Learn medical definition of problem	To cooperate with any social help offered	To take some responsibility for learning to cope with their problems	To cooperate with therapist; understand their interpretation of problem	Whole family has aduty to participate in therapy process	To recognize their social obligations outside being deviant/ill

Table 6.1 (continued) Summary definitions of the nature of the six key models of mental disorder

Questions addressed	Models/ elements	Medical (organic)	Social (stresses)	Cognitive-behavioural	Psychotherapeutic	Family interactions	Conspiratorial
	Rights of society	To restrain those who are at risk of harming themselves or others	Limited rights, rights, society should be proactive in preventing stress	To restrain/ sanction those who break social rules	Not used in this description of this model	To help when when families becomes dysfunctional	No right to politically define acceptable behaviour
	Duties of society	To empathize and provide proper medical facilities for care	To acknowledge the problem and change so as to reduce social stress	To provide places for their training and therapy	To build therapeutic partnerships with people to listen and respect their views as individuals	To provide facilities for dysfunctional families. To give carers more direct support	To respect the rights of individuals and to tolerate difference

important guide to meaning, then how can anyone presuppose that the variance covered by the explicit theories in our models-grid will correlate (or even associate) with the way individuals think/respond at an implicit level? To put this point another way, why should the models implicit in practice bear any relation to those described in the literature? Secondly, given the nature of the explicit/implicit divide, how can we be sure that directly asking people (professionals, patients, or informal carers) about mental disorders will do any more than elicit their explicit views as currently defined by the politically correct expectation that everyone should 'sign up' to the so-called 'biopsychosocial' model? Thirdly, social reaction research within the social sciences has demonstrated that people's preconceptions about terms/referents such as 'mental disorder', 'mental illness', 'insanity', etc. are value-laden (Wolffe *et al.* 1996) and although this is a problem inherent within the subject matter itself (Bean 1985), the very fact that people hold different beliefs and attitudes towards such labels will make it impossible to identify common implicit model patterns across groups. For example, the term mental disorder does not constitute a common experimental stimulus as it is not similarly defined by everyone involved in the study. In fact, the term may encourage subjects to think of a range of different qualifying behaviours from anxiety to xenophobia making it impossible to compare implicit views across different groups; the implicit models held for schizophrenia are unlikely to be the same for depression and so on. Finally, a growing volume of research within medical sociology has recognized the existence of differential power relationships operating during clinical encounters between various practitioner groups, and between practitioners and patients (Lupton 1994) which may distort the responses given by research participants and so make it difficult to 'capture' the real usage of language as it is employed by distinctive multi-agency groups.

In order to satisfy the potential difficulties raised by the first point stated above a measuring instrument organized around a series of 12 open-ended questions was developed which respondents answered after reading a case vignette describing a person (Tom) who may be experiencing mental health difficulties.

Each question related to one of the 12 dimensions (diagnosis/definition, interpretation of behaviour, labels, aetiology, treatment, etc.) used to differentiate the six models (see Table 6.1, Column 2). For example, the open-ended question concerning the dimension 'aetiology' was: what do you think caused Tom to behave like this? Ultimately, the subject's response could have been related to any of the six explicit models presented in the model-grid or it could have referred to aetiological issues outside the scope of this pre-defined framework. For example, one respondent, a patient, felt that Tom had become a 'born-again Christian … had found religion' and that this had caused him to 'have strong thoughts about his experiences', suggesting some form of spiritual model.

Thus, as the open-ended questions acknowledge that the list of explicit material contained within the models-grid may not be an exhaustive representation of all possible models, or dimensions within each model, the empirical measure avoids the complication of making prejudgements about the importance (if any) of each model and is more likely to yield results which reflect the patterns of the models implicitly used in practice. Furthermore, in order to circumvent the claim that the results are likely to be more artefact than real, and to ensure that we obtained informal/implicit opinions, our respondents were kept naïve as to the existence of different models until after the research was complete. Moreover, the respondents' open-ended qualitative responses were only thematically related to the particular descriptors of the formal/explicit model dimensions presented in Table 6.1 following a series of extensive coding and independent recoding procedures, which produced a strong Kappa Index coefficient of 0.81 (Cramer 1998) demonstrating a high level of stability/reliability within our coding process.

6.3.3. Using a case vignette as a research stimuli

The second and third potential difficulties – that respondents may simply proffer an explicitly populist 'catch all' view of mental disorder and that the use of value-laden terms such as 'mental disorder' as research referents are unlikely to provide a stable enough baseline across respondents for comparative purposes – raised a number of methodological obstacles.

Asking superficial/market research type questions – such as what do you think causes mental disorder? – is only ever likely to produce surface-level responses. The interviewee will be aware of the sensitive nature of the subject and so their response is likely to be sufficiently neutral in order not to upset these sensibilities. To overcome this, we needed to develop a research design which would encourage the respondent to actively engage with the process, to feel concerned about what they were being asked, to believe that their professional or life experiences mattered – in short, we needed to make the research experience seem as real as possible. To do this, we developed a descriptive vignette which contained summary case notes about a person named Tom (see Appendix A). Respondents were then asked questions, with a view to eliciting their true opinions about Tom. Case vignettes generate a more realistic context (Colombo 1997; Hall *et al.* 1993) by presenting the illusion that the interviewee was faced with an actual person who was experiencing real difficulties and who needed their help. As one psychiatrist put it: 'This Tom could be any one of a number of my patients'. After reading the vignette an informal carer said: '... this could be my daughter', and a service user responded by stating: 'Some of this stuff... well, it's like looking in a bloody mirror' (Pat1: 05).

Employing a case vignette as the stimuli within the research design also helped overcome the methodological difficulty associated with the use of non-specific and stigmatizing referents such as 'mental disorder' or 'a person with schizophrenia' (the third point). More specifically, the description of Tom avoided the use of prejudicial labels such as schizophrenia and mental illness and was designed so that respondents may proffer a view beyond the notion that Tom is experiencing problems with his mental health. For example, the first question asked of respondents was: Do you think that there is anything wrong with Tom? Furthermore, by ensuring that everyone received the same case vignette we could be more confident that a baseline stimulus was in place, which in turn would empirically justify attempts to compare responses across different multi-agency groups.

6.3.4. Recruitment of participants: developing a level playing field

The final methodological difficulty stated above refers to the fact that, given the nature of the power differences operating between multi-agency groups, it would not be possible to 'capture' the real usage of language as employed by certain groups, especially patients.

However, the aim of philosophical fieldwork is to obtain a fully representative set of data on language use across the study's multi-agency groups. To achieve this, those involved should as far as possible be free to speak for themselves, reflecting their own implicit models rather than directly or indirectly reflecting the models of others.

Our sampling design, therefore, sought to develop a level playing field amongst the respondents. This was attained by: Firstly, ensuring that the research sample included representatives from the key agencies – psychiatrists, social workers, community psychiatric nurses, patients with long-term schizophrenia, and informal carers – involved within community-based MDTs. The final sample included 100 respondents, with 20 subjects representing each of the five key participant groups operating within MDTs in an East Midland's catchment area.

Secondly, establishing a Research Advisory Network comprising of representatives from each group involved in the study and ensuring that they were consulted at all stages in the design and development of the study. This proved to be a fruitful strategy: feedback on initial drafts of the case vignette and semi-structured interviews led to significant changes which more accurately reflected the concerns of all participants.

And, thirdly, by recruiting participants from each multi-agency group directly through their own constituent organizations rather than through the hierarchical structure of a particular MDT. This method ensured that all those involved in the research had a greater chance of participating without feeling influenced by other team members. For example, if patients were accessed via their consultant psychiatrists, the subordinate nature of the relationship between these two groups may prejudice the results.

Overall, the sampling design strategy of developing a 'level playing field' amongst the respondents appears to have encouraged a sense of 'ownership' in the research amongst the participants through enabling them to engage in a project which seems 'real' and meaningful to them.

6.4. Results

6.4.1. Data coding using the models-grid

The models-grid is a convenient and intuitively powerful way of structuring and presenting the empirical data on implicit models of mental disorder.

Once the participants had read the case vignette and responded to the 12 open-ended questions, each of which respectively related to the 12 dimensions (diagnosis, behaviour, labels, aetiology, etc.) used to differentiate the six models, the data was coded.

Responses were coded in terms of their agreement with the model definitions given in Table 6.1. Because participants were asked to focus their responses on dealing with the particular problems faced by a single case, 'Tom', most made statements committing themselves to a single model, as may be seen in the following response: 'Well to this type of problem there is strong evidence of a genetic contribution and Tom's family history... seems to support this. So in this case, Tom probably has schizophrenia, which has a genetic basis' (Psych-12). This response was coded as agreeing (+) with the medical model theme for aetiology (see Table 6.1).

Some participants' responses, however, were more general, referring to several models. For example, two models were clearly identifiable in the following response: 'There are likely to be several factors really. One of which must be some sort of genetic vulnerability which was somehow triggered, possibly by cognitive factors such as Tom's developmental delay' (Psych-10). This response was coded as agreeing with a medical model ('must be some sort of genetic vulnerability') and a cognitive-behavioural model ('possibly cognitive factors such as Tom's developmental delay'). On occasion, respondents explicitly disagreed with a model; in such cases the response is identified with a minus sign (-). Up to three model themes could be identified and coded. The questions were also tested to ensure that they produced reliable and valid data (Colombo *et al.* 2003).

In order to gain a clearer understanding of shared decision-making in practice, the research team developed a second research instrument based on the Critical Incident Technique (CIT) (Flanagan 1983). This qualitative measure involved asking each subject to recall two critical incidents involving inter-agency co-operation: one which worked successfully, and another which was less successful. The questions used were open-ended and encouraged participants to specify as precisely as possible: (*a*) the multi-agency groups they had most difficulty/success working with, (*b*) the type of incident in which these difficult/successful relationships were likely to become apparent, and (*c*) their views on what factors contributed to the failure or otherwise of multi-agency working within the context of each of these particular incidents. Data from this assessment were used to help interpret the implications of model differences, particularly in terms of how such differences might contribute to our understanding of power relations within clinical encounters and, in turn, processes of inter-agency cooperation.

6.4.2. Six models of mental disorder

6.4.2.1. Table 6.2: summary of each multi-agency group's overall percentage support for each of the six models of mental disorder

Table 6.2 provides an overview of each multi-agency group's implicit level of support for each of the six models of mental disorder. The differences between practitioner groups are apparent: psychiatrists and community nurses clearly favour the medical approach (91.25% and 60.83%, respectively) while social workers show strong implicit support for the social model (47.5%). Disparity within the patient group is also highlighted with patients(1) supporting a medical definition of their situation (57.53%) while those within the patients(2) group rejected this model (6.41%) in preference for a more psychotherapeutic interpretation of their problems (46.79%). Separation of the patient sample into two different groups was established on the basis of results obtained from a series of chi-square tests, which were carried out on the frequency of responses in order to check for consistency of implicit support for model patterns within each multi-agency group. However despite these differences, each patient group's percentage agreement scores suggest some degree of implicit unity across a range of perspectives. In the case of informal carers, support is shown for the medical and family models (39.17% and 24.17%,

Table 6.2 Summary of each multi-agency group's overall percentage support for each of the six models of mental disorder

Models CMHT Group	Medical	Social	Cognitive- behavioural	Psycho- therapeutic	Family	Conspiratorial
Psychiatrists	91.3	7.9	11.8	5.4	6.3	17.1
Social workers	8.8	47.5	7.5	36.7	1.3	21.6
Community nurses	60.8	25.1	13.3	19.6	0.0	20.4
Patients(1)	57.6	29.8	8.3	26.2	0.0	26.2
Patients(2)	6.4	41.0	7.7	46.8	0.0	27.6
Informal carers	39.2	18.8	22.1	7.1	24.2	18.8
Mean % support for model	44.0	28.4	11.8	23.6	5.3	22.0

Notes: Percentage calculation = groups overall support for each model/total possible support for each model ×100

respectively), though judging from the spread of scores within this group, subjects appear less committed to any particular approach.

Across all multi-agency groups, most overall support is given to the medical view (40.47%) while few subjects made reference to either the cognitive-behavioural or family models (8.64 and 4.58, respectively). The results, however, may have been different if a case vignette describing the symptoms of a mental disorder other than schizophrenia were used. Further research will be able to verify this point. A more detailed picture of the implicit model patterns supported by each sample population, as defined across each model dimension, is presented elsewhere (Colombo *et al.* 2003). For the purposes of this chapter only the models-grid for psychiatrists, approved social workers, and patients are presented. The qualitative responses underlying the numeric values displayed in the component-cells of these tables are comparable with the cell content explicitly defined in Table 6.1 presented earlier.

6.4.2.2. Tables 6.3, 6.4, 6.5, and 6.6 on psychiatrists, social workers, and patients

6.4.2.2.1. Psychiatrists

The results in Table 6.3 show that psychiatrists support all 12 elements of the medical model. Their qualitative responses maintain the view that Tom's

Table 6.3 Models-grid showing the number of psychiatrists supporting each of the six key models of mental disorder across 12 dimensions

Models elements	Medical	Social	Cognitive-behavioural	Psychotherapeutic	Family	Conspiratorial
Diagnosis	20					
Behaviour	20		8			
Labels	20			9		10
Aetiology	20	3	9		8	
Treatment	20		4	1	2	
Hospitals	20	12				16
Community	18					
Prognosis	20		1			
Patient rights	17					15
Society rights	15	4	2			
Patient duties	15		4			
Society duties	14			3	5	

behaviour '... is presenting the key signs and symptoms of schizophrenia or perhaps a psychotic episode' (Psych, 10). That this mental illness has an underlying '... biological, probably a genetic predisposition' (Psych, 02) which is more likely to have been precipitated by cognitive-behavioural factors such as Tom's developmental delay than specific social events. Their argument being that: 'Tom's money difficulties and problems with his business are just as likely to result from, as be the cause of, his schizophrenia' (Psych, 11). The stigma associated with mental illness labels was implicitly acknowledged as well as the psychotherapeutic principle to treat Tom as an individual.

Medication, administered '... and monitored at least initially within hospital' (Psych, 09) was viewed as essential to a good prognosis. They also saw the relationship between hospital and community as part of a '... continuing process of care – a seamless service' (Psych, 16).

Psychiatrists recognized that Tom has civil rights and believed that he should be entitled to empathy, understanding, and care under the 'sick' role. They also implicitly agreed that Tom has a duty to learn about the medical definition of his problems.

6.4.2.2.2. **Approved Social Workers (ASWs)** Table 6.4 shows that approved social workers implicitly supported 9 of the 12 elements within the social

Table 6.4 Models-grid showing the number of approved social workers supporting each of the six key models of mental disorder across 12 dimensions

Models elements	Medical	Social	Cognitive-behavioural	Psychothera peutic	Family	Conspiratorial
Diagnosis				12		
Behaviour		8		15		
Labels		10		14		13
Aetiology	4	15	8	13		
Treatment	5	10		14		
Hospitals		10				16
Community	9	12		7		
Prognosis	5	16		2		
Patient rights		12				16
Society rights	10	15				
Patient duties	2	6	10			7
Society duties	4			11	3	

model and 6 model elements within the psychotherapeutic approach. Only 3 elements were specific to a single model: diagnosis, prognosis, and society duties.

More specifically, Tom's behaviour was implicitly defined within a psychosocial framework in which his 'mental distress' or 'emotional difficulties' were viewed as the product of: 'unresolved psychological stresses stemming from his childhood' (ASW:08) such as: 'the trauma of his uncle's death' (ASW:11), 'physical and sexual abuse... probably bullied at school' (ASW:17), and 'poor communication skills which have been compounded by current social difficulties relating to his job, financial circumstances, and family relationships' (ASW:10).

As a consequence, ASWs showed little direct support for medical treatment and hospital care, but instead felt that Tom's prognosis would be greatly improved if modalities of support and care were made available within the community specifically designed to address these 'distressing' issues. In particular, subjects talked about the need for: '... psychotherapeutic help to deal with his (Tom's) unresolved problems' (ASW:08), '... social welfare... and help with his business' (ASW:11). These issues were also reflected in their support for the social rights of patients.

6.4.2.2.3. **Patients** Judging from the models-grid presented in Table 6.5, the implicit views of patients(1) closely relate to the medically based approach adopted by psychiatrists. Respondents within this group agreed with 8 of the 12 elements within this model, including the use of labels such as schizophrenia for prescribing medication and assessing the seriousness of Tom's mental illness.

Patients(2) showed implicit support for 8 out of 12 elements within the psychotherapeutic model and 6 elements within the social model, forming an implicit pattern more supportive of the psychosocial approach adopted by social workers (see Table 6.6). Their support for elements within the medical model was minimal and in some cases showed strong disagreement. The use of illness labels, for example, was strongly rejected on the grounds that: 'They take away your identity as an individual and even deny you access to some types of (non-medical) care' (Pat2:03).

The interviewer observed, albeit intuitively, that the mental health problems of patients in the first sub-sample appeared more serious; respondents seemed more withdrawn and preoccupied during the interview and found it difficult to concentrate. Furthermore, respondents in the patients(1) group had experienced mental health problems – a diagnosis of schizophrenia – for longer

Table 6.5 Models-grid showing the number of patients (1) supporting each of the six key models of mental disorder across 12 dimensions ($N = 7$)

Models elements	Medical	Social	Cognitive-behavioural	Psychothera peutic	Family	Conspiratorial
Diagnosis	7					
Behaviour	5			5		
Labels	5			4		7
Aetiology	6	6				
Treatment	7		1	6		
Hospitals	6	6				6
Community	5	5				
Prognosis	7					
Patient rights	7					7
Society rights	1	7				
Patient duties	2	1	6			2
Society duties	3			7		

Table 6.6 Models-grid showing the number of patients (2) supporting each of the six key models of mental disorder across 12 dimensions (N = 13)

Models elements	Medical	Social	Cognitive-behavioural	Psycho-therapeutic	Family	Conspiratorial
Diagnosis				13		
Behaviour		9		11		
Labels	10			10		11
Aetiology		12		13		
Treatment			2	13		
Hospitals						11
Community	8	11				
Prognosis		9				
Patient rights		8				13
Society rights	8	10				
Patient duties	3		10			8
Society duties		5		13		

than respondents in the patients(2) group with a median of 9 and 4 years, respectively. Thus the severity and length of a patient's illness may be a factor influencing their implicit model differences.

In terms of rights and duties a complex implicit pattern emerged in which both sub-samples simultaneously accepted and rejected the 'sick' role status and society's right to restrain those who are a danger to themselves or others.

6.5. Discussion

The aim of this discussion will be to draw out the key findings on implicit models of mental disorder, and demonstrate how conflicting practitioner and patient perspectives may generate subtle, yet significant, poor quality working practices during the course of adopting a multi-agency approach towards the community-based treatment, management, and care of people who experience long-term schizophrenia. Within this context, only the results appertaining to psychiatrists, approved social workers, and patients will be considered.

6.5.1. Power relations and implicit models of mental disorder

It is important to recognize at the outset that empirical evidence produced elsewhere clearly demonstrates that clinical decision-making between various practitioners and between practitioners and patients takes place within an implicitly predefined power relationship organized around a 'hidden agenda' that promotes as predominant a medical interpretation of mental disorder (Busfield 1986; Lupton 1994). This is a supposition which prevails despite the fact that there are many plausible explanations of mental disorder. The fact that one particular view has priority may possibly rule out consideration of other accounts which may be crucial to the process of effective shared decision-making within multi-agency teams.

Thus, while the medical approach may be the most dominant in mental health practice, this fact alone does not necessarily justify why it should stand as conceptually superior to other perspectives. Yet our evidence suggests that because of its perceived superiority, especially amongst psychiatrists, the decision-making process is often reduced to little more than a highly contestable process in which each group's alternative implicit model has to compete for recognition and authority alongside the traditionally dominant medical perspective. Ultimately, it is within this context that inter-agency decision-making is likely to lead to unethical practices.

6.5.2. Implicit models and unethical practice between psychiatrists and approved social workers

The complex interplay between conflicting implicit perspectives and differential power relationships as the source of unethical practice was clearly demonstrated by the implicit models and critical incident findings obtained from psychiatrists and ASWs. In this study, the empirical data shows that psychiatrists believe Tom's behaviour should be medically defined and managed within hospital through the 'sick' role, while social workers understand the problem within a psychosocial context and are concerned about re-establishing Tom's social identity (job, finances, etc.) and safeguarding his civil rights.

As a consequence of these underlying ideological differences, our evidence suggests that communication over 'patients who aren't clear cut' can on occasion bring to the surface a 'a smouldering power struggle' between mental health and social services in which: '... each service tries to gain control of the situation through pushing their own perspective' (Psych:11), resulting on occasion in the development of serious inter-agency conflicts and poor working practices. For example, our critical incident data showed that during the course of making decisions over sectioning patients under the Mental Health Act, social workers occasionally attempt to use their power in this area to control the influence of the medical approach, motivated by the perception that their role is: '... to be frank... to clip the wings of psychiatrists' (ASW:07). Equally, psychiatrists were suspicious of social workers' decisions stating that: '... they sometimes delay or simply turn down a Section just to prove a point' (Psych:17). As a result, social workers sometimes felt that decision-making on occasion was reduced to instances of 'blackmail', with the actions of some psychiatrists being interpreted as deliberately withholding mental health resources until a section was approved: '... until I agreed to hospital care for a client, CPN input was denied and so I was on my own dealing with him (the patient)' (ASW:19). Several psychiatrists also accused social workers of taking patient's civil rights too far and '... often dropping out of Care Plans too early, leaving patients to manage their problems without any real support... which can so easily lead to cases of relapse' (Psych:14).

In some respects, the very practice of sectioning patients promulgates and promotes these entrenched ideological and power conflicts making the practice itself unethical. Surely common sense dictates that notions about developing ethically sound practices based on shared decision-making, especially between practitioners and patients, are likely to remain at best a myth and at worst a cruel misconception if clinical encounters continue to be influenced by the implicit belief that medicine should have the right and power to control patients by aggressive means such as the use of involuntary admission and compulsory treatment orders. Moreover, the notion that the ASWs job is to 'protect the civil rights of patients' is equally misconceived as it simply promotes an adversarial agenda which may result in practitioners promoting and protecting the self-interests of a particular profession. For example, the management and care of patients may be reduced to negotiating and reconciling practitioners' entrenched differences instead of developing solutions that are genuinely valued and shared by all those involved in the decision-making process.

6.5.3. Implicit models and unethical practice between psychiatrists and patients

To some extent, decision-making within a medical context is not problematic as patients, especially those who are very unwell, may wish to relinquish responsibility for their illness, accept the 'sick' role status (Parsons 1951) and rely upon the asymmetrical power differential operating within the clinical encounter in order to be told by a 'professional' what is wrong

(Mechanic 1979). These patients, may feel so anxious, tired, and confused that they do not want, or have the energy to become empowered and take control, and at least initially welcome psychiatric interpretations of their treatment and care: 'My psychiatrist says I've got schizophrenia... she gives me lots of advice about my illness and is helping me get better' (Pat1:04).

The data from our patient sample suggests, however, that this unequal power relationship, promoting a medical interpretation of mental health problems, is seen as a temporary status, which if allowed to continue unchecked runs the risk of promoting unethical working practices with patients.

Difficulties arise when patients are no longer prepared to adopt the 'sick' role on the grounds that they perceive it as demeaning to their own self identity: 'They (psychiatrists and CPNs) don't talk to you – have a conversation. Just say, how are you? How do you feel? That's all I get in ten years of knowing me.' (Pat1:05), become disillusioned about the benefits of medication: '... doctors are always over optimistic about what it can actually do'(Pat2:17), or more generally feel unable to identify exclusively with a medical definition of their problems.

It is at this point shared decision-making can become unethical as psychiatrists' implicit support for the medical perspective only equips them with the professionalism to define as meaningful, clinical encounters with patients that take place within the boundaries of the 'sick' role. If patients are not happy with their ascribed status as sick, then an unsatisfactory power dynamic comes into being, which prevents reciprocal relations and provides no mechanism for incorporating patient judgements or agency within the decision-making process. For example, our data suggests that discussions about treatment are often not concerned about different types of medical and non-medical treatment, but about 'dosage' of medication and presented as a *fait-accompli*: 'I'm always prepared to have a full and frank discussion with patients about (drug) treatments we might try and (in terms of dosage) their possible side-effects' (Psych:18).

Respondents, therefore, felt compelled to accept medication and many talked about being made to feel uncooperative if they refused, or were ignored: '... as if you are out of touch with reality if you insist on something different to medication' (Pat2:11). Moreover, evidence from psychiatrists suggests that these 'professional patients' are perceived as attempting to undermine medical power by: '... knowing exactly how things work and often playing one practitioner off against another in order to get what they want' (Psych:15). Ultimately, such action could also be construed as constituting little more than 'soft' resistance to medical dominance compared to the options of empowerment available to the physically unwell (Silverman 1987).

Many patients recognized the positive value of holding on to the status of a 'sick' person, such as not being seen as culpable for having mental health difficulties. However, respondents also felt that their right to the privileges associated with this role should not be conditional upon first having their problems 'fitted-up' to medical labels such as schizophrenia. The potentially unethical implication here is that having your circumstances exclusively associated with medical vicissitudes such as labels not only 'define everything about you' so that people (practitioners and the public) see the label rather than the person, but in some cases has had the unintended consequence of denying patients access to alternative forms of treatment and care such as psychotherapy as: '... psychologists won't touch you if you're schizophrenic' (Pat2:15).

Moreover, the potential for unethical practice becomes even more apparent if we acknowledge the Foucaultian claim that power relations within the medical encounter operate on a more subtle level and so can be both repressive and productive (Armstrong 1982). Within this context, any attempt at widening patient participation, to account for their implicit perspective, while still operating within a medically defined decision-making process may actually disadvantage patients further.

On the one hand patients are unconsciously encouraged, via the 'sick' role along with its associated rights and obligations, to become passive recipients of care while on the other, via notions such as patient empowerment and social inclusion, they are being subjected to contradictory messages encouraging them to take on more responsibility and see this as an important civil right.

The potential for unethical practices as a result of attempts to merge these implicit ideological differences was evident across a number of incidents involving shared decision-making. For example, patients described being 'terrified' of participating in Ward Round or Care Plan meetings because they were uncertain of their role and never felt part of the process, instead: '... you're just assessed, ignored or patronised and told what "the team" has decided is for the best' (Pat2:20).

Ultimately, it could also be argued that developing initiatives empowering patients to take control of the medical encounter by having their own implicit perspective recognized makes little sense, as this would redefine the natur e of the practitioner–patient relationship to such an extent that it would destroy the purpose and role of medicine itself: Why should people bother to seek medical advice if a psychiatrist's expert knowledge is considered to be of no greater value than the perceptions offered by patients?

6.5.4. Future directions: reconciling implicit models, power relations, and good ethical practice in shared decision-making

Judging from our empirical findings on the nature and influence of implicit models, and in the absence of conclusive scientific facts about mental disorder, it can be argued that medical dominance in the field of mental health may be defined as resulting from occupational control over several other conflicting interest groups. This power is reinforced by recognition from all groups that medicine is a socially valued skill, which affords considerable benefit. However, as this chapter has shown, its influence may encourage the establishment of unethical working structures and practices by restricting autonomy and choice for both practitioners and patients.

Ultimately, patients should be able to work within MDTs by being recognized and valued as part of that team. Moreover, redefining the balance of power within the decision-making process does not mean that the purpose and role of medicine would be destroyed. Instead, team decisions regarding the treatment, management, and care of a patient's specific mental health needs should be reached through an informed consideration of a range of options that may or may not include medical solutions.

Towards such a goal, multi-disciplinary training initiatives should be established that use the models-grid heuristic developed by this research to help improve communication skills through encouraging, at least initially, the conscious recognition amongst practitioners and patients that there exists a dynamic heterogeneity of models. In turn, this consciousness raising exercise would ensure that MDTs (including patients) are better equipped to identify and value a wide range of mental health perspectives and so be able to make more informed and ethically sound judgements about what is the most appropriate course of action within a specific case.

Ongoing work in this area needs to continue to update and modify the explicit model's framework established in this chapter and more closely evaluate the interrelationship between implicitly held models and power relations as an emergent force influencing processes of shared decision-making within community-based MDTs, and their impact on ethical practice.

References

Armstrong D (1982). The doctor-patient relationship: 1930–1980. In P Wright and A Treacher, eds. *The problem of medical knowledge: examining the social construction of medicine*. Edinburgh University Press, Edinburgh.

Austin JL (1956/57). A plea for excuses. Proceedings of the Aristotelian Society, 57, 1–30; Reprinted in AR White, ed. (1968). *The philosophy of action*. Oxford University Press, Oxford.

Bandura A (1986). *Social foundations of thought and action*. Prentice Hall, Englewood Cliffs, NJ.

Bean P, ed. (1985). *Mental illness: changes and trends*. Wiley, Chichester.

Becker S and Silburn R (1999). *We're in this together: conversations with families in caring relationships*. Carer National Association, London.

Bracken P and Thomas P (1999). Home treatment in Bradford. *Open Mind*, 95, 11–14.

Clunis (1994). *The report of the enquiry into the care and treatment of Christopher Clunis North East Thames and South East Thames Regional Health Authorities*. HMSO, London.

Colombo A (1997). *Understanding mentally disordered offenders: a multi-agency perspective*. Ashgate, Aldershot.

Colombo A, Bendelow G, Fulford KWM and Williams S (2003). Evaluating the influence of implicit models of mental disorder on processes of shared decision making within community-based multi-disciplinary teams. *International Journal of Social Science and Medicine*, 56, 1557–70.

Cramer D (1998). *Fundamental statistics for social research*. Routledge, London.

Department of Health (1999a). *National service framework for mental health: modern standards and service models*. Department of Health, London. Available at www.doh.gov.uk/nsf/mentalhealth

Department of Health (1999b). *Still building bridges: the report of a national inspection of arrangement for the integration of care programme approach with care management*. Department of Health, London.

Dunn S (1999). *Creating accepting communities: report of the mind inquiry into social exclusion and mental health problems*. MIND, London.

Flanagan JC (1983). The critical clinical incident technique. *Psychological Bulletin*, 51, 327–58.

Fulford KWM (1995). *Moral theory and medical practice*. Cambridge University Press, Cambridge.

Fulford KWM (1998). Mental illness, concepts of. In R Chadwick, ed. *Encyclopaedia of applied ethics*, Vol. 3, pp. 213–33. Academic Press, London.

Fulford KWM, Thornton T and Graham G (forthcoming). *The shorter Oxford textbook of philosophy and psychiatry*. Oxford University Press, Oxford.

Giddens A (1975). *Positivism and sociology*. Heinemann, London.

Goffman E (1961). *Asylums*. Penguin, Harmondsworth.

Goffman E (1963). *Stigma: notes on the management of spoiled identity*. Prentice Hall, New York.

Hall P, Levings J and Murphy C (1993). A comparison of responses to the mentally ill in two communities. *British Journal of Psychiatry*, 162, 99–101.

Lupton D (1994). *Medicine as culture*. Sage, London.

Mechanic D (1979). *Future issues in health care: social policy and the rationing of medical services*. The Free Press, New York.

Parsons T (1951). *The social system*. The Free Press, New York.

Rogers A and Pilgrim D (1996). *Mental health policy in Britain: a critical introduction.* Macmillan, Basingstoke.

Sainsbury Centre for Mental Health (1998). *Key to engagement: review of care for people with severe mental illness who are hard to engage with services.* Sainsbury Centre for Mental Health, London.

Siegler M and Osmond H (1966). Models of madness. *British Journal of Psychiatry,* **112**, 1193–203.

Silverman D (1987). *Communication and medical practice: social relations in the clinic.* Sage, London.

Wittgenstein L (1958). *Philosophical investigations*, 2nd edn. Basil Blackwell, Oxford.

Wolffe G, Pathare S, Craig T and Leff J (1996). Community attitudes to mental illness. *British Journal of Psychiatry,* **168**, 183–90.

Chapter 7

Empirical ethics in action in practices of dementia care

Minke Goldsteen

7.1. Introduction

In the last decade of the twentieth century there was increasing interest in empirical approaches to the discipline of bioethics. The issue was raised of how to combine empirical research and ethical theory. How does this 'marriage' come about and what does it look like? Different approaches to bioethics have different implications for the relationships between ethical theory and empirical data. In this chapter I will not discuss these different positions in detail; instead I will take a specific research project as a case-study and reflect on the concrete process of doing empirical ethics research. What does empirical ethics research look like? What kind of phases does such a process have? What kinds of choices need to be made? What kinds of problems might occur?

I will begin by giving a short overview of the developments in the discipline of ethics, and more specifically of health care ethics, in order to sketch the context in which the research was carried out and to make clear my own position with regard to approaches to empirical ethics. I will then turn to the actual practice of doing empirical ethics. I will discuss the issue of how empirical data and ethical theory were combined in the research study, which is the focus of this chapter: *Practices of responsibility in the care of the chronically ill.* In this study we made use of the theoretical perspective of the American philosopher Margaret Walker (Walker 1998). I will argue that theory plays various roles and that theory is interwoven into the whole research process. I will examine the process of analysis and give examples of what kinds of results this study offers. Finally I will draw out some conclusions relevant to the general question of what is 'empirical ethics'.

7.2. Developments in health care ethics

Over the last century the discipline of health care ethics has gone through several transformations. Until the 1960s medical ethics was taken as ethics of professionals, and in particular of doctors: it was a matter for physicians only. Doctors decided how to handle ethical issues on the basis of internally formulated professional codes and rules. After the 1960s a change took place in the thinking about the role and function of ethics. Professional ethics was replaced by a more socially oriented ethics. The emphasis changed towards general ethical theories that were considered to be a reflection of the moral opinions existing in society. Medical ethics was seen as a practice that applies these general ethical theories and rules to problems and dilemmas within medicine in order to bring about solutions to dilemmas or prescriptions about how to handle problematic situations. Ethical analysis and reflection was no longer the exclusive preserve of doctors and other health professionals, but was properly exercised by 'experts' outside health care such as philosophers, theologians, sociologists, lawyers, and historians. This development has been described as 'the turn to applied ethics' (Ten Have *et al.* 1998).

In the last decade of the twentieth century new developments became salient. The way in which ethical theories were used within applied ethics, and the relationship between theory and practice that underlay the 'applied ethics' perspective, came increasingly under attack. Applied ethics is normative in that it makes the assumption that theories prescribe how a certain (health care) practice ought to be carried out. One of the objections raised against this normative assumption is that in our society there is no general shared moral paradigm – at most there are certain 'moral understandings' (Walker 1998). Critics argue that it is difficult to give convincing reasons for choosing a specific ethical theory or moral principle when considering a moral dilemma. Another objection to the assumption that theories prescribe what should be done in a particular practical situation is that this approach is not sufficiently sensitive to the complexity and fickleness of the daily practice of health care. There is a big gap between ethical theories and concrete situations, making it problematic to apply abstract rules and principles (Ten Have and Lelie 1998). Critics of the 'turn to applied ethics' argue that applied ethics does not ask critical questions, and does not pay attention to the specific context in which ethical issues arise nor to the moral experiences of people involved and the tragic character of many ethical dilemmas in medicine (Van Tongeren 1988; Zwart 1992; De Vries 1993; Kater 2002). The role of ethics, according to these critics, is far more closely bound to the details of specific situations than traditional models of applied medical ethics allow.

In line with these ideas about the role and function of ethics and in reaction to this traditional conception of applied ethics, several alternative approaches have been developed, such as care ethics, virtue ethics, hermeneutical ethics, and narrative ethics. These alternative approaches share two features: they are context-based and they all focus on the experiences and ideas of those involved in a particular 'practice', such as medical or nursing practice. This contrasts with traditional applied ethics which takes (external) ethical theory, rather than practice, as the starting point (Ten Have *et al.* 1998). The focus of the alternative approaches on the internal morality of a practice has made empirical research and empirical methods – quantitative as well as qualitative – an important part of research projects that originated from a contextual perspective. The empirical ethical study presented in this chapter is set up from a context-based perspective. In the following section I will discuss what such a perspective implies for the process of carrying out research.

7.3. Empirical ethics in action – a case-study

The title of the study that will be described here is *Practices of responsibility in the care of the chronically ill.* This study involved semi-structured interviews with both professional and informal caregivers of elderly people with dementia. The philosophical theory used to inform the design and analysis of the empirical data was provided by the work of the American philosopher Margaret Walker. According to Walker morality is situated in social practices and especially in practices of responsibility.

Before discussing the question of combining ethical theory and empirical research, I will give a brief outline of the background and aim of this research project, and a short introduction to the philosophical ideas of Margaret Walker.

7.3.1. Practices of responsibility – background and aims of the research

Progressive dementia is a growing problem in our society. In the Netherlands, for example, over 175 000 people are currently afflicted with a dementing disorder and it is estimated that in 45 years time there will be more than 400 000 people with dementia (Gezondheidsraad 2002). Dementia is characterized by cognitive impairment that often involves disturbances in memory, mood, behaviour, and character. The most common cause of dementia is Alzheimer's disease. Dementia has radical consequences for people's lives: for the lives of relatives as well as for those with dementia.

The process of dealing with dementia raises moral issues and challenges for those involved. In our study *Practices of responsibility in the care of the chronically ill* we focused on one such issue: the way responsibilities are determined in the care of people with dementia. Currently in Dutch health care there is a great deal of debate about continuity and integration of care, that centres on the question of who is doing what – what is my responsibility as a professional caregiver or as a family member, and who coordinates the process of care? Health care organizations are developing programmes and protocols that set out standards of care as well as the tasks and responsibilities of health care institutions. But formal arrangements in terms of rules, guidelines, and programmes of care with different packages of tasks for different caregivers can be at odds with the way in which people define and deal with responsibilities in daily practice. The lack of fit between the formal and the actual can result in problems for the people concerned. The aim of our study was to provide more insight into this issue and to give recommendations about how to deal properly with moral aspects of the division of responsibilities in the care of people with dementia.

We decided, therefore, to carry out an empirical study and to interview family caregivers of patients with dementia ($N = 10$) and one or two of the professional caregivers who were closely involved in each of these particular situations ($N = 15$). In studying the literature in order to prepare our fieldwork and to devise an interview scheme, we were introduced to the ideas of the American philosopher Margaret Walker. Her ideas offered a useful theoretical framework to study practices of responsibility. Empirical research, in our view, always requires a prior theoretical perspective, or at least some prior theoretical presuppositions. For example, there needs to be some theoretical standpoint from which to define what is being studied and how certain choices are made; and why a particular phenomenon is identified and described rather than something else. We therefore decided to make our theoretical perspective explicit and to be transparent in our endeavour to justify the choices that we made.

7.3.2. Walker's theory on moral understandings

In her book *Moral Understandings* Margaret Walker describes morality as situated in social practices, which makes morality fundamentally interpersonal (Walker 1998). People construct and maintain moral orders together with those with whom they interact. This process takes place against a background of (moral) understandings about what people are supposed to do, expect, and understand. The way people define who they, and others, are (identity), what they care about (value), and to whom they are related (relationships), produces normative expectations that they have for all their interactions with others. These ideas and the normative expectations that are embedded in them play an important role in our understandings of how responsibilities are assigned and realized: 'It is in practices of responsibility that we make each other accountable to certain people for certain states of affairs, we define the scope and the limits of our agency, affirm who in particular we are, what we care about and reveal who has standing to judge and blame us. In the way we assign, accept or deflect responsibilities we express our understanding of our own and others' identities, relationships and values. At the same time, as we do so, we reproduce or modify the very practices that allow and require us to do this' (Walker 1998, p. 16).

Walker considers it as the task of ethics to give a reflective analysis of forms of moral life by studying how moral concepts and judgements inhere in, and are reproduced by, interactions between people. With regard to responsibilities, Walker argues for the development of 'geographies of responsibility' by which something can be said about how responsibilities are assigned and assumed in daily life. These 'geographies' should try to map the characteristics of our practices of responsibility by following the interactions between people and by following the trajectories of individual human actions. In this way a picture – a 'moral landscape' – can be developed showing how, through these individual actions, shared understandings are regulated about who is asked to take care of someone, and who has to account for something in certain situations or for certain results (Walker 1998).

These ideas about mapping the characteristics of our practices of responsibility might give the impression that Walker is defining responsibility in terms of more or less stable and fixed institutionalized practices that structure the way people think about things and deal with situations. To a certain extent Walker would accept this. She argues that within a society there do exist shared moral understandings, otherwise it would not be possible for people to live together. But she also states that these practices of responsibilities are dynamic in the sense that they are changing and growing: people struggle with the meaning of their responsibilities and argue with each other about them. Walker considers 'responsibility' as a concept that is given meaning within different contexts and relationships. For this reason it is not very helpful to talk of 'the' concept of moral responsibility. Smiley – to whom Walker refers – states in her book *Moral Responsibility and the Boundaries of the Community* that there is no universal concept of 'responsibility', but that responsibility is a social construct (Smiley 1992). She shows how assigning and judging responsibilities is shaped and defined by normative, often moral, expectations people have towards each other and by existing distributions of power. These normative expectations are not so much directed towards people in general, but towards certain individuals, in certain roles, relationships, and contexts. These kinds of processes are dynamic and dialectic; in response to actual tendencies or problems in the community or with the introduction of new 'facts' people influence and change each other's thoughts and expectations about who is responsible for what, and why.

7.3.3. **Various roles of theory**

Walker's theoretical perspective raises the question of how to work out her ideas in the context of an empirical ethical study. I will argue, based on my experience, that an ethical theory plays various roles within an empirical ethical research study.

In the first place, from an ontological point of view, one could argue that the choice to use a certain ethical perspective (theory) already implies an idea about how one as a researcher thinks about the nature of empirical research and the relationship between theory and practice. When we look at Walker's work, we see that she is not offering a normative theory in the sense that she states what kinds of responsibilities people have and should fulfil. Walker's ethics of responsibility is more meta-ethical. She argues for the value of an analysis of how morality is constructed in practices of responsibility and for studying what people are actually doing when they deal with responsibility: 'An empirically saturated reflective analysis of what is going on in actual moral orders needs to be supplied by many kinds of factual researches including documentary, historical, psychological, ethnographic and sociological ones' (Walker 1998, p. 11). Using Walker's ideas as the theoretical framework in this study leads us to consider the practice itself – the field of care for people with dementia – as the source of morality, and to be sceptical about the idea that there are universal ethical theories from which can be prescribed how practices ought to be and how people ought to behave. Consequently, the research focused on the experiences, opinions, and actions of those involved in the practice of care for people with dementia.

In the second place a theory can also inform us about the research methodology. The theoretical ideas of Walker when applied to our research interests suggest a research method that is aimed at articulating experiences, opinions, and actions of people. Although in her book *Moral Understandings* Walker gives no concrete methodological guidelines about how to gain insight into a social practice, she gives some directions about how to set up the research in stating that moral thinking is narrative in pattern: 'The idea is that a story is the basic form of representation for moral problems. We need to know who the parties are, how they understand themselves and each other, what terms of relationship they obtain, and perhaps what social or institutional frames shape their options' (Walker 1998, p. 110). And: 'People make sense of, or give significance to, events in their and others lives, including their own and others' actions, by embedding them in some story or other' (Walker 1998, p. 120).

In line with these ideas, we decided to carry out in-depth open interviews with people involved in the care of people with dementia that enabled the participants to talk about whatever they thought was important. Because of the centrality of the concept of responsibility in Walker's approach we asked participants about their expectations of themselves and others with respect to their roles as carers, and, at the end of the interviews we asked explicitly how participants understood and defined their responsibilities. In this way we collected interview material with detailed accounts about people's experiences around the care of people with dementia.

A third role of a theoretical framework is that it informs decisions about the analysis of the material and the articles that are written on the basis of this analysis. In fact theory forms the perspective from which one examines the empirical material. The research question in this study was how responsibilities are defined and attributed by the people involved in the care of people with dementia. Although we stayed close to the empirical data, we were aware that our theoretical framework informed both our choice of a focus on responsibility and our understanding of this concept as well as how we structured our research publications. Alvesson and Skoldberg formulate this point as follows: 'It is thus not so much that objective data talk to the theory (data are after all constructions and dependent on perspective); rather the theory allows the consideration of different meanings in empirical material' (Alvesson and Skoldberg 2000, pp. 249–50). Our perspective, derived from Walker's theoretical position, led to the focus of the analysis on how people see themselves (identity), how people relate to each other (relationship), and what people expect from each other (normative expectations). These are also the main themes in the written articles; they form stepping stones, sometimes explicit, sometimes more implicit throughout our accounts of the interpretations of responsibility.

These various roles of theory within our empirical research study give an idea about how theory and empirical data are integrated within the whole research process. In our opinion, ethical theory and empirical data are not two separate things but work interdependently throughout the research study. Theory is not as prominent in every phase of the research, but is particularly prominent in the phase of analysis and writing.

7.3.4. Analysing identity, relationships, and normative expectations

In this study there were 25 interview transcripts and more than 300 pages of text. We started our analysis by reading all the transcripts, underlining striking statements, and writing some first remarks in the margin of each interview. An analysis was then performed at three different levels: first, content analysis; second, linguistic analysis; and third, an analysis of the structure of the respondent's story. In this third analysis, fragments of the interviews were labelled and our ideas and lines of interpretation were written down together with these fragments. Walker's concepts of identity, relationship, and normative expectations helped us to focus our analysis but the codes we chose derived from the content of the material rather than directly from the theoretical framework. In this way an analysis document of each interview was created that could be used for further analysis. In the next phase the process of writing about practices of responsibility started. At this point Walker's theoretical ideas played a more prominent role: they offered a structure for writing about responsibilities. In one of our papers ('What is it to be a daughter? Identities under pressure in dementia care' Goldsteen *et al.* 2005) we first presented the story of a 40-year-old woman and her 73-year-old mother who is becoming demented. In the second part of the article we reflected in more detail on her story and focused on the way the identity of this family member was put under pressure and changed during her mother's illness. Thus we used Walker's idea that personal identities (Who am I and who is the other?) colour the normative expectations that people have towards themselves and other people in specific situations. These expectations can be described as normative because they have to do with ideas about how to handle, in a concrete situation, the questions What should be done by whom and to whom? We were able, using this approach, to say something about the ideas that people have about their own, and other people's, responsibilities in the process of care. In the case of the 40-year-old daughter and her mother with dementia, for example, there is a normative clash at some points during care, between the expectations of the daughter and the professionals with regard to who is supposed to do what in the care of the mother. The daughter says:

> No, I am not a nurse, I am not a caregiver, it is my mother and I want her to get the best care possible. But should this be arranged? I don't know. From the beginning, I had to sort this out all by myself. I thought, aren't there people who have done this already? Couldn't they tell me what to do? But no, somehow this never happened, not at the Regional Individual Needs Assessment Agency (RIO) and not at the Regional Institution for Ambulatory Mental Care (RIAGG) ...

According to the daughter she was dragged into all kinds of consultations, for example when her mother became agitated at the day-care centre:

> Umm, yes we got involved in these consultations again and again, we had to ... I: And did you like this or ...? R: Actually no, because I also didn't know what I had to do with this. I mean, I only have one mother and I've never been through anything like this, a mother who is becoming demented, so ... And they're the ones who have experience with this; I mean, it wouldn't be the first time that someone became agitated at the day care centre, I think.

In the analysis of this interview material we draw the conclusion that defining herself as a daughter and not as a caregiver is a reason for this woman to assign to the professional caregivers the responsibility for organizing appropriate care and for making treatment decisions. However, the professionals see the daughter as her mother's spokeswoman and expect her to act according to this role. In other cases too there were differences between family views of their responsibilities and professional views. For example professionals of a domestic care institution considered the daughter of a woman with dementia to be responsible for managing a whole variety of small problems that arose in the care of her mother such as providing clean towels and replacing a lost key to her mother's house. This particular daughter did not feel comfortable with these tasks and requests, although she did not have clear ideas about who should have been responsible.

The stories of the respondents show that people define their identity – and thus their responsibilities – in different ways. In the first case that was mentioned, the woman sees herself as a daughter. In another case a participant compared her role with that of being a mother, even though she was the wife of the person with dementia.

> I consider myself as responsible in any way, also for his mental and physical health. Maybe it is wrong to say it in this way but like you were used as a mother to go to a general practitioner with your children, I also now want to stand beside him. The responsibility of the health caregivers is also big. They are the experts and they need to see things and take care that something is done about it. But I would like to know this and I would like to have this explained to me.

The fact that she refers to her role as being that of a mother in this situation reveals something about this woman's expectations towards herself, and it legitimizes her attitude towards, and her way of dealing with, this situation. Just as a mother guides a child in most circumstances, this woman wanted to handle most situations involving her husband with dementia. One implication of this is that professional caregivers should explain to her what is happening and what kinds of decisions need to be made, and that she, for her part, can express her own ideas and doubts.

7.4. Reflection and conclusion

The results of the empirical ethical study described in this chapter provide a detailed description and a critical analysis of how different attributions of identity between family members and professional caregivers can lead to difficulties and misunderstandings in the distribution of responsibility in the care of people with dementia. What is the value of this kind of empirical ethical research? We believe that this research is valuable for both normative ethics and for clinical practice.

With regard to normative ethics, from Walker's perspective no clear answers can be given about what exactly is morally appropriate in these kinds of situations: for example what care do children owe their parents with dementia? We believe, as does Walker, that morality is situated in social practices and that there are no universal ethical theories which determine how practices ought to be and how people ought to behave. But does this mean that how people act and what they say is therefore morally adequate, and that we are not able to draw normative conclusions from our analysis? Our view is that detailed description and critical analysis of situations such as caring for someone with dementia expose misunderstandings and disagreements about what happens, what participants think is going on, and what some parties think that others think. An understanding of the views and perspectives of people who have experienced, for example, caring for a parent with dementia challenges others to evaluate and rethink their own ideas and moral presumptions about how to deal with this situation. Walker's ethical perspective does not give clear answers about what exactly is morally adequate in these kinds of situations, but the analysis of our interview material shows how important it is to search for answers to this question within the specific context. For example, the care someone ought to give to his father or mother with dementia is determined by the context. In other words it is connected with how he understands himself and who he takes his parents to be, taking into account the present relationship between them and what they have valued throughout the history they have shared. If the stories of family members make one thing clear it is that one cannot determine beforehand what it means to be a 'good' husband, wife, daughter, or son in relation to a person with dementia.

The study described in this chapter is also valuable for professional caregivers in clinical practice. The research has shown that there are differences, which are generally unarticulated, between families and professionals about ethical issues, specifically about roles and responsibilities. It is important for professional caregivers to take into account that family members will often have different ideas about who they are (e.g. what it means to be a daughter) and consequently about what their responsibilities are. They should also be aware that family members might have different views from their own concerning professional caregivers' responsibilities. These differences are not always in the direction of each group assuming that the other group has more responsibilities. One of our participants was a woman who considered her responsibilities to be greater than the professionals did. As a result the woman required more information from the professionals than they realized in order for her to be able to discharge what she saw as her responsibilities. Unless these views of family members and professionals are explicit, there is a danger that care will be sub-optimal because of unexplored and unacknowledged differences of view. A way for professionals to become sensitive to these matters is by listening attentively to the stories of family members – particularly to the way families express issues of identity and responsibility in their stories – and by openly discussing these issues with them and making these issues regularly recurrent themes within consultations. Professional caregivers can start these kinds of conversations, for example by asking family members what they think they owe their relatives with dementia in this specific situation and who they think should be responsible for what, in caring for their relative. It is important that they do not confine themselves to general statements, but focus on the concreteness of the situation.

In this chapter I have described an example of research involving an 'exploration' of empirical-ethics-in-action. I hope to have given an idea of an approach to reflective analysis of morality in practices of dementia care. Because of its focus on experiences, opinions, and actions of people involved in a certain practice, empirical ethical research offers insights into the moral landscape that is inherent in a social practice. In this way research in empirical ethics can contribute to the discussion about what might be called a good moral practice.

Acknowledgements

Research, on which this article is based, was supported by a grant from the Dutch Organization for Scientific Research (NWO). The study was conducted in collaboration with the 'geheugenpoli' and Faculty of Medicine of the Maastricht University Hospital. We gratefully acknowledge the contributions of the family caregivers and the health professionals, in particular the ones who helped recruit participants to the study.

References

Alvesson M and Skoldberg K (2000). *Reflexive methodology: new vistas for qualitative research*. Sage Publications, London.

American Psychiatric Association (1994). *Diagnostic and statistical manual of mental disorders*, 4th edn. Author, Washington DC.

De Vries GH (1993). *Gerede twijfel: over de rol van de medische ethiek in Nederland*. De Balie, Amsterdam.

Gezondheidsraad (2002). *Dementie*. Gezondheidsraad, Den Haag.

Goldsteen M, Abma T, Oeseburg B, Verkerk M, Verhey F and Widdershoven GAM (2007). What is it to be a daughter? Identities under pressure in dementia care. *Bioethics*. **21**, 1–12.

Kater L (2002). *Disciplines met dadendrang: gezondheidsethiek en gezondheidsrecht in het Nederlandse euthanasiedebat 1960–94.* Aksant, Amsterdam.

Nelson HL (2001). *Damaged identities, narrative repair.* Cornell University Press, Ithaca.

Nelson HL (2002). What child is this? *Hasting Center Report,* **32**(6), 29-38.

Nelson HL (2003). *On the mend: narratives of repair.* Manuscript, unpublished.

Ritchie K and Lovestone S (2002). The dementias. *The Lancet,* **360**, 1759-66.

Smiley M (1992). *Moral responsibility and the boundaries of community.* University of Chicago Press, Chicago.

Ten Have HAM and Lelie A (1998). Medical ethics research between theory and practice. *Theoretical Medicine,* **19**, 263-76.

Ten Have HAMJ, Meulen RHJ ter and Van Leeuwen E (1998). *Medische ethiek.* Bohn Stafleu Van Loghum, Houten.

Van der Scheer L and Widdershoven GAM (2004). Integrated empirical ethics: loss of normativity. *Medicine, Health Care and Philosophy,* **7**(1), 71-9.

Van Tongeren P (1988). Ethiek en Praktijk. *Filosofie en Praktijk,* **3**(9), 113-27.

Walker MU (1998). *Moral understandings: a feminist study in ethics.* Routledge, New York.

Widdershoven GAM (1999). Ethiek en empirisch onderzoek. *Kennis en Methode: Tijdschrift voor Empirische Ethiek,* **23**, 145-54.

Widdershoven GAM (2000). *Ethiek in de kliniek.* Boom, Amsterdam.

Zwart HAE (1992). Is medische ethiek ethiek? *Tijdschrift voor Geneeskunde en Ethiek,* **2**(2), 34-7.

Chapter 8

Family carers, ethics and dementia: an empirical study

Clive Baldwin

8.1. Introduction

It is estimated that there are currently approximately 750 000 people in the UK living with dementia (Alzheimer's Society 2006) and that the vast majority of these are cared for by family members. Caring for people living with dementia can be burdensome; indeed for many years the focus on research into the experience of carers was on just that, the burden they carried (see for example, Burns and Rabins 2000; Gruffydd and Randle 2006). This research explored the facets of this burden: social, psychological, financial, and emotional.

Over the last 20 years there has been an upsurge of interest in the ethical issues facing people caring for those living with dementia. Using the data prepared by Baldwin *et al.* (2003) for their review of ethical issues in dementia between 1980 and 2000, it can be seen that 40% of the articles concerned with ethical issues for family caregivers were published in the period 1995–2000, compared with only 14% in the first 5-year period. Indeed, even a far less systematic search on a single database (*PubMed*) for the period 2001–05 suggests that this trend is continuing, with a further 41 articles being retrieved.

In personal accounts of caring, matters of value – indicating the ethical issues – arise spontaneously (see for example, Butterworth 1995; Cross 1997). Furthermore, the onset and progression of dementia often challenges previously held beliefs, values, hopes, desires, morals, and relationships, turning traditional morality on its head. And because the progression of dementia can be unpredictable and uneven and its manifestations uncertain, ethics in daily life tend to be messy and, in comparison with the well-formed and well-articulated ethical frameworks that find their way into textbooks for the medical professions, relatively ill-defined or articulated and under-researched. In this everyday ethics is reminiscent of the postmodern ethics Baumann describes:

> Human reality is messy and ambiguous – and so moral decisions, unlike abstract ethical principles, are ambivalent. It is in this sort of world that we must live; and yet, as if

defying the worried philosophers who cannot conceive of an 'unprincipled' morality, a morality without foundations, we demonstrate day by day that we can live or learn to live, or manage to live in such a world, though few of us would be ready to spell out, if asked, what the principles that guide us are, and fewer still would have heard about the 'foundations' which we allegedly cannot do without, to be good and kind to each other (Bauman 1993, p. 32, cited in Haimes 2002, pp. 105–6).

The challenge to researchers, in understanding the moral lives of carers in the messiness of every day life, is to develop a way of researching ethics in daily life, a way that:

- does not predetermine what the ethical issues are
- locates ethics in the lived experience of the participants
- can identify features of the process of ethical decision-making
- can get behind what people say about themselves – the presentation of self – to explore how and possibly why these presentations are produced and the impact the process of production of moral reasoning and action
- can capture the ethical concepts/thinking used by family carers
- remains true to the experience of participants and rings true to the experience of others in similar situations.

The research project described here attempted to address these issues, with varying degrees of success. This chapter will focus on the methods and the reasoning behind these rather than the findings of the research, detail of which must wait for another time.

8.2. **Empirical research, ethics and family carers**

Until recently bioethics has been primarily a philosophical inquiry but with the rise of evidence-based medicine and the engagement in research of clinical ethicists, with their medical knowledge and ethical vocabulary, institutional, practice-based positions, and interests, there has been some movement towards developing an empirical ethics that draws on the methods and insights of the social sciences (see, Borry *et al.* 2005, Borry *et al.*, Chapter 4 of this volume). This movement is seen by some (see, for example, Goldenberg 2005) as an attack on the normative and analytical methods of bioethics. For others, it is a welcome development, providing new material for and insight into bioethical theory and practice. I do not intend here to enter into this debate, although I will indicate later how the study reported here may contribute to it. Here, my purposes are far more humble – to indicate how the research study may contribute to our understanding of the moral lives of carers and the empirical ethics enterprise.

According to (Borry *et al.* 2004b) ethical reflection proceeds in three steps: the description of the moral question, the assessment of the moral question, and the evaluation of the decision-making. Empirical research can contribute to each step in this process playing a role 'in answering the reality-revealing questions (what, why, how, who, where and when), in assessing the consequences and in proposing alternative courses of action' (Borry *et al.* 2004b, p. 41). In this way of thinking, it makes a great deal of sense to engage directly with practitioners to develop our understandings of the ethical concepts, reasoning, and environment in which health care decisions are made (see, for example, Dierckx de Casterle *et al.* 2004).

Empirical ethics is still, however, a minority enterprise, with only 15.4% of studies in the nine major ethical peer-reviewed journals in 2003 using an empirical design (Borry *et al.* 2006). Furthermore, it has been indicated by Baldwin *et al.* (2003) that the majority of research into ethics has been conducted by professionals, about professionals, for professionals and that, despite the fact that informal carers provide the vast majority of care to people living with dementia, research in this area is both a minority interest within an already minority interest and what research has been undertaken has generally taken as its starting point issues of interest to professionals. Indeed, to date, there are only two studies that report on ethical issues spontaneously raised by family carers (Pratt *et al.* 1987; Hughes *et al.* 2002a,b).

The research reported here goes some way to increasing our understanding of the moral lives of family carers in that it was designed to identify and explore areas needful of ethical reflection, the concepts utilized by carers in that reflection, the ethical reasoning of carers, and the ethical environment in which carers endeavour to provide care.

8.3. **Background to the project**

The study reported here grew out of previous work by Hope and Oppenheimer (1997) in which it was noted that family carers often used the 'language of morality' to describe their situations and actions.

A small pilot study was then designed, interviewing ten family carers (see Hughes *et al.* 2002a,b). This study supported Hope and Oppenheimer's original insight and identified a range of ethical issues facing family carers. On the basis of this pilot study application was made to the Quality Research in Dementia programme of the Alzheimer's Society for funding to undertake the first systematic study of the ethical issues facing family members caring for a relative living with dementia. The project ran from January 2001 to December 2004.

8.3.1. **Participants**

Participants were recruited through personal contacts, voluntary sector agencies, consultants' lists, and word of mouth. Recruitment and interviewing, using purposive sampling, continued until data saturation was reached. In all 62 carers were interviewed. Of these, 60 granted consent to allow use of one or both of the interview transcripts. Details of participants can be found in Table 8.1.

8.3.2. **Methods**

The purpose of the research was to explore the ethical issues facing family carers from their perspective. Because ethics in everyday life may not be well articulated, it was important to utilize methods that allowed for both the exploration of issues that were raised directly by participants and issues that had been reported in the literature but not mentioned spontaneously by the participants. In attempting to do so, it was also important to frame the research in such a way as to avoid, as far as possible, the intrusion of pro-

Table 8.1 Details of participants (consenting to allow use of transcripts $N = 60$)

Gender	Male	27
	Female	33
Relationship to person living with dementia	Wife	14
	Husband	20
	Son	4
	Daughter	15
	Partner	3
	In-law	3
	Other	1
Age range of participants		38–93
Ethnicity	White British	54
	Asian	3
	Chinese	1
	Irish	1
	Other (White Muslim)	1
Place of residence of person with dementia at time of first interview[a]	Home with spouse	19
	Own home	1
	Carer's home	1
	Residential or nursing care	24
	Not applicable (Deceased)	12
Current/former carer (self-defined)	Current	46
	Former	14

[a]$N = 57$. Two daughters and two couples were interviewed about their parents.

fessional/academic ethical concepts and thinking into the research process. It was further assumed that access to ethical issues and decision-making would be gained through an exploration of the everyday experience of care-giving – as this would be the concrete, lived location in which ethics would be realized:

> ... empirical ethics states that the study of people's actual moral beliefs, intuitions, behaviour and reasoning yields information that is meaningful for ethics and should be the starting point for ethics (Borry *et al.* 2004a, p. 1).

Given that qualitative methods are particularly well suited to exploring perspectives, experience, and context (see, Chandros Hull *et al.* 2001), it was decided to undertake open-ended, narrative interviews as the starting point, leading to more focused questions in the second interview and ending with questions on specific ethical issues derived from the literature. While possibly unacceptable to purists such as Glaser (1992) this amended form of grounded theory had several advantages for the purposes of this research.

- It allowed access to the lived experience of participants while not restricting the data to the spontaneous responses of participants.

It allows for previous knowledge of relevant theory and research – necessary, by the way, to secure research funding as such applications require the location of the proposed research in the current understandings of the subject.

- It acknowledges, as per Strauss and Corbin (1998) that the researcher's view (and/or that of the Steering group) may conflict with that of the participant and as such may limit the understanding of the lived experience of caring. In order to address this, the second interview provided the opportunity to clarify, expand, or amend statements made earlier and for the researcher to check out his understanding of the situation with the participant.

- In drawing on both lived experience and responses to questions on specific, previously identified ethical issues the research attempted to navigate between the positions of the normative ethics generally found in the literature and extreme relativism in which ethics is little more than individual preference for a way of acting.

The interview schedule was established via six pilot interviews with carers who then went on to be involved in the full study. The interviews were audio taped and, where permission was granted, videotaped. The interviews were transcribed from the audio tape and checked against the video recording, noting any features of body language and facial movements that lent meaning to the text of the interview. The transcripts were anonymized and returned to the participants for checking accuracy and meaning. The agreed transcripts were then analysed by members of the Steering Group for issues that seemed to involve an ethical dimension and/or the use of the 'language of morality'. On the basis of these pilot interviews, and a review of the literature, interview schedules for two interviews were drawn up. The first interview started with the invitation to 'tell us about your experience of caring for your relative, starting from the time you first suspected that something might be amiss'. Broad areas of possible interest were identified from the pilot interviews as a checklist for open-ended questions should these areas not be covered within the spontaneous narrative of the participant. These broad areas covered: diagnosis, relationship with professionals, relationships with family and friends, difficult decisions, turning points, information, advice to other carers, and anything else the carer might want to add.

Following transcription and agreement/consent the transcript was examined for indicators of ethical issues, language, or reasoning. For example, the use of the language of morality: ought, should, duty responsibility; or feelings of guilt, obligation, and so on. This analysis formed the basis of the second interview schedule, aimed at seeking explanation, clarification, and expansion of aspects of the transcript that were thought to indicate an issue of or for ethics.

The schedule for the second interview also contained a series of questions concerning more specific areas not covered in the first interview and a series of questions concerning ethical issues identified from the literature.

The two interviews were designed to move from the general to the specific in order to avoid imposing a focus too early. Transcripts were subject to constant comparison and a coding tree established and revised during the course of the project. The Steering Group, consisting of the authors and three carers appointed by the Alzheimer's Society, were involved in the establishment and review of the interview schedule and coding tree.

8.4. **A summary of findings**

This is not the place to go into detail regarding the findings of the study – for the focus of interest is the contribution of the study to empirical ethics. It is, however, necessary to provide a summary of the findings as a prelude to that discussion.[1]

---

[1] For a brief discussion of the study, see Baldwin *et al.* (2004).

8.4.1. Identifying the ethical issues

Family carers reported a wide range of areas that gave rise to ethical concern (see Table 8.2). Across the interviews all of the areas below were raised within the narrative responses of participants and not in response to questions on specific issues identified by the researchers. Where the issues were not raised in this way, participants were asked for their personal experiences of the issues or their view of those issues if they did not have that particular personal experience. In this way, we attempted to ensure that we had covered the range of areas of ethical concern as experienced by family carers.

It is worth just noting here that while many of these areas appear in the literature on ethics and dementia such as advance directives (e.g. Vollman 2001), feeding (e.g. Hoefler 2002), and informed consent (e.g. Fellows 1998), others appear less frequently, if at all: for example, what to do with a relative's pets and belongings, the negotiating and balancing of competing demands and the taking over of tasks.

8.4.2. Moral principles/concepts

Just as professionals utilize moral principles as tools in clinical practice, so too family carers utilize moral principles as navigational guides in determining the best course of action. The range of concepts utilized by carers in this research bore some resemblance to those found in current bioethical discourse (such as best interests, independence/autonomy, fairness, or justice) but also included

Table 8.2 Ethical issues reported by carers

Advance directives	Feeding	Planning issues
Assessment	Financial issues	Professional ethics
Care and control	Friends	Quality of life
Chaging relationships	Genetics	Research
Communication	Inappropriate behaviour	Residential care
Competing demands	Information	Resource allocation
Confidentiality	Informed consent	Safety
Denial	Legal issues	Self, personhood
Diagnosis	Loss	Services
Driving	Medication	Taking over tasks
Drug treatments	Negative feelings	Treatment
End-of-life issues	Patients' rights	Truth-telling
Family issues	Pets and belongings	Wandering

principles that are less commonly, if ever, found in professional publications (faithfulness or loyalty, love, being true). The way in which these principles were deployed varied but in most interviews there was some combination of quasi-bioethical and more specifically lay principles.

8.4.3. The basis of moral action

While carers referred to moral principles as factors in their decision-making (for example, best interests and independence) these principles were not *a priori* principles (as in the principlists approach of Beauchamp and Childress 2001) but realized in various forms and in various degrees within broader frameworks. A number of frameworks were identified across the transcripts: duty/responsibility; reciprocity; mutuality; and sacrifice. As in the pilot study (Hughes *et al.* 2002a) a significant proportion of carers spoke of their sense of duty towards the person they were caring for. For spouses this 'duty' was sometimes, but not always, couched in terms of their marriage vows; for children in terms of filial responsibility. This duty was sometimes, but again not always, experienced as a burden. For others, it was a matter or conscience, that they could no other without failing to be true to themselves and their relatives. But as Hughes *et al.* (2002a) state: 'the sense of duty towards the person with dementia displayed an imperative quality: it was not something the carer could shirk' (p. 244).

The sense of reciprocity was strong amongst many carers, primarily spouse carers. One carer put it this way:

> ... we had four sons which she, me being away working she took responsibility, most of the responsibility for bringing them up and you know she was a very loving and very capable mother and wife. ... And to me it's been no problem to look after her because I find that I think she deserves it and so it's, I suppose a labour of love really but I don't find it a heavy burden. ... and so I just accept it as something to be done and look after her as I'm sure, well as I know she looked after our four sons and she would look after me if the situation were reversed (Participant 2).

While the notion of reciprocity has been noticed elsewhere (Pratt *et al.* 1987), the notion of 'mutuality', being in it together, has not. This mutuality took the form of 'what happens to one of us, happens to both of us', and it is something that is met together, as a team. In this, there are echoes of a more social definition of dementia (in contrast to the more usual biomedical definition) and an indication of how the best interests of the person with dementia and the carer are inextricably entwined.

A fourth framework was that of sacrifice. While it was clear that the vast majority of carers had sacrificed something (in the sense of giving up things and activities in order to be able to care for their relative) for a number of carers this sense of sacrifice was an important, and not necessarily negative, part of what it meant to be a carer, that is, part of the identity of being defined as such:

> ... most of the time looking after somebody you love is an enjoyable experience because, because you love them you're doing your best for them, it's not, it's not like somebody who's coming in to care for them, they're yours and you're doing the caring.

> But on the other side it is tiring and at times it is very tiring and sometimes you just want to sit down and go to sleep but you can't because that person needs you from the minute they wake up to the minute their eyes close, they need your attention and that's what you have to do, you have to give them one hundred per cent in everything. You don't have to think about yourself and your needs because they don't come into it and that's the way I saw it. If you love them, you give them one hundred per cent and forget yourself for the time being. Whether I did forget myself I don't know, but I done the best I could and from what people have said, I didn't do a bad job so I was quite pleased with that (Participant 8).

8.5. **The contribution of the study to the enterprise of empirical ethics**

The above study was the first systematic study of the ethical issues facing family carers from their perspective. As such it extends our understanding of the experience of family carers and the notion of 'ethical burden' (see, Schneider *et al.* 1999). The study also contributes to the field of empirical ethics in a number of ways.

First, the project was designed to elicit the range of ethical issues faced by family carers in caring for a relative living with dementia through purposive sampling and continuing until data saturation. The main limitation on this element of the study is the lack of participants from black and minority ethnic (BME) groups. While every attempt was made to recruit participants from such groups, as with other studies this proved difficult. Although approximately 10% of participants described themselves in terms other than White British, the numbers from any one group were very small (usually just one). The ethical issues raised by participants from BME groups were not significantly differently from those of the White British participants but, given the very small numbers from any one group it is impossible to make any reliable statement as to whether the range of issues identified in the study is the same or different from those facing carers in BME groups. This is an area for further research.

As stated above, the range of issues experienced as having an ethical aspect included but was not restricted to areas already identified as such and reported in the literature. Not all carers viewed all areas as having ethical import and responses amongst carers to the issues raised varied greatly. For example, in the area of medication some carers saw covert administration of medication as an ethical issue as it infringed or impacted upon their notions of truth, choice, and healthy relationships, while others saw it as merely a practical decision of how to administer necessary medication.

Identifying the range of issues (what counts as an ethical issue) and the varying responses of family carers, while important in itself and for enhancing the understanding of professionals in their dealings with family carers, also sensitizes us to the possibility of multiple perspectives on ethics. This does not, however, imply that 'anything goes' – for, as Van der Scheer and Widdershoven (2004) state: 'The meaning which practitioners [In this case, family carers – CB] give to their situation and the reasons they have for their actions are relevant issues for ethical consideration because they already contain a normative evaluation of the situation' pp. 72–3). In this way empirical research can indicate where normative analysis is needed – making this embedded normative knowledge explicit – and thus enrich practical experience through the development of guidelines for the improvement of practice (Van der Scheer and Widdershoven 2004). Further (normative) analysis of the data from the project may help provide guidelines for family carers giving impetus to changing or improving practice and helping to reduce uncertainty and anxiety.

Second, the study generated data that helps us understand how the ethical perspectives of family carers may differ from those of professionals. Not only are there areas that carers identify as having ethical import that professionals do not, but the ways these issues are thought about may also differ significantly. In the first place the principles used as navigational tools and the bases for moral action amongst carers may be different than those currently predominant in bioethics. These principles, their deployment in practice and the bases for moral action can thus be a source of philosophical analysis and reflection, thus contributing to ethical theory and practice. For example, the notions of faithfulness or being true are different from the professional notion of fidelity; the notions of reciprocity and duty mean something very different for family carers than the professional duty of care; and the notion of mutuality can be interpreted as being in stark contrast to the individualism found in bioethical principalism (see: Beauchamp and Childress 2001).

In addition, the contexts in which everyday actors resolve ethical dilemmas differ greatly between professionals and lay people. This difference has been noted by Edwards (1993) with regard to assisted conception, where 'everyday actors are seen to have other cultural reference points through which they resolve such difficulties. In this case, that which is usually presented as an issue of medical ethics, is seen by everyday actors as an issue of family ethics. That is, the "same" ethical issues are located in different contexts by different sets of actors and are accordingly seen to have different implications and meanings' (Haimes 2002, p. 104). For family carers, decisions were not simply seen as medical or social care decisions but as having an impact on family and friends, on past and future relationships and on one's sense of Self. Witness:

> I can remember the first time we took her to respite, I can remember walking out the door and feeling a real cad because we'd left her there and that wasn't my mother it was my mother in law but I really felt quite a cad at having left her in this home (Participant 5).

In its small way this study contributes to our understanding of such differences.

A third way in which this study can contribute to the field of ethics is to examine the ways in which family carers present themselves as moral agents (moral identity) and thus attempt to act ethically in detailed, contextualized dilemmas. The way the two interviews were structured facilitated access to data relevant to each of these areas of interest. By inviting participants to tell their story in their own words, for as long as they wished (interviews lasting from approx. 20 min to 6.5 h) we attempted to access the detail of carers' lives. The limits of interviews as windows onto experience notwithstanding, this approach generated a mass of data about the detail of carers' lives. The initial narrative was an important backdrop against which to examine the ethical issues peculiar to individual carers. By being able, on the whole, to revisit the transcript with the participant after initial analysis, we were able to amend errors, clarify ambiguities, check out initial interpretations, and explore issues in more detail. In this way we have access to the lived experiences of carers in their attempts to inhabit a moral world.

In terms of establishing moral identity, carers utilized differing configurations of principles and moral frameworks, positioning themselves in relation to both the dementia and professionals. In the same way that parents in Baruch's research (Baruch 1981) sought to position themselves as having behaved morally in adverse situations, some carers also distinguished between lay and professional worlds and the worlds of people living with dementia as having different standards and criteria of reasonableness. As one carer said:

> Yeah I think there's some huge experience out there; out in the real world, people learn all sorts of practical ways of managing. And some of it doesn't necessarily sit *easily* with professional ethics but you're dealing with people, the patient is someone with, without a memory, not necessarily without a brain. I think the most frightening

thing when you watch this is the thought that you might have, where you might be ending up is with something that's thrashing around that's trying to make sense out of no information.

And I'm not sure that the classic ethics of the medical profession actually apply. I suppose in the crudest sense if you're going to sit in a, in the world, if you're going to manage a patient with dementia and you're going to sit in their world you're going to lie to them. Because in accepting their reality you are denying yours. And when you deny reality in *our* world you're seen as lying or not telling the truth or not telling it as it is.

And I think recognising that untruth is a, untruth in that sense is a fundamental part of the management process may not sit entirely easily with conventional ethics. If that is so then in this area you have to revise your thoughts about conventional ethics. You have to manage patients in their world (Participant 52)

Just as carers identified differences between lay and professional worlds, they recognized the differences between their own situation and those of others, generally expressing reluctance to offer all but the most general advice to other carers:

I would qualify *all* that by saying, 'Only you are the carer for the person you are caring for. And only they are the sufferer. We *are* all different. We all have different ways of doing things. Have the courage of your convictions' (Participant 21).

At the same time as eschewing advice to others, however, carers generally do not seem to subscribe to a relativist position. There seem to be some principles or concepts that guide individuals that they see as applying not just applying to themselves but having a somewhat more normative status. These principles or concepts (dignity, respect, person) however, seem to be more related to notions of personhood than principle-based ethical frameworks and as such are resonant of personalism (see, for example, Schotsmans 1999) in giving value to relationships, uniqueness, commitment, and solidarity. The point here, however, is that empirical research can identify what work such principles and concepts do in practice, generating the need for further analytical work in determining the status (normative or otherwise) that those principles.

Finally, the project can contribute something to debate as to the role of empirical research in the field of ethics. Haimes (2002) believes that empirical work can contribute on three levels

It provides the data on particular substantive issues, that is, the 'facts' about what people say or do on particular topics. This in turn provides data on how individuals and groups think and act ethically; that is the 'how' and the 'why' of what people say and do, that fall outside the frameworks of formal philosophy. In addition, the empirical work demonstrates and refines techniques for gaining access to the 'what', 'how' and 'why' of ethical behaviour (p. 112).

The project described here has, in some small way, contributed to each of these three levels. Through accessing the lived experience of family carers it has enhanced our understanding of what the ethical issues and how carers think about these issues. But more than that, it has identified concepts (such as being true, faithfulness, and mutuality) that might benefit from philosophical analysis and reflection. In turn, the results of that analysis and reflection can be returned to the field of practice in the form of guidelines and recommendations for practice. In so doing it illustrates the potential of the cyclical model of empirical ethics outlined by Hope (2004).

8.6. **Concluding remarks**

The onset and progression of dementia can turn the moral world of carers upside down. In the face of such upheaval carers attempt to create an inhabitable moral world through the application of a range of (sometimes revised) ethical principles within a framework of meaning drawn from relationships, shared histories, and other socio-cultural reference points. These principles and reference points may be different to those of health care professionals but are not necessarily or generally as adverse or hostile to them as the quote from Participant 52 above would suggest, as the deployment of similar, if not identical, principles indicate:

> But when I was looking after my wife I didn't need any help, she, was the one, so everything really was gravitated toward providing or doing whatever was in her best interests, you know (Participant 33).

> ... but its only in recent months that I've realised that it *is* possible to, to maintain something of the independence that, uh, she had before, uh, by giving her choices in, in often very small matters, but sometimes in quite, quite large matters, and always, always consulting her about things (Participant 7).

In drawing on principles and bases to justify their actions carers attempt to present themselves as having tried to act with probity – in Baruch's terms as 'morally adequate' (Baruch 1981) – in the face of both adversity and the inadequacies of previously held moral beliefs. (For example, taking action that might constrain or be against the wishes of the person living with dementia the action may be justified in terms of safety or best interests.) It is possible, however, to find resonances of many different ethical theories both within and across transcripts: principalism, the ethics of care, narrative ethics, consequentialism, deontology, personalism – though this is not the language of family carers. This moral positioning is important in understanding the realization of values by everyday actors, not as the application of a neatly worked out theoretical stance but as a unique and flexible configuration of values, principles, theory, and experimentation. Essentially everyday ethics is a performative practice, a realization (making real) of values and ethical principles in social context.

In identifying ethical issues and the values and reasoning behind ethical decisions the project has enhanced our understanding of the moral lives of family carers of people with dementia and has provided rich data for further ethical analysis. In so doing, it has illustrated the potential of the cyclical model of empirical ethics and, hopefully, contributed in some small way to the field.

References

Alzheimer's Society (2006). Facts about dementia. Alzheimer's Society website: http://www.alzheimers.org.uk/Facts_about_dementia/index.htm (Accessed September 2007).

Baldwin C, Hughes J, Hope T, Jacoby R and Ziebland S (2003). Ethics and dementia: mapping the literature by bibliometric analysis. *International Journal of Geriatric Psychiatry*, **18**(1), 41–54.

Baldwin C, Hughes J, Hope T, Jacoby R and Ziebland S (2004). Ethics and dementia: the experience of family carers. *Progress in Neurology and Psychiatry*, **8**(5), 24–8.

Baumann Z (1993). *Postmodern ethics*. Blackwell, Oxford.

Baruch G (1981). Moral tales: parents' stories of encounters with the health profession. *Sociology of Health and Illness*, **3**(3), 275–96.

Beauchamp TL and Childress JF (2001). *Principles of biomedical ethics*, 5th edn. Oxford University Press, New York.

Borry P, Schotsmans P and Dierickx K (2004a). Editorial. Empirical ethics: a challenge to bioethics. *Medicine, Health Care, and Philosophy*, **7**(1), 1–3.

Borry P, Schotsmans P and Dierickx K (2004b). What is the role of empirical research in bioethical reflection and decision-making? An ethical analysis. *Medicine, Health Care, and Philosophy*, **7**(1), 41–53.

Borry P, Schotsmans P and Dierickx K (2005). The birth of the empirical turn in bioethics. *Bioethics*, **19**(1), 49–71.

Borry P, Schotsmans P and Dierickx K (2006). Empirical research in bioethical journals. A quantitative analysis. *Journal of Medical Ethics*, **32**(4), 240–5.

Burns A and Rabins P (2000). Carer burden in dementia. *International Journal of Geriatric Psychiatry*, **15**(S1), S9–13.

Butterworth M (1995). Dementia: the family caregiver's perspective. *Journal of Mental Health*, 4(2), 125–32.

Chandros Hull S, Taylor HA and Kass NE (2001). Qualitative methods. In J Sugarman and DP Sulmasy, eds. *Methods in medical ethics*, pp. 146–68. Georgetown University Press, Washington.

Cross P (1997). Carers: the carers' own perspective. In R Jacoby and C Oppenheimer, eds. *Psychiatry in the elderly*, pp. 403–9. Oxford University Press, Oxford.

Dierckx de Casterle B, Grypdonck M, Cannaerts N and Steeman E (2004). Empirical ethics in action: lessons from two empirical studies in nursing ethics. *Medicine, Health Care, and Philosophy*, **7**(1), 31–9.

Edwards J (2003). Explicit connections: ethnographic enquiry in north-west England. In J Edwards, S Franklin, E Hirsch, F Price and M Strathern, eds. *Technologies of procreation*. Manchester University Press, Manchester.

Fellows LK (1998). Competency and consent in dementia. *Journal of the American Geriatrics Society*, **46**(7), 922–6.

Glaser BG (1992). *Basics of grounded theory*. Sociological Press, Mill Valley.

Goldenberg M (2005). Evidence-based ethics? On evidence-based practice and the "empirical turn" from normative bioethics. *BMC Medical Ethics*, November. Accessible online at: http://www.biomedcentral.com/1472–6939/6/11. (Accessed September 2007).

Gruffydd E and Randle J (2006). Alzheimer's disease and the psychosocial burden for caregivers. *Community Practitioner*, **79**(1), 15–8.

Haimes E (2002). What can the social sciences contribute to the study of ethics? Theoretical, empirical and substantive considerations. *Bioethics*, **16**(2), 89–113.

Hoefler JM (2000). Making decisions about tube feeding for severely demented patients at the end of life: clinical, legal, and ethical considerations. *Death Studies*, **24**(3), 233–54.

Hope T (2004). How can empirical research reflect and inform medical ethics? Contribution to investigating ethics and mental disorders meeting 30 June–1 July 2004. Report available from: http://www.wellcome.ac.uk/assets/wtx025115.pdf (Accessed September 2007)

Hope T and Oppenheimer C (1997). Ethics and the psychiatry of old age. In R Jacoby and C Oppenheimer, eds. *Psychiatry in the elderly*, pp. 709–35.Oxford University Press, Oxford.

Hughes JC, Hope T, Reader S and Rice D (2002a). Dementia and ethics: the views of informal carers. *Journal of the Royal Society of Medicine*, **95**(5), 242–6.

Hughes JC, Hope T, Savulescu J and Ziebland S (2002b). Carers, ethics and dementia: a survey and review of the literature. *International Journal of Geriatric Psychiatry*, **17**(1), 35–40.

Pratt C, Schmall V and Wright S (1987). Ethical concerns of family caregivers to dementia patients. *The Gerontologist*, **27**(5), 632–8.

Schneider J, Murray J, Banerjee S and Mann A (1999). Eurocare: a cross-national study of co-resident spouse carers for people with Alzheimer's disease: I – factors associated with carer burden. *International Journal of Geriatric Psychiatry*, **14**(8), 651–61.

Schotsmans P (1999). Personalism in medical ethics. *Ethical Perspectives*, **6**(1), 10–20.

Strauss A and Corbin J (1998). *Basics of qualitative research: techniques and procedures for developing grounded theory*. Sage Publications, Thousand Oaks, CA.

Van der Scheer L and Widdershoven G (2004). Integrated empirical ethics: a loss of normativity? *Medicine, Health Care, and Philosophy* **7**(1), 71–9,

Chapter 9

The advance directive conjuring trick and the person with dementia

Julian C. Hughes and Steven R. Sabat

9.1. Introduction

In an ideal world philosophers would approach their work without prejudice or preconceptions. Of course, this is not how the world is. But, as Wittgenstein once suggested, it may be the seemingly innocuous moves that cause problems. Wittgenstein asks how philosophical problems arise and suggests:

> The first step is the one that altogether escapes notice...But that is just what commits us to a particular way of looking at the matter... (The decisive movement in the conjuring trick has been made, and it was the very one that we thought quite innocent.) (Wittgenstein 1968, p. 308).

The innocent move immediately has us heading in a particular and problematic direction.

Concerning philosophical problems, Wittgenstein famously wrote:

> These are, of course, not empirical problems; they are solved, rather, by looking into the workings of our language, and that in such a way as to make us recognise those workings: *in despite of* an urge to misunderstand them. The problems are solved, not by giving new information, but by arranging what we have always known. Philosophy is a battle against the bewitchment of our intelligence by means of language (Wittgenstein 1968, p. 109).

Hence, Wittgenstein suggests that philosophy is not empirical; but philosophical problems are solved by looking at how language works in its ordinary setting. The philosophical mistake (often leading to a dilemma) is frequently the first step – the conjuring trick – which involves abstracting language from its ordinary setting.

In this chapter we shall look at what people actually say in order to illuminate and suggest ways to solve real ethical and practical problems in connection with dementia. In the next section we shall set out these problems. Then we shall outline the empirical method used and discuss our analysis of the resulting data, which comprises conversations involving people with dementia. Finally, we shall show how the qualitative data contributes to the solution of the ethical and practical problems. And we shall briefly consider the relevance of this empirical work to philosophy.

9.2. **The problems**

The ethical problem we shall discuss arises directly from practice in connection with the use of advance directives by people who develop dementia. The problem is that someone might have stipulated something in an advance directive presupposing that the state of dementia would at some point be unbearable. But this might turn out not to be the case. The ethical problem is then whether the stipulations of the advance directive should continue to hold sway.

This problem has become familiar in the literature. There is, for instance, the debate between Ronald Dworkin and Rebecca Dresser. Dworkin (1993) proposed that 'critical interests' (which concern our longer term commitments and interest in the shape of our lives as a whole) should take precedence. Hence, advance directives, typically expressing a person's concerns about how life ends, should be honoured as a way of respecting the person's autonomy and well-being. Dresser (1995), on the other hand, emphasized the need to respect the person's current views and wishes, that is, the person's 'experiential interests'. At the extreme it is argued that the previously expressed views are not necessarily the views of the same person (Dresser 1986).

This is certainly the concern expressed by Hope (1994) in his discussion of Mr D, who had changed so profoundly once he had dementia that his wife said he was not the same man as the one she married. Although the case and the discussion around it raise concerns about advance directives (Louw and Hughes 2005), it also raises a deeper philosophical problem about personal identity (McMillan 2006). The issue of advance directives, therefore, raises profound questions about our views of the person with dementia (Hughes 2001; Hughes *et al.* 2006a).

Jaworska (1999) contributed a sophisticated critique of the Dworkin–Dresser debate by proposing that people with dementia might still be valuers, even when dementia is quite marked. As valuers, Jaworska argued that people with dementia can still exhibit the capacity for autonomy and generate critical interests. Jaworska's assault on Dworkin was sophisticated in that she was able both to undercut his argument by extending the conceptions of autonomy and well-being to take account of the possibility and significance of valuing, and to show, using real cases, that people with dementia are still valuers. However, whilst this allowed her to show some sympathy for Dworkin's analysis, it also meant that on the grounds of real experience, she was more prone towards Dresser's view that the person here and now should be given full attention. Thus she was inclined to favour the person's contemporaneous interests over previously expressed (advance directive) views:

> So long as the person is still a valuer, current decisions on her behalf ought to take seriously her current values (Jaworska 1999, p. 137).

Meanwhile, Widdershoven and Berghmans (2006) describe the case of Mrs P who has an advance directive stating she wishes her life to be ended if she is incompetent and unable to take care of herself. The problem in the case was that Mrs P was disconsolate, yet became distrustful of staff who discussed the advance directive with her. It was then difficult for her carers to know what her real wishes were at the time and, in part, this was because her values were opaque, even if they could be interpreted.

The issue of advance directives in dementia seemingly raises problems regarding the use of the concepts of 'self' or 'person'. We can look at these problems in three related ways:

1 **The ethical then and now question**: There is an 'ethical problem' concerning critical and experiential interests. This has sometimes been formulated as a distinction between the 'then-self' and the 'now-self'. The ethical problem is whether to give precedence to the wishes and interests of the 'then-self' or the 'now-self'.

2 **The philosophical self question**: Underlying the ethical problem is a 'philosophical concern' about the nature of personhood. Is the person with an advance directive the same person he or she was before? This philosophical problem raises questions of a practical nature. How is the person's selfhood maintained in the face of cognitive impairment and the sort of psychosocial disintegration that is typical of dementia?

3 **The practical interpretation question**: Finally there is the 'practical difficulty' of knowing how to interpret a person's advance directive in concrete circumstances where the person's abilities to communicate or express opinions is diminished and where the stipulations of the advance directive cause concern to those now caring for the person.

9.3. Method

To answer the ethical and philosophical questions it would be possible to conduct a solely conceptual argument. However, Wittgenstein encourages us to look in more detail at what people say and do. The view that is often ignored in dementia research is the view of the person with dementia (Cotrell and Schulz 1993). Hence, the approach here has been to engage people with dementia in discursive dialogue over time with the aim of understanding their meanings, concerns, and interests. The benefit of this empirical work is that it enriches our appreciation of the factors that should be relevant; moreover, it has the added benefit of providing ways to approach the practical difficulties of interpreting advance directives.

In the case examples that follow, the people in question had been diagnosed with dementia of the Alzheimer's type (AD) according to standard criteria (McKhann *et al.* 1984). In each case, the person with dementia was engaged in conversation once or twice a week for 2 to 4 hours per week, for a period of 4 months to 2 years. Conversations involved issues that were of concern to the people with dementia, including their subjective experience of the disease. Time was also spent discussing aspects of the individuals' past lives in order to gain insight into their values, attitudes, and dispositions. This provided a larger context in which to understand their present experiences, and helped to establish a trusting and genuine relationship. Each conversation was tape recorded and transcribed verbatim, including mispronunciations, poor syntax, and the like. Further details about the cases presented can be found in Sabat (2001). The overall aim of the project was to encourage a better understanding of the experience of dementia from the inside, from the perspective of the person with dementia. The implications of this, *vis-à-vis* advance directives, are drawn out here.

9.4. Interpretation and analysis

We shall present data relevant to the three types of question separately. However, it should be recalled that the different questions reflect aspects of the same problem to do with the 'self' or 'person'.

9.4.1. The ethical then and now question

The case of Dr M, a retired, female academic with a doctorate and a masters qualification in social work, provides an example of a person with dementia whose interests in being able to use language effectively and in maintaining her intellectual abilities were well established. These same interests persisted even though she (*a*) had been diagnosed as being in the moderate to severe stage of the disease at the time of the recorded conversations; (*b*) evidenced severe word-finding problems; (*c*) could not sign her name, was unable to perform simple calculations, copy a design, or recall the date, month, or year; (*d*) was unable to use eating utensils, and had striking difficulties with dressing and grooming and no longer drove a car. In the following extract, she discussed the frustration she experienced as a result of her word-finding problems, given that she had possessed extraordinary linguistic ability throughout her life.

SRS: You're not just any ordinary person who has some problems finding words. You're a person for whom words, words to you are kind of like a musical instrument.

Dr M: Um hum, um hum. That's exactly right.

SRS: And so the kind of frustration you feel would be greater than for a person whose focus in life was not so literary. That could give you cause for a lot of grief.

Dr M: I think the issue is, that is, for me maybe especially this day for some reason or other, but for last, maybe four years, that I am not satisfied with myself because what I want isn't here. I've, uh, thinking of it and it makes me angry as well as, that is part of the... and I guess that is what is happening now. Don't you think?

Dr M could not feel 'unsatisfied' if she no longer maintained an interest in and valued greatly, the ability to express herself with the linguistic grace that was such an important part of her life prior to the onset of AD.

In the next extract, she expresses this interest even more blatantly:

Dr M: I don't know how you go through the various steps, but I want to have a, a feel that when I talk, that when I caw, talk, I, I can talk.

SRS: Um hum.

Dr M: I can't always do that.

SRS: Um hum, well, you're doing it pretty well right now.

Dr M: No, but when I haven't, we're just talking uh,

SRS: Light

Dr M: Light, light stuff, and even light sa stuff are problems because I miss and word and I can't find it.

SRS: Um hum.

Dr M: And I'm probably able to do it as other people can, but uh, not it that good, it's not good enough for me.

In order for Dr M to evaluate her present linguistic ability as being 'not good enough for me', her standard for being 'good enough' had to have been coeval with the standard that she held and maintained in decades of life prior to the time of the conversation above.

As part of her professional training Dr M learned a great deal about the functioning of support groups and group therapy. At the time of the extract presented below, she was a member of a support group for people with AD and was dissatisfied with the manner in which the group leaders were managing the group dynamics.

Dr M: Um anyhow, they they were talking about how they could make it organized. I had for about uh maybe five days, five days of the time, five times had that not they didn't have that. I couldn't put that in them. I knew exactly what they should do and uh and I, I, at least I don't mean I was perfect. I mean there's a way of bringing in and uh and so I say I watched them and I help, I saw what was going on, and I was not a hero... see we don't know each other's backgrounds at all and there were and our experiences are different and I don't know how to... nobody says uh, what that's a problem. What do you do doctor?

> SRS: Let me see if I understand here. You, you see an opportunity to give some
>   constructive criticism.
> Dr M: Well, ya. It's peoples are not all there at the same time. It's not well organized.
> SRS: And you have some thoughts about how to organize it.
> Dr M: Ya, but it's not my role.

Dr M's evaluation of the group leaders' work was based upon her previously established understanding and professional expertise. She wanted to be helpful, as befitting someone trained to be a therapist, but she rightly recognized that it was not her role to instruct or criticize the group leaders.

Her desire to be helpful was often apparent during the 2-year association with SRS and is exemplified in the following extract from a conversation about the interactions that occurred at a support group meeting that SRS had attended. Having spoken to the group once before, SRS was asked to return, and he had expressed his delight to Dr M.

> Dr M: I knew that! I knew that, I knew that it gives you just what you're looking for.
>   So uh, and I think it gives, gives the group some. You repeated, I mean I
>   repeated what you had said in a sense.
> SRS: Yes indeed! I think we learn more about what people do (when we observe
>   them) in very rich social settings.
> Dr M: Um hum, and you can have it for the next, uh... paper
> SRS: That's right!

Dr M was well aware of SRSs interest in elucidating the remaining intact cognitive abilities of people with AD and understood that the support group provided him with fertile ground for this research. She expressed, in her last comment in the extract above, her delight that he could use the information gained from the group dynamics in 'the next...paper'. She demonstrated her lifelong interest in communicating knowledge through published papers and she expressed her understanding, as a fellow academic, that SRS might wish to pursue this course.

9.4.2. Analysis: Dr M – then and now

A large part of the advance directive 'problem' stems from the then and now dichotomy, which potentially leads to a clash of the past and present selves. As we have seen, however, Dr M's speech reveals the extent to which her 'then' remains present in her 'now'. There is a very ordinary sense in which talk of how a person was then and how a person is now seems reasonable. This mirrors the way in which Dworkin's (1993) talk of critical and experiential interests makes sense. Indeed, he is pointing to an important distinction in terms of how we estimate and rank the features of our lives. Nevertheless, the conjuring trick has taken place. We start to think of separate selves precisely because we have allowed talk of 'then-selves' and 'now-selves'. The language of 'then' and 'now' bewitches us into thinking of separate entities. Dr M, however, demonstrates continuity between her selves; moreover, she shows how her previous self is still present and part of her present self. There simply is no dichotomy. And, very clearly, she is still (as Jaworska (1999) suggested) someone who values things about her self and the world.

All of this has been well put by Stephen Post:

> The radical differentiation between the formerly intact or 'then' self and the currently demented or 'now' self, as put forward by some commentators, is simply a misrepresentation of the facts. The reality is that until the very advanced and even terminal stage of dementia, the person with dementia will usually have sporadically articulated memories of deeply meaningful events and relationships ensconced in long-term memory. It is nonsense to bifurcate in any strong sense the self into 'then' and 'now', as if continuities are not occasionally quite manifest. This is why it is essential that professional caregivers be aware of the person's life story, making up for losses by providing cues toward continuity in self-consciousness. Even in the advanced stage of dementia... one finds varying degrees of emotional and relational expression, remnants of personality, and even meaningful non-verbal communication (as in the reaching out for a hug) (Post 2006, p. 231).

None the less, there is a potential criticism that might be levelled at these thoughts. It could reasonably be argued that, at some stage, there will no longer be the requisite continuity between Dr M's past and present and, therefore, it may make no sense to talk of her being able to manifest her past (critical) interests in her present. Indeed, the threat posed to psychological continuity by dementia is precisely the threat highlighted by Hope (1994). Continuity and connectedness were the psychological features by which Parfit (1984) characterized personal identity; hence the argument that a loss of psychological continuity and connectedness equates to a loss of the self. It may simply be said that Dr M is not yet ill enough to raise the ethical problem of then and now.

In the next section we shall discuss this criticism further. It is important to note, however, that on standard tests of cognitive function and activities of daily living Dr M was found at this time to be in the moderate to severe stage of AD. Nevertheless, as the quotations above show, she is able to demonstrate an accurate, layered, and rich appreciation of her past and a fine sensitivity to how her past relates to her present. This in itself should alert us to the possibility that the talk of 'then' and 'now' is, at least, possibly tricky.

9.4.3. The philosophical self question

Aspects of Social Construction Theory (Harré 1983, 1991) may be employed as heuristic devices to identify facets of selfhood in a person suffering from dementia and show that the loss of certain aspects of selfhood may be traced to dysfunctional social interactions rather than to the neuropathology of the disease.

From the constructionist point of view, selfhood is expressed in public discourse (conversation as well as behaviour), and can be analysed into three different forms. The self of personal identity, Self 1, is expressed through the use of personal pronouns such as 'I', 'me', 'myself', 'my', 'mine', 'our'. One could also point to oneself to express one's personal identity. We experience this aspect of selfhood through our single point of view on the world: the one continuous experience of events that forms the narrative or our lives. Thus we take responsibility for our actions, index (locate for others) feelings and experiences as being our own, and tell autobiographical stories. In principle, a person could suffer from amnesia yet still have an intact self of personal identity as demonstrated in conversational discourse.

Self 2 comprises a person's past and present physical and mental attributes and beliefs about those attributes. One's height and weight, eye pigmentation, one's sense of humour, religious and political convictions, educational achievements, vocational pursuits, are examples of physical and mental attributes. A person may have beliefs about his or her attributes, which may have long histories or be more recent (such as being diagnosed with AD).

Self 3 is made up of the various different personae that we construct in the social situations in which we live. Each persona involves a specific pattern of behaviour which is, in many ways, distinct from the others. One and the same person may display patterns of behaviour that are quite different from one another, such as the dedicated teacher, the deferential child, or romantic spouse. Each persona requires for its existence the cooperation of at least one other person in our social world. Thus, the Self 3 personae are extremely vulnerable in ways that Self 1 and aspects of Self 2 are not. If others view the person with dementia as being 'defective', 'burdensome', and the like, the only Self 3 persona which the afflicted person would be able to construct would be that of the 'dysfunctional patient'. Under these conditions, there could be, potentially, a loss of Self 3 personae. Such a loss would hardly be caused by the neuropathology of the disease, but rather by the lack of cooperation from others.

In the case of Dr M we have already seen a number of examples of the persistence of her Self 1 through her use of first person indexicals. In addition, her Self 2 attributes include holding two advanced degrees, being a retired university professor, having great respect for the elegant use of language, having a diagnosis of AD in the moderate to severe stages, her embarrassment about that attribute, her word-finding problems and her negative reactions to them, and the like.

The case of Mrs D illustrates the social dynamics involved in the persistence of Self 3, the multiple social personae or identities. Mrs D was a 70-year-old, married woman who was diagnosed with probable AD (McKhann *et al.* 1984) in the moderate to severe stage. She could not name the day of the week, the date, the month, the season, year, the city, nor the county. She had a number of sensory-motor problems, such as difficulties in picking up eating utensils, getting food to her mouth, imitating the movements of instructors during exercises. She underestimated her age, had difficulties in discriminating right from left and in finding her way to the bathroom at the day centre she attended 2 days each week. Although she did have frequent word-finding problems, her ability to use spoken language was not as compromised as was her recall and sensory-motor skills. She was a high school graduate who was raised in a show business family and loved to tell jokes and sing songs.

When asked if she would relate some of the significant experiences in her life, she said,

> The only thing I can think of is when someone came and told me, 'come, there's a problem here'. It was all about Alfat, Alfased, no, it's not Alfased, Alzheimer's.

She was quite aware of the effects of the disease: 'It's a hell of a disease'. And when she experienced word-finding problems, she would often comment, 'This is the Alzheimer's right now carrying on'.

Unlike Dr M, who preferred to avoid neuropsychological testing, Mrs D frequently volunteered for extensive testing as a subject in drug studies at the National Institute of Health (NIH). For Mrs D, this was a way for her to construct an aspect of her social identity, that of 'helpful volunteer'. She said,

> That was the nicety of it, cause I could have said, 'no', but believe me, if I can help me and my (fellow) man, I would do it.

For Mrs D, frequent errors on tests did not carry the same meaning that they did for Dr M, and so she pursued this avenue of being of service to others. Likewise, at the adult day centre, she was known as the 'life of the party', for her ability to make others laugh by telling jokes, for engaging others in song, and for helping the staff with the process of integrating new people into the group with her outgoing, warm personality. She was also quite sensitive to the moods of others, often providing sympathy and solace to those experiencing difficulty. In fact, she referred to her role at the day centre as 'her work', often insisting that her husband hurry to take her there lest she be 'late for work'. For some time, Mr D believed his wife to be suffering from a delusion caused by AD about having a job, until it became obvious to him that she was referring to her role at the day centre. She was quite clear about her job:

> Some of them are in bad shape, you know, that they couldn't remember a thing. I would try to help them. That's what you have to do almost if you want to get along... I would work, you know, with somebody just to keep them happy.

Mrs D's discourse indicates an intact self of personal identity through her use of first person pronouns and an intact social identity, of which she was proud, and which she maintained with the cooperation of others at the day centre and at the NIH. At home, however, Mrs D's social identity was confined to that of 'dysfunctional patient' by her loving husband who, quite innocently, would not enlist her help around the house; nor would he discuss with her some of his own problems because, in his words, 'she wouldn't understand'. Having negatively positioned his wife (see Sabat 2006), Mr D innocently created a situation in which his wife could not offer him comfort and sympathy as she did for so many others at the day centre. Thus, the Self 3 of a person with dementia can be quite vulnerable, but that vulnerability inheres in social dynamics rather than in neuropathology alone.

9.4.4. Analysis: Mrs D's philosophical self

Let us return to the criticism that perhaps Mrs D (like Dr M), despite the diagnosis of a moderate to severe AD, was simply not ill enough to show the sort of psychological discontinuities that would raise doubts concerning the intactness of her self. In passing, it is again worth considering Post's (2006) words, which suggest that it may only be in the terminal phase of the disease that the person lacks the required sense of a previous self. This is likely to be the same in most diseases, not just in dementia; yet it might be part of the conjuring trick to presume that even in the terminal phase of a disease the self no longer exists. Thinking about Self 3 is a way of seeing the trick.

To revert to the unanswered question, might Mrs D cease to have selfhood at some stage of her illness? Well, we already know that she is markedly impaired by AD in a number of regards. If the key criterion for personhood is recall memory, we would have to say that her personhood is already deficient. But what would such a statement mean when applied to a woman who is as socially adept and gregarious as Mrs D? Might we not, for the sake of equity, if this were to be allowed, have to say that others (without dementia) who lack Mrs D's social accomplishments are deficient in some other respect in terms of personhood? The truth is that we flourish as persons in innumerable ways and to stipulate that only some manifestations of our flourishing should be regarded as tokens of personhood is to restrict our own possibilities. That is to say, we need a broad view of what it is to be a person (Hughes 2001). Social constructionism encourages such a view: it draws attention to the extent that we are situated in various ways as human agents.

Mrs D emphasizes the extent to which selfhood is maintained by social interaction. Her interactions at the day centre give her a purpose, but more than this (at a conceptual level) they are a manifestation of her embeddedness in 'webs of interlocution' (Gillett and McMillan 2001, p. 162). At some point it might be argued that she can no longer participate in these 'webs of interlocution' (McMillan 2006); but it might equally be argued that elements of her personhood could then be held in place by these networks of human intercourse. These might be regarded in terms of interconnecting narratives that help to maintain personhood; or they might reflect a type of situated agency, according to which personhood is a function (in part) of the embedded understandings we share just by our participation in human nature (Aquilina and Hughes 2006).

So we can argue that, even in the terminal stages of any disease, the individual's personhood is still maintainable by others. For, the possibilities of personhood are uncircumscribable (Wiggins 1987). They are certainly not confined to recall memory as suggested by one interpretation of Parfit (1984). Despite deficits in recall, Mrs D demonstrates herself to be a situated embodied agent (Hughes 2001). Moreover, we also see another possibility, which is that her personhood depends on others. On the one hand she can be positioned, at the day centre, as a useful asset to the group; whilst, on the other hand, at home she can be positioned as dysfunctional. The heuristic value of social constructionism (Thornton 2006) is that it alerts us to the possibilities of Mrs D's remaining capacities as a person.

The first step in the conjuring trick is the one that tends to equate personhood with a particular capacity, typically the capacity to recall things. But the capacity to relate to people – 'I would work, you know, with somebody just to keep them happy' – with the intention of improving their emotional state is, arguably, at least as important. Another aspect of the conjuring trick, which we are too easily prone to miss, is the tendency to view matters through the spectacles of the biomedical model (Downs *et al.* 2006). Just as the person is regarded quintessentially as requiring psychological continuity and connectedness, so too a deficit in 'memory' (by which is usually meant 'recall' or 'episodic' memory) is taken to reflect a dysfunctional brain. The enormous significance of brain disease leads to the possibility of malignant positioning (Sabat 2006). This possibility, as well as the possibility that the psychosocial environment might be enabling and restorative, emphasizes the extent to which, as in the African doctrine of *ubuntu* (Battle 1997),[1] a person exists, *qua* self, through other people. Mrs D exemplifies these possibilities: through her interactions with others she shows how her values and her continuing ability to value can be demonstrated and encouraged.

---

[1] We are indebted to Dr Stephen Louw for drawing the theology of *ubuntu* to our attention.

9.4.5. **The practical interpretation question**

It is often difficult to understand what a person with dementia is saying. In many cases, however, taking 'the intentional stance' (Dennett 1987) aids understanding. Then one can use what psycholinguists call 'indirect repair', in which one actively inquires about the speaker's intentions, sometimes rephrasing so as to determine if one understood the speaker's meaning correctly. The following extract illustrates this. Dr B was a retired, male academic diagnosed with a moderate to severe AD. This conversational extract concerns Dr B's subjective experience of AD and demonstrates indirect repair:

> Dr B: When I leave something with hiatus I think maybe I get, I wouldn't say disturbed, but it, it, it, screws up the rhythm.
> SRS: Oh, so if you're in the middle of thinking about something...
> Dr B: Uh huh
> SRS: And you get distracted...
> Dr B: Yeah
> SRS: Then you lose what you wanted to say?
> Dr B: Yeah, but um, I can, uh, wait for a little while
> SRS: Um hum
> Dr B: And uh, I get, and uh, I get rejuvenation, and uh, up it comes.
> SRS: So there are times when you get distracted and you lose track of what you wanted to say, but if you wait a little while, it comes back?
> Dr B: Ya, it'll sort of creeps in.
> SRS: That's really good... it's helpful to know that.
> Dr B: What does it mean?
> SRS: It means that you... (he interrupts)
> Dr B: Is this of any value?

Dr B could easily be positioned as being confused. Here we see, however, SRS 'repairing' or elaborating on what Dr B meant when he said 'I leave something with hiatus'. He is talking about what happens when he gets distracted: he loses the thought, but it then might come back to him later ('I get rejuvenation, and... up it comes'). The point about 'rejuvenation' might have been missed if the initial point had not been correctly interpreted by SRS. Strikingly, Dr B then questions whether what he is saying is 'of any value', meaning to the research project, which he knew he was engaged upon with SRS. Thus he demonstrates, as elsewhere in his conversations, his recall (despite his dementia) of (what he referred to as) 'the project' and the obvious importance he attaches to this sort of academic work. This in itself is a sign of the persisting value he attaches to intellectual pursuits. It is clear that communication between people with dementia and healthy others can be facilitated and thereby improved (Sabat 2001); but it is also clear that the person with dementia must be thought of, positioned as, someone who is trying to say something in order for the process of facilitation to occur in the first place.

On another occasion, when Dr B was very ill and in hospital, he was very upset, angry, and emotional during a discussion with SRS. At one point he said:

> Dr B [crying]: When can channa, channa, channa, my favourite [says youngest son's name three times], what, what can I come? What can I want? Come what I come, come what I come, come what I come. She was, was in, in there. She was in one too.

All of this seems to make little sense. However, SRS was very familiar with Dr B and his family, and accordingly, could guess Dr B's concerns. He was aware that Dr B would be missing his wife and would feel out of control in hospital. The accumulated history and contextual knowledge enabled SRS to facilitate some meaningful and potentially therapeutic dialogue (see Sabat 2001, pp. 286-90).

9.4.6. Analysis: meaning-making and the practice of interpretation

It may be allowed that the dichotomy between the 'then-self' and the 'now-self' is an artefact created by language; it may be allowed that the embodied self exists as a situated agent, with personhood held to some extent by others; yet it might still be argued that, in severe dementia, the self is simply too inaccessible, leaving us with an uncertainty, not only (conceptually) concerning the self, but also (practically) concerning what might be best for him or her. The possibility of 'indirect repair', as shown in conversations with Dr B, is but one way in which greater attention to people with dementia might reveal their meanings, including the things they value.

More broadly, Dr B's case demonstrates the utility of co-creating meaning. If the person with dementia is truly inaccessible, then a process of co-creating or re-creating his or her meaning, bearing in mind the need to take a broader view of what it is to be a person, will need to occur. This will involve talking to all those concerned with the person, and crucially it will involve talking with the person himself/herself. It is in this context that an advance directive becomes valuable. However the breadth of the person's concerns – revealed by paying attention to the broader aspects of the person's narrative, which is embedded in a social and cultural context, which may involve particular moral and spiritual attitudes – should mean that the advance directive is regarded as just one item (potentially an important one) contributing to the overall picture.

The difficulty in Widdershoven and Berghmans's (2006) case of Mrs P was that some staff were finding it difficult to establish the sort of therapeutic relationship with her that would allow a broader interpretation of her current values and concerns so as to accommodate her past and present wishes. However, inasmuch as the staff had elicited some information concerning things she valued, such as privacy, there was the possibility that they could move towards an engagement with her that would allow further interpretation. In order to make sense of her current view of the world (meaning-making) a good deal of interpretation would be required. This involves a process of filling in the gaps that surround her, in terms of her story, her beliefs, and her values.

In the case of Dr B we see the importance of two things: first, the need for people with dementia to remain engaged in relationships (which may be called 'therapeutic', or perhaps simply 'meaningful'); secondly, the benefits of and requirement for 'indirect repair' as a specific technique for co-creating meaning. Of course, these two aspects interrelate: where the quality of the relationship is good, and the healthy interlocutor is patient and takes the intentional stance, there is a greater chance that interpretations will tend to be meaningful.

The conjuring trick here is one of which Wittgenstein himself was well aware. It involves seeing meaning in a particular way. Put briefly (but see Taylor 1985; Hughes *et al.* 2006b), it involves regarding meaning as a type of designation, where items in language pick out items in the world. As such, 'When can channa, channa, channa, my favourite... what, what can I come'?, seems on the face of it meaningless. However, understood in a context in which meaning-making is possible, where previous knowledge of the person allows successful interpretation, the words show sense. Understanding requires a grasp of the idea that meaning is use: meaning is itself situated; it is understood against 'a very complicated filigree pattern... the whole hurly-burly' (Wittgenstein 1980b, p. 624, 629) that forms the background against which we make our judgements and interpretations.

9.5. Conclusions

In *Culture and Value* Wittgenstein wrote:

> 'If we look at things from an ethnological point of view, does that mean we are saying that philosophy is ethnology? No, it only means that we are taking up a position right outside so as to be able to see things *more objectively*' (Wittgenstein 1980a, p. 37).

This suggests that philosophy is not ethnology, but philosophers look at things as ethnologists do. Like the ethnologist, the philosopher (Wittgenstein suggests) must be a careful observer; but the philosopher observes (and describes) afresh language itself. This again is similar to the ethnologist whose task will often be to record what people actually say. The ethnologist's approach is to observe language in its ordinary setting; it is the opposite of abstracting. It is best achieved from the outside, because the tendency to abstract is a tendency that lurks in language (it bewitches us). The area of interest is the same for the philosopher and the ethnologist: it is the hustle and bustle, the hurly-burly of human existence (Hughes and Fulford 2005). It is the detailed patterning of the human world, quintessentially shown in human language, which needs to be described and seen afresh without bewitchment.

This study has used an ethnographic approach inasmuch as it has involved an objective observation of human beings as revealed by their conversation in their ordinary settings. From this we can glean a host of empirical observations about how people with dementia feel themselves to be regarded or about how they feel in themselves. This leads to an uneasy comparison, because in truth people with dementia are much like other people in terms of their feelings, yet they can easily be (and often are) positioned as, in various ways, inadequate. Wittgenstein's comments about philosophy (cited earlier) being a matter of 'looking into the workings of our language' suggest how studying the conversations of people with dementia can be useful philosophically.

At one level, this is firsthand data about personhood, which underpins the problems we highlighted at the start of the chapter. We have seen how language can bewitch us into thinking of the self as existing in different compartments of 'then' and 'now'. In reality, as shown by how people talk, we do not make these splits: we are the persons that we now are, which involves being as we once were, but which does not involve being different persons to the persons we once were, even if it does involve being different. Nor does our natural talk show signs of reducing personhood to one particular capacity. Ordinary language is not in this regard simple; if anything, it shows the complexity of our thoughts about personhood. And reflecting on human exchanges in this way also demonstrates the extent to which, in order to understand one another, we readily rely upon context. These are lessons for philosophers from the qualitative data of this research.

At another level, this sort of empirical work has relevance as a means to solve the ethical, philosophical, and practical problems with which we began. 'The problems are solved', said Wittgenstein, 'not by giving new information, but by arranging what we have always known' (Wittgenstein 1968, p. 109). The 'ethical then and now question' concerned whether to give precedence to the wishes and interests of the 'then-self' or the 'now-self'. The innocent move is the one that talks of different selves; but, as the case of Dr M makes plain, there is no dichotomy: the previous self is present and part of the present self. The 'philosophical self question' concerned the nature of personhood. Mrs D demonstrates how selfhood is, in part, maintained by social interaction. We saw that the first step in the conjuring trick is the one that ignores the extent to which we, as persons, are situated in multifarious fields: personhood is not any one particular capacity. The 'practical question of interpretation' is answered by grasping the extent to which meaning, as in conversations with

Dr B, is co-created. All of these insights are gained by looking at how language is actually used in a context where meanings are embedded in human interaction. And human interaction is what the ethnologist observes; so too must the philosopher, but for a different purpose.

The purpose of the philosopher's observations is to hold us back from the 'decisive movement in the conjuring trick' (Wittgenstein 1968, p. 308). With respect to advance directives, the tricks that split up or attempt to simplify our complex notions of the self or person are demonstrated by the observation of real people with dementia who converse, interrelate, and interact in particular social and cultural circumstances. This whole approach should alert us to alternative conjuring tricks, for it emphasizes our historical embeddedness. The trick is the assumption that the advance directive maintains the person's autonomy or self-direction. But a person's direction at any one time is a reflection of history; future history cannot be foretold. Not only can we not be certain how things will go, but there is also the possibility of a mistake in the present when the advance directive is drawn up. The thing that might have been regarded in the past as 'severe dementia' may turn out not to be the reality of 'severe dementia'; and how things are in 'severe dementia' will itself depend on the person's particular history.

All of this does not suggest that advance directives are otiose. Rather, it suggests that an advance directive should be regarded as only one item to be weighed up in the context of a person's life. What is required, as Jaworska (1999) suggested, is an estimation of what the person values now; but the reality is that – as interconnecting, cultural and historical selves – our values are inherently embedded in our narrative lives.

In order to understand fully the place and function of advance directives in people's lives we should observe, over time, how the meanings and intentions of people change: from the time of drafting to when the advance directive is executed. This would require a new (and methodologically complicated) empirical study. It is likely that the meanings and intentions would change, but this would not be because the individuals concerned had ceased to exist or had turned into different individuals. To think such things requires the type of bewitchment that allows the first move of the conjuring trick. No, the changes in our meanings and intentions simply reflect the more ordinary fact that none of us floats free from our historical and cultural embedding in a world of change.

References

Aquilina C and Hughes JC (2006). The return of the living dead: agency lost and found? In JC Hughes, SJ Louw and SR Sabat, eds. *Dementia: mind, meaning, and the person*, pp. 143-61. Oxford University Press, Oxford.

Battle M (1997). *Reconciliation – The Ubuntu theology of Desmond Tutu*. Pilgrim Press, Cleveland, OH.

Cotrell V and Schulz R (1993). The perspective of the patient with Alzheimer's disease: a neglected dimension of dementia research. *Gerontologist*, **33**, 205-11.

Dennett D (1987). *The intentional stance*. MIT Press, Cambridge, MA.

Downs M, Clare L and Mackenzie J (2006). Understandings of dementia: explanatory models and their implications for the person with dementia and therapeutic effort. In JC Hughes, SJ Louw and SR Sabat, eds. *Dementia: mind, meaning, and the person*, pp. 235-58. Oxford University Press, Oxford.

Dresser R (1986). Life, death, and incompetent patients: conceptual infirmities and hidden values in the law. *Arizona Law Review*, **28**, 373-405.

Dresser R (1995). Dworkin on dementia: elegant theory, questionable policy. *Hastings Center Report*, **25**, 32-8.

Dworkin R (1993). *Life's dominion. An argument about abortion and euthanasia*. Harper Collins, London.

Gillett G and McMillan J (2001). *Consciousness and intentionality*. John Benjamin, Amsterdam.

Harré R (1983*). Personal being. A theory of individual psychology*. Blackwell, Oxford.

Harré R (1991). The discursive production of selves. *Theory and Psychology*, **1**, 51-63.

Hope T (1994). Personal identity and psychiatric illness. In A Phillips Griffiths, ed. *Philosophy, psychology and psychiatry*, pp. 131-43. Cambridge University Press, Cambridge.

Hughes JC (2001). Views of the person with dementia. *Journal of Medical Ethics*, **27**, 86-91.

Hughes JC and Fulford KWM (Bill) (2005). Hurly-burly of psychiatric ethics. *Australian and New Zealand Journal of Psychiatry*, **39**, 1001-7.

Hughes JC, Louw SJ and Sabat SR, eds. (2006a). *Dementia: mind, meaning, and the person*. Oxford University Press, Oxford.

Hughes JC, Louw SJ and Sabat SR (2006b). Seeing whole. In JC Hughes, SJ Louw and SR Sabat, eds. *Dementia: mind, meaning, and the person*, pp. 1-39. Oxford University Press, Oxford.

Jaworska A (1999). Respecting the margins of agency: Alzheimer's patients and the capacity to value. *Philosophy & Public Affairs*, **28**, 105-38.

Louw SJ and Hughes JC (2005). Ethical issues. In A Burns, J O'Brien and D Ames, eds. *Dementia*, 3rd edn., pp. 230-4. Arnold Health Sciences, London.

McKhann G, Drachman D, Folstein M, Katzman R, Price D and Stadlan EM (1984). Clinical diagnosis of Alzheimer's disease: report of the NINCDS-ADRDA work group under the auspices of the Department of Health and Human Services task force on Alzheimer's disease. *Neurology*, **34**, 939-44.

McMillan J (2006). Identity, self and dementia. In JC Hughes, SL Louw and SR Sabat, eds. *Dementia: mind, meaning, and the person*, pp. 63-70. Oxford University Press, Oxford.

Parfit D (1984). *Reasons and persons*. Oxford University Press, Oxford.

Post S (2006). Respectare: moral respect for the lives of the deeply forgetful. In JC Hughes, SJ Louw and SR Sabat, eds. *Dementia: mind, meaning, and the person*, pp. 223-34. Oxford University Press, Oxford.

Sabat SR (2001). *The experience of Alzheimer's disease: life through a tangled veil*. Blackwell, Oxford.

Sabat SR (2006). Mind, meaning, and personhood in dementia: the effects of positioning. In JC Hughes, SJ Louw and SR Sabat, eds. *Dementia: mind, meaning, and the person*, pp. 287-302. Oxford University Press, Oxford.

Taylor C (1985). Theories of meaning. In *Human agency and language. Philosophical papers I*, pp. 248-92. Cambridge University Press, Cambridge.

Thornton T (2006). The discursive turn, social constructionism, and dementia. In JC Hughes, SL Louw and SR Sabat, eds. *Dementia: mind, meaning, and the person*, pp. 123-41. Oxford University Press, Oxford.

Widdershoven GAM and Berghmans RLP (2006). Meaning-making in dementia: a hermeneutic perspective. In JC Hughes, SL Louw and SR Sabat, eds. *Dementia: mind, meaning, and the person*, pp. 179-91. Oxford University Press, Oxford.

Wiggins D (1987). The person as object of science, as subject of experience, and as locus of value. In A Peacocke and G Gillett, eds. *Persons and personality: a contemporary inquiry*, pp. 56-74. Blackwell, Oxford.

Wittgenstein L (1968). *Philosophical investigations*, 3rd edn. Blackwell, Oxford.

Wittgenstein L (1980a). *Culture and value*. In GH von Wright and H Nyman, eds.; trans. P Winch. Blackwell, Oxford.

Wittgenstein L (1980b). *Remarks on the philosophy of psychology*, Vol. II. In GH von Wright and H Nyman, eds.; trans. CG Luckhardt and MAE Aue. Blackwell, Oxford.

Chapter 10

Interference in psychiatric care: a sociological and ethical case history analysis

Marian Verkerk, Louis Polstra, and Marlieke de Jonge

10.1. Introduction

When, in the early 1970s, initial efforts were made in the Netherlands to modify the old 1884 Lunacy Act (Krankzinningenwet) and establish what was later to become the Psychiatric Hospitals (Compulsory Admissions) Act (BOPZ) a debate arose concerning the morality and legality of coercion and pressure on psychiatric clients (Berghmans 1992). The debate is still ongoing and has been given new impetus by the evaluation of the BOPZ (Berghmans 1997; Raad voor de Volksgezondheid en Zorg 1997). Since the 1970s various studies have been conducted in the Netherlands on aspects of coercion in psychiatric care (Berghmans *et al.* 2001).

The debate on coercion and pressure is largely based on ethical concerns. In the case of clients who do not constitute a serious danger to themselves or to others but are in a worrisome situation, the BOPZ does not permit any form of coercion. Despite this provision, pressure on such clients – for instance, to take medication – can be an option. The use of various types of coercion with chronic psychiatric clients also requires an ethical assessment, in which preference should be given to the notion of a 'trajectory' rather than a single, isolated decision. In other words, the ethical justification for coercion cannot be seen as separate from the care process of which it is part (Verkerk 2001). The decision to apply coercion should be regarded as a situated, moral decision, tailor-made, as it were, depending on the circumstances of those involved in the situation and the possibilities open to them.

It is precisely this social context of coercion that is the subject of this chapter. To that end we make use of the sociologist Giddens' structuration theory. Giddens states that every action contains within itself the characteristics of the social system. We use a case study to attempt to reveal the influence of the mental health care system on the act of pressure. The data for this case were assembled within the framework of the study 'Drang als dwangpreventie' (Pressure as Prevention of Coercion).[1] The data sources consist of two interviews with a chronic female psychiatric client, a social psychiatric nurse and a nurse.[2] The case analysis starts with a description of the care system as the context within which pressure was applied. This is followed by a reconstruction of two episodes of care and pressure each ending with a short analysis. Our final considerations take us back briefly to the importance of sociological analysis and its relation to ethical judgements. We begin the chapter with a brief definition of 'coercion' as we understand it.

10.2. **Coercion and pressure**

Coercion is distinguished from pressure by the extent to which it influences the client's freedom of choice. When coercion is applied, the client is no longer free. The client cannot escape the caregiver's intervention. In the case of pressure the client can choose, though some options are made either (un)attractive or conditions are attached to certain choices. Coercion and pressure are designed to bring about an activity or situation that is not the *prima facie* wish of the client. The literature sometimes draws a distinction between weak and strong pressure (Henselmans 1993; Pols 2000). 'Weak' pressure is expressed as persuasion while 'strong' pressure has the characteristic of 'on the pain of', and is thus mainly in the form of 'if A then B'. Examples: 'if you take your medication I will find you a place to stay' or 'if you fail to take your medication you will be compulsorily hospitalized'. In this chapter we focus on the so-called strong pressure variant.

Since 'pressure' implies a *prima facie* conflict with the right to freedom of choice and control, good reasons must be present to justify it. Indeed, in principle there is always tension between pressure and respect for the client's autonomy. Thus when coercion is applied, reasons are required to justify limiting another's autonomy (Berghmans 1997; Verkerk 1999, 2001). Moreover, it does not necessarily have to be the caregiver who exerts influence on the client's freedom of choice: third parties can also apply the pressure. Thus, for

---

[1] This study was commissioned by the Netherlands Organization for Scientific Research (NWO).

[2] In the context of the study 15 clients, 13 (social-psychiatric) nursing staff, 2 psychiatrists, and 2 managers, all from four different teams, were interviewed. For the case study presented here, use was made of two interviews with a chronic female psychiatric client, a social-psychiatric nurse, and a nurse. There was a time lag of 5 months between the interviews. The interviews were semi-structured and were typed out word by word.

instance, a housing association can make the client's acceptance of professional help a condition for granting accommodation. In such a situation the housing association applies the pressure rather than the caregiver. In this case it is usually the caregiver who implements the ruling. Here too, moreover, it is the caregiver who always carries the moral responsibility of determining whether the offer of assistance under such conditions is justified.

10.3. **Giddens' structuration theory**

Giddens attempts to build a bridge between theories which analyse how social systems function (but in which there is little room for individual action) and theories that take individual activity into account but lack a framework to analyse the influence of the system on that activity.

According to Giddens, while an individual's activity is structured by the social system, it is not determined by it. Individuals are 'knowledgeable' actors, 'knowledgeable' here meaning familiarity with the rules of structure, otherwise he would not be able to function within the system in conformity with the rules. Such familiarity is generally to be found in daily, routine activity, but can be made discursive by what Giddens calls the 'reflective monitoring of action'. The care system is produced by activity in conformity with the system's structure rules. However, familiarity with the structure rules makes it possible to act otherwise in a conscious fashion, whereby the system is no longer reproduced or changed.

In his book *The Constitution of Society* Giddens (1984) distinguishes three sets of rules that structure activity: (*a*) Meaning making: In every interaction certain meanings are expressed. What is a carer? What is appropriate care? What is a disquieting care avoider? What is the GGZ (Dutch National Mental Health Care organization)? What is autonomy? What is pressure? What is collaboration? What is socialization?; (*b*) Norms: Norms governing proper treatment also structure activity: the right to privacy, the right to self-determination, honesty, and reliability; (*c*) Power: Giddens defines power, following Parsons, as the capacity to attain a particular outcome. Power is delineated by the access to various sources of help, e.g. knowledge, possessions, and respect.

Structuration theory does not provide an explanation of the working of a system or of human activity, but merely offers an analytical framework. The concrete content of the structure rules differs from system to system. The analytical framework can be applied to interview material because every account of pressure given by an interviewee contains not only unique information about the event itself, but also information about the structure rules governing the care system in which the pressure is (re)produced.

10.4. **The worlds of treatment and counselling**

The GGZ institution studied divides the care it offers to chronic psychiatric clients into treatment and social counselling. This division leads to a division of labour between treatment and counselling teams. We are thus dealing with two subsystems, for convenience called 'worlds'. In order to describe these worlds we use the previously mentioned characteristics that structure activity: (*a*) meaning making; (*b*) norms; and (*c*) power.

The central meaning making component of the treatment world is the treatment of the client's psychiatric disorder. Treatment focuses on the removal of the psychopathology and its negative consequences and consists, among other things, in the prescription of medication, psycho-education and discussions designed to provide insight. Good care implies, among other things, that diagnostic tests are used to establish a diagnosis and its accompanying prognosis, and upon which a treatment plan is established and implemented (Romme 1999).

The right to participation and partnership (norms) in the drawing up of the treatment plan has its legal foundation in the Wet Geneeskundige Behandelingsovereenkomst (Medical Treatment Act – WGBO).

In the practice studied the social psychiatric nurse (SPN) holds the key position (power). The treatment is mainly given in the SPN's large surgery. The clients come by appointment and must report to the reception and wait in the waiting area. The SPN makes home visits if necessary. Within the system the SPN regulates the stream of information going to the psychiatrist. Intensive contact with the client means that the SPN has access to information required for the treatment. The SPN interviewed works 32 h per week and has a caseload of approximately 65 clients. The psychiatrist has approximately 300 clients in his caseload and works 16 h per week.[3]

In a formal sense only psychiatrists can prescribe medication, but they are dependent upon information supplied by the SPN such as symptoms shown by the client, reactions to medication, and so on. In addition, the psychiatrist has another, legal power base. He is legally responsible for the treatment plan. If the treatment required should happen to go beyond the limits of the treatment plan, e.g. during a crisis, the SPN discusses the matter with the psychiatrist or the crisis service doctor. The psychiatrist's power position is hereby recognized and reproduced, but the key position held by the SPN has

---

[3] Since the psychiatrist had no recent contact with the client and the coercion was implemented by the SPN in her capacity as therapist, no interview was held with the psychiatrist.

in practice led to identification with the psychiatrist's power position. This has also led to the SPN bearing the title of therapist (meaning making).

Access to the treatment world is in the hands of the treatment team that puts forward the client's name. In the counselling world the client is linked to a member of the nursing staff. Counselling means advising, supporting, and helping the client to maintain or improve his quality of life as regards self-care, accommodation, social contacts, work/daily routine, finance, and treatment (taking medication).

In the counselling world involvement with the daily ups and downs in the client's life is regarded as important. This involvement is a strong motive for taking action. The nursing staff member is part of the client's real-life world.

Just as in the treatment world we can speak of an inequality of power between helper and client. Clients are dependent on the services offered by counsellors in order to be able to keep going. Within the counselling world, however, activity is not strictly organized, which means that the clients partly determine the activities undertaken by the nursing staff. For instance, in the mornings counsellors spend their time making home visits and on administrative matters. The door is shut and clients can only come by appointment. In the afternoons the door is open and clients are free to come and have a cup of coffee or tea, to chat, pick up money, or discuss things with counsellors. It is not known beforehand which or how many clients will turn up or what their motives for their visit will be.

Both treatment world and counselling world are familiar with staff problems. The treatment team is understaffed. Counsellors frequently change jobs. A number of counsellors are following in-service training with the aim of finding work elsewhere as an SPN or therapist. The manager we interviewed stated that staffing policy (recruitment, prevention of burnout, staffing numbers) is a constant source of concern.

The division of the care system into treatment and counselling means that, as far as pressure is concerned, its application occurs in the interactive triangle of client, therapist, and counsellor.

10.5. The case of Mrs G

Mrs G is a 47-year-old Surinamese-Hindustani woman. She suffers from schizophrenia and has regular psychotic episodes that lead to a great deal of disturbance in her immediate vicinity, self-neglect, and debts. Mrs G attaches importance to a good appearance. She refuses to take her medication because it causes her to put on weight. According to her therapist she is well aware that failure to take her medication can result in her becoming psychotic but she allows it to happen anyway.

Her current therapist has worked with her for 2 1/2 years. The monthly consultations deal with whatever is occupying Mrs G's mind, things she is finding difficult and her medication. A few times a week, in the interests of social contact, Mrs G attends the walk-in session organized by the counselling team. Her regular counsellor helps with her financial affairs and with the completion of various forms and other paperwork.

At the start of the care process, 2 1/2 years ago, the counsellor decided to apply the following form of pressure: 'only if Mrs G took her medication (Semap) would she be given the sleeping pill for which she asked'. In the beginning the counsellor maintained this policy but abandoned it after returning from maternity leave, partly because the pressure variant turned out to have had little effect. Moreover the counsellor's colleagues had not continued the pressure during her absence, something she blames on a lack of attention and effort on their part. During the first session the therapist told of her experience with the pressure variant she had developed.

10.5.1. Episode 1

In order to be able to recognize the start of a psychotic episode the therapist and the counsellor together had intensive discussions with Mrs G about possible portents, such as 'messing about' with money. The new pressure variant was: 'if Mrs G refuses medication during the onset of a psychotic episode, the therapist will ask for an RM (Rechterlijke Machtiging = court order)'. All the information was gathered together in the treatment plan, to which Mrs G gave her assent. The therapist came to apply this form of pressure 'because I too deeply regretted the fact that during that period we had destroyed everything she had built up. And I discussed it with her in these terms. It keeps getting so out of control and so much is being lost. I find that a great pity'. The loss had to do not only with a collapsing social network – friends, neighbours, children, and grandchild – but also with a loss of self-esteem as a consequence of eroticizing behaviour during the psychosis. Her counsellor puts it in the following terms: 'Particularly when she was better again and looked back on the episode. At that point she admitted being terribly ashamed of what had happened, how the neighbors reacted, what her balcony looked like. This was extremely traumatic for her ... And it's very humiliating, or can be. That's how she experienced it'.

The aim of the new form of pressure is to prevent an escalation of the crisis situation – as happened in the past despite the old pressure variant. According to the therapist there are no other alternatives. The pressure variant that goes 'if you get your medication from the therapist you will get money from the counselor', a variant sometimes used at this GGZ institution, is not permissible according to the therapist. Carers do not have the right to claim property belonging to the client. Moreover, what the client does with her money is her own responsibility.

10.5.1.1. Analysis of episode 1

Pressure is part and parcel of the treatment world, both regarding the targets and the means. The treatment plan is indicative for the activities undertaken by all involved, including the counsellor (definition power). The task of the counselling world is mainly to give off signals. But this relationship does not lead to tension between the two worlds. Indeed, the 'normative framework' for applying pressure is shared, as are the shared responsibilities: the handing out of medication belongs to the therapist's domain while the social counselling is left to the nursing staff.

Mrs G's past made clear that medication was the best therapeutic method of treating the psychosis. Combating the psychosis was not the only aim: in addition pressure is legitimized by pointing out the client's loss of self-esteem and social network. Self-esteem and social network are regarded as partially determinant for the client's identity. Limitations are placed on the client's freedom of action in order to prevent her identity being damaged.

The client's assent is important for the legitimacy of the pressure. Both therapist and counsellor attach great importance to this since it expresses the client's autonomy. Discussion of the pressure variant is regarded as part of the treatment strategy itself. Indeed, insight into the clinical picture is thereby gained. This means that the pressure variant is not only a component in a particular form of treatment but is also part of the treatment process itself.

In both this pressure variant and the previous type the means – medication and court order – are in the hands of the treatment world. In this case, therefore, no use is made of means available to the counselling world. It should be noted here that the therapist has relative autonomy in the choice of treatment strategy.

In the next episode the distinction between treatment and counselling does lead to tensions.

10.5.2. Episode 2

In the period between the two interviews Mrs G's foster mother died. At the insistence of her family Mrs G was flown to Surinam, where she became psychotic and locked herself in a room. On her return she was prepared to take her medication without protest, a fact interpreted by the therapist as an effective result of the pressure applied, while the counsellor disagreed, believing that Mrs G's assent had to do with the nature of the psychosis. And although Mrs G was agitated – throwing things out of the window – she was not manic. 'She was extremely upset and it could be that that led to another situation different from the previous psychosis'. Although the treatment plan (and the pressure it contained) is a constantly recurring subject of discussion with Mrs G, the interview demonstrates that she does not really understand why she is being given Semap: 'I don't know, don't know why I'm being given it. I don't know'.

Following the psychotic episode Mrs G continues to collect her medication from the RIAGG (Regional Institute for Ambulant Mental Health Care). Other factors characterizing this period are repair to the damage caused, particularly in renewed contact with Mrs G's children. Prior to Mrs G's psychosis her daughter had given birth to a baby. This strengthened the fragile bond between mother and daughter. During her psychosis she had been rude about her daughter's in-laws, which had lead to a temporary break in the relationship with her daughter. The counsellor says that she sometimes discusses the matter with Mrs G and talks about the sorrow it causes her. The therapist is more reticent in this regard and has avoided the subject after one conversation. The same difference applies to the subject of the management of finances. The counsellor is worried about the way the money is being spent. The therapist is not concerned since all fixed expenses are automatically paid by the treatment team and the way the housekeeping money is spent is the client's own responsibility. The counsellor thinks that the therapist should keep a closer eye on the social dimensions of existence. The therapist is of the opinion that the counsellor feels too great a responsibility for the client. They discuss this on a regular basis, the therapist taking on the role of supervisor. 'If she can discuss it at all then she can also solve it. And it is important that she and I agree what to do about it'. Where the therapist thinks that everything has been discussed, the counsellor retains a feeling of dissatisfaction and lack of recognition. 'You don't want it to turn into a fight, because that's not in the client's interests... Nor do we want to allow ourselves to be sort of provoked into it but we regard a few things as important and we're keen to do them for people. But we'll have to be tougher negotiators'.

10.5.2.1. **Analysis of episode 2**

Mrs G fails to give clear reasons for taking her medication. In the second interview she herself does not say that she had been to Surinam and had become psychotic. Whatever the case, the pressure and the treatment plan were not changed after the second psychosis. The therapist perceives a clear relationship between the taking of the medication and the treatment plan with its pressure factor. Mrs G seems to assent in a routine way to the pressure agreement contained in the treatment plan.

The therapist's actions focus on combating the psychotic episodes with the use of medication. Problems in other areas of life play a subordinate role in the therapist's professional ideas on identity. The therapist believes that it is the client's own responsibility to solve these problems or to ask for help in dealing with them. By way of contrast, the counsellor seems to be more receptive to the other, more social problems. Evidently she expects of herself that she should bear some responsibility in the matter. An active, involved approach is a part of good social work in the social counselling world. The therapist rejects this, as already stated, from her view on good social work. Both parties recognize this conflict around good social work, but the balance of power is in the therapist's advantage. Because of this the meaning making and the counsellor's (professional) norms are subordinated to those of the therapist. It is remarkable that there seems to be no real exchange between therapist and counsellor regarding the norms for good social work and for the meaning making in the care provided for Mrs G. To 'preserve the peace' the counsellor goes along with the therapist's strategy but the conflict continues to smoulder below the surface.

10.6. **Sociology and ethics**

We have here tried to reveal the influence of the care system on normative aspects of pressure by way of a case history analysis based on the sociologist Giddens' structuration theory.

Our analysis shows firstly that the care system is divided into a number of subsystems. A major reason for this would seem to be efficiency. A social psychiatric nurse can work more efficiently when freed from time-consuming organizational affairs. It is more economical in commercial terms to have these matters attended to by less qualified and cheaper staff. The same argument applies to the division of roles between SPN and psychiatrist. Division of labour of this type is not unique and can be found in many mental health care organizations. However, the division of labour has all kinds of unintended side effects, one of the most important being that the SPN is placed in the position of therapist. The SPN is thereby given activities and responsibilities for which she is not legally qualified and which she should only be allowed to exercise under supervision of a doctor. Yet there is such an acute shortage of doctors and psychiatrists in the mental health care system that such supervision is impossible.

The dominant subsystem, that of the therapists, is receptive to needs for care ensuing from psychiatric disorders. Chronic psychiatric clients require this help in many areas of life. The counselling team was created to provide for the needs in other areas of life. This team is, as it were, the caring component in the care system. The subsystems have different normative frameworks for good social work, between which the balance of power is not equal. The counselling team lacks the self-awareness that would enable it to enter into a dialogue with the therapists. The therapists do reflect on their actions as such, but not on their power position. As a consequence, there is no real exchange of ideas between therapists and counsellors regarding norms and meaning making. The colliding views on good social work are therefore not explored further. The discourse is more of a monologue on the part of the more powerful subsystem. This causes the conflict, felt but not expressed, to be reproduced unconsciously and unintentionally.

The paucity of reflection on the position of power also brings about a limited interpretation of the client's needs. Attention is mainly focused on care needs directly linked to the psychiatric disorder. Other care needs are subordinate. In this way the care system runs the risk of the client not feeling helped. Some withdraw and become care avoiders. This is a reason for the care system to proceed in a more active way, including the use of pressure. For example, in the second episode Mrs G had to be given 'extra' motivation to take her medication. The reproduction of pressure is the unintended consequence of the care system's limited capacity for response.

With the aid of Giddens' structuration theory the influence of the context as system could be demonstrated. This revealed the fact that the therapist's power position affects not only the way the system's actors make meaning but also determines the norms regarding good social work and the legitimizing of pressure. The professional's power position is not an achievement of the individual therapist, but is part of the nature of the care system. In turn the system is influenced by all kinds of social developments, such as scarcity on the labour market, the calls for increased security in society, for the reduction of social disturbance, for cost management and so on. Inside and outside the care system, therefore, all kinds of normative conditions affect the primary care process.

This sociological analysis of pressure has consequences for the ethical analysis and assessment of pressure. Pressure should not be regarded as an isolated action, the ethical acceptability of which must be determined. For the justification of pressure, it does not suffice to analyse the situation as a conflict between two principles – namely beneficence on the one hand and respect for autonomy on the other hand (Verkerk 2001). This definition of the moral problem fails to illuminate the social and institutional context of the action. One should also take into account power relationships that cause the views of some caregivers to prevail while those of others only occupy a marginal position. A normative assessment of the exercise of pressure requires that the view of all parties involved is taken into consideration. The normative perspective of the world of treatment and that of the world of counselling are both relevant to the moral issue of how to justify coercion.

The nature of good care, including the use of certain pressure variants, is not given, but is the result of negotiations between the various parties involved who, in turn, also reflect on their mutual positions in the overall system. The SPN in this case history was unreflective and unaware of her own dominant position. As a result any real exchange of ideas about norms and meaning making between the nurse and the counsellor was absent. This sociological fact has consequences for the normative evaluation of the practice under consideration. It implies that the exercise of coercion in the case was based on a normative framework, which was one-sided. From a normative perspective, practice could be improved by readjusting the power balance and involving other perspectives into the discussion about good care.

Giddens' sociological theory not only enables us to illuminate normative aspects of the practice of coercion in psychiatry, it also shows the need for ethical theories, which take into account social relationships. Care ethics is one of the theoretical approaches that aim to take the social character of ethics seriously. The political scientist Joan Tronto describes good care as a practice in which care is given and received in an attentive, responsible, competent, and responsive manner. According to Tronto current practices of care are characterized by inequalities in power and responsibility. Instead of sweeping such conflicts under the carpet, from the start it is necessary to choose this inherently conflictive characteristic of care as the starting point for an ethical analysis (Tronto 1993). This makes care-ethical insights relevant for cases such as the use of pressure in mental health care (Verkerk 1999, 2001).

References

Berghmans RLP (1992). *Om bestwil: paternalisme in de psychiatrie*. Thesis Publishers, Amsterdam.

Berghmans RLP (1997). *Beter (z)onder dwang?* Achtergrondnota geschreven in opdracht van de Raad voor de Volksgezondheid en Zorg bij het RVZ-advies Beter (z)onder dwang. Raad voor de Volksgezondheid en Zorg, Zoetermeer.

Berghmans RLP, Elfahmi D, Goldsteen M, Widdershoven GAM (2001). *Kwaliteit van dwang en drang in de psychiaterie*. GGZ Nederland, Utrecht/Maastricht.

Giddens A (1984). *The constitution of society: outline of the theory of structuration*. University of California Press, Berkeley.

Henselmans H (1993). *Bemoeizorg. Ongevraagde hulp voor psychotische patiënten.* Eboron, Delft.

Pols J (2000). Macht en dwang in psychiatrische hulpverlening. In J Graste and D Bauduin, eds. *Waardevol werken: ethiek in de geestelijke gezondheidszorg,* pp. 130-48.Van Gorcum, Assen.

Raad voor de Volksgezondheid en Zorg (1997). *Beter (z)onder dwang?.* Raad voor de Volksgezondheid en Zorg, Zoetermeer.

Romme M (1999). THEORIE – Psychose: bron van kennis. *Deviant: tijdschrift tussen psychiatrie en maatschappij,* **6**, 24-7.

Tronto J (1993). *Moral boundaries, a political argument for an ethics of care.* Routledge, London.

Verkerk MA (1999). A care perspective on coercion and autonomy. *Bioethics,* **13**(3-4), 358-68.

Verkerk MA (2001). Over drang als goed zorgen: een zorgethische benadering. *Tijdschrift voor Geneeskunde en Ethiek,* **11**(4), 101-6.

Chapter 11

Providing good care in the context of restrictive measures: the case of prevention of obesity in youngsters with Prader–Willi syndrome

R.H. van Hooren, H.W. van den Borne,
L.M.G. Curfs, and G.A.M. Widdershoven

11.1. Introduction

It is only in recent years that empirical data have been systematically collected in order to help develop or adjust ethical theories. Instead of attempting to clarify and explain moral dilemmas with the help of ethical theories, principles, and rules, an increasing number of ethics projects study specific care practices with the aim of explicating those moral rules and convictions that are intrinsic to these practices (ten Have and Lelie 1998). This chapter reports one such project, a study of the ethical aspects of the prevention of obesity in young people with Prader–Willi syndrome. In this study both a qualitative and a quantitative approach were used to gather data. We will compare the qualitative and quantitative approaches and analyse the differences between them.

The conflict between providing good care and respecting the client's autonomy is central to caring for people with Prader–Willi syndrome. Achieving autonomy is an important goal in human life in general, and is no less important in the lives of people with intellectual disability. Recent developments in the care of people with intellectual disability emphasize the promotion of self-determination, freedom of choice, and responsibility. However, caregivers may sometimes feel frustrated by this focus on autonomy. They may be confronted with situations in which there is a conflict between providing high-quality care and respecting the client's autonomy. It is not always easy to decide what to do when a client's wishes and interests conflict. Should one respect the autonomy of the intellectually disabled person, or should one protect them against the adverse consequences of their choices?

These conflicts are prominent in the care of people with Prader–Willi syndrome (PWS). This genetic disorder is associated with mild to moderate intellectual disability (Whittington *et al.* 2004). Excessive appetite is a prominent feature of PWS and this can easily lead to overeating. It has been suggested that in PWS the normal satiety response is impaired and delayed (Holland *et al.* 1993), possibly through a hypothalamic dysfunction (Swaab *et al.* 1995). This overeating frequently leads to obesity, which can be severe and may cause serious health problems. Should caregivers leave the persons themselves to choose how much to eat, or should they intervene to protect them against the adverse consequences of their eating?

One of the mothers interviewed in a study we undertook expressed this dilemma as follows:

> In some countries, it is said, let them eat themselves to death, then at least they have had a happy life. This is very radical. Can we ever determine that overeating will make them happy? If we look at our daughter, we are glad that she is not too fat. She seems to be happy when she is able to run a little, can play a ball game, take part in walking contests and fits in a normal bathing suit and so on. She does not have to be beautiful, if only she is able to feel comfortable with herself. Well, that already is quite a battle, and for that it is necessary that people decide for her what she can and cannot eat.

Empirical ethics aims, amongst other things, at developing normative theories which do justice to the complex and unique character of situations and practices (van der Scheer *et al.* 2004). In this chapter we explore the complexity of the care practice of dealing with the prevention of obesity in persons with Prader–Willi syndrome. We stress the importance of developing a normative framework within this specific practice, relevant to the problems that emerge within this context. We believe that a framework which is developed on the basis of empirical data will provide more perspectives on, and approaches to, the moral conflict between respecting autonomy, and providing good care than those which emerge from purely theoretical debates alone.

11.2. **The qualitative study**

Since little was known about the care practice of dealing with the prevention of obesity in people with Prader–Willi syndrome, we began with a qualitative study. Parents, and professional caregivers, were interviewed about their views on the prevention of obesity, and on the practical ways in which they tried to manage the situation in everyday life. The interviews combined an open approach, encouraging the interviewees to give a narrative about their experience of caring, with more structured questions following the stories told by the interviewees. The structure was organized around several themes: daily social intercourse, food practice, interaction in general, and social environment.

These qualitative interviews were conducted with 23 parents and 14 professional caregivers of 18 persons with PWS. Nine (age range 8 to 17 years) out of these 18 people with PWS lived at home and nine (age range 13 to 38 years) lived in a group home. Initial contacts with parents and professional caregivers were made in cooperation with the Centre for Clinical Genetics in Maastricht, and with the Dutch Prader–Willi Parent Association. The interviews were recorded on audiotape and later transcribed with the consent of the participants.

11.2.1. The narrative analysis

The interviews were first analysed using narrative analysis of the transcripts as a whole. This analysis was not structured but involved a comparison of all the cases as a whole with each other at a general level. We looked at the differences in the ways parents, professional caregivers, and the children or adults with Prader–Willi syndrome communicated, and what kind of attitudes were apparent. Interviews were coded. Codes were grouped, compared, and categorized into themes. In this first qualitative analysis (van Hooren *et al.* 2002) we found that none of the caregivers opted to leave the choice for food intake entirely to the person with Prader–Willi syndrome. Neither did they simply intervene without taking into account the wishes of the individual with the syndrome.

> *Interviewer*: Do you think it is necessary to lock the kitchen?
> *Father*: No, not in our case. We want him to learn to cope with it himself. We can talk about it with him very well, and he also is fairly wise. That doesn't mean he never takes something out of the cupboard secretly.
> *Mother*: We try to stimulate as much as possible her own responsibility. For example, she needs to take care of her homework herself, we don't go after that. By stimulating her own responsibility in all these other areas, so that she feels she is being trusted, we try to ensure that she can cope with food in a better way.

In these examples autonomy is promoted, not by giving freedom of choice, but by fostering self-understanding and self-development. The focus is not on negative freedom, but on positive freedom (Berlin 1969). Negative freedom refers to freedom of choice without external interference. Positive freedom refers to a perspective of autonomy that is not a matter of individual self-determination, but of self-realization through the support of others. Being dependent is therefore not the opposite of being autonomous; individual autonomy can be enhanced through dependency on others.

The data show that the process of care cannot adequately be seen in terms of choosing between respecting autonomy through securing freedom of choice on the one hand, and paternalism on the other. That is too crude. The stories indicated that caregivers see other options and act in other ways. As a starting point we used the four kinds of physician–patient interaction outlined by Emanuel and Emanuel (1992). These authors define not only a paternalistic and an informative model (which are based on the traditional dichotomy between paternalism and autonomy in terms of self-determination) but add two further possible approaches to the physician–patient model: the interpretive model and the deliberative model.

In the interpretive model, the physician helps to elucidate the patient's values, and to make clear what she or he actually wants. This model assumes that the patient's values are not always fixed and known to the patient. The deliberative model, like the interpretive model, sees the aim of the physician–patient interaction as being to help the patient determine and choose the best values for his health. But unlike the interpretive model, the values of the patient not only need to be clarified; they are also open for development and revision through moral discussion and deliberation.

We analysed the interviews with parents and professional caregivers in terms of these four models. The focus was not on discrete decisions, but on the general patterns of interaction between caregivers and people with Prader–Willi syndrome. The focus was not merely on rational but also on emotional aspects. The results showed that there were few examples that clearly corresponded to the informative model. According to this model a caregiver would fully inform the person with PWS of the dangers of overeating, but leave the choice of eating behaviour up to that person. The accounts given by the caregivers often had a paternalistic tone. In addition, however, there were also elements in the stories showing that the process of care was directed towards fostering self-understanding or moral development. The stories were never totally in accordance with only one model, although one of the models was quite often dominant within a specific interview. Thus, cases of paternalism, of interpretive interaction and of deliberative interaction could each be distinguished.

This narrative analysis showed that the care practice of prevention of obesity in persons with Prader–Willi syndrome goes beyond the dichotomy of either respecting the individual's choice or of acting paternalistically. The stories make clear that most caregivers are not inclined to leave decisions to the person with Prader–Willi syndrome alone. On the other hand, neither do they always act paternalistically. Caregivers are also interested in fostering self-understanding and moral development. They do this in ways less rational than are presupposed by Emanuel and Emanuel. The analysis, however, shows that the theoretical models of Emanuel and Emanuel can help to understand the practice of care for persons with Prader–Willi syndrome, but also need to be adjusted to do justice to specific elements of this practice.

11.2.2. Grounded theory analysis

In addition to this narrative analysis of the data in terms of types of interaction between caregiver and care receiver, we carried out a structured analysis of the interviews, using the constant comparative method as described in grounded theory[1] (Strauss and Corbin 1990). The purpose of this structured analysis was to aid the development of concepts and theory (van Hooren *et al.* 2005). The interviews were coded, and the codes were grouped, compared, and categorized into concepts. This analysis resulted in a theoretical framework consisting of three layers: values, conditions, and interventions (see Table 11.1). First, several values emerged. These values characterize what caregivers saw as important and what motivated them in their behaviour towards the child or client. Second, conditions were found that either interfered with or enhanced these values. These conditions reflect social contexts and situations. Third, interventions were found that caregivers apply in order to realize their values. In Table 11.1 an overview is given of this theoretical framework. The arrows show the direct connections between elements of the three layers.[2]

Several techniques were used in order to establish the different aspects of trustworthiness (Lincoln and Guba 1985). Prolonged engagement and persistent observation[3] increased the chance that the research had high credibility. Peer debriefing, a review process in cooperation with colleagues and experts was carried out during the period of data analysis. The colleagues and experts had experience in grounded theory, health, ethics, and the Prader–Willi syndrome. Thick descriptions of cases were used to ensure transferability.

---

[1] The constant comparative method of grounded theory was only used as an analysis tool for the interview transcripts. The grounded theory approach usually also entails a constant (re)adjustment of the interview scheme during data collection, on the basis of the findings of the earlier interviews.

[2] See van Hooren *et al.* (2005) for an elaborate explanation of this framework and its elements.

[3] Prolonged engagement means that the investigator invests sufficient time in examining empirical material in order to become totally familiar with it. This means knowing exactly which respondent said what and in which context, etc.

The technique of persistent observation need not be direct visual observation but can also be observation of written data, which is the case here. The purpose of persistent observation is to identify those characteristics and elements in the situation that are most relevant to the problem or issue being pursued, and focusing on them in detail.

Prolonged engagement provides scope; persistent observation provides depth (Lincoln and Guba 1985).

Table 11.1 Theoretical framework grounded theory analysis

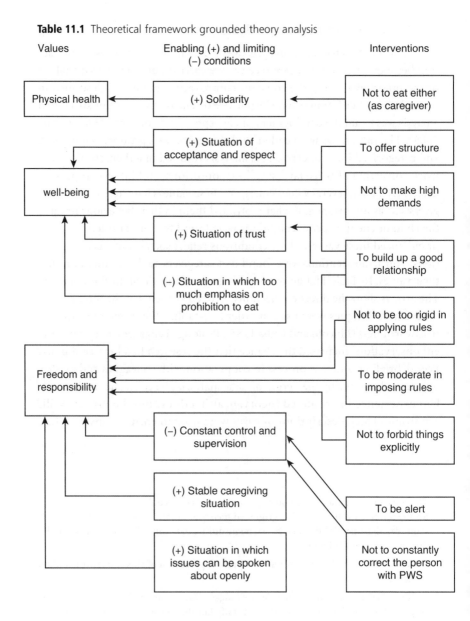

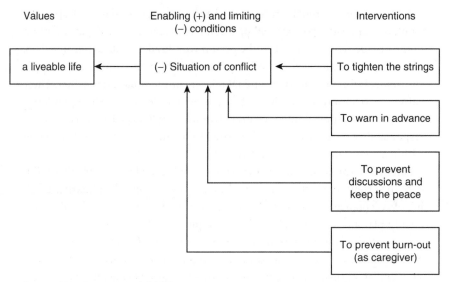

Source: Van Hooren *et al.* 2005

Regular dependability audit meetings took place in order to guarantee the dependability of the different steps in the research process. In addition, regular confirmative audit meetings were held to guarantee the corroboration of the data. These meetings were also held with the experts, who read the transcripts of the interviews and checked the coding, categorization, and interpretation of the data. These checks resulted in only small adjustments in each step of the process. The construction of a three-layer framework (Table 11.1) resulted from the discussions with experts.

Various different values play a role in the care of people with Prader–Willi syndrome. A primary value is the health of the child or client. This is not surprising, as the urge to overeat can lead to significant obesity and hence damage to the person's health. In addition to this value on health, parents and professional caregivers consider it important for the person with Prader–Willi syndrome to feel good. Parents are happy when the child feels comfortable. Professional caregivers emphasize that the client needs to have a good quality of life. Thus, although it is important to try to prevent obesity, this should not be done at the expense of everything else. Happiness is more than health. A further value that caregivers considered important is that the person with Prader–Willi syndrome learns to lead his own life: a central value is freedom. This freedom is not conceived as being able to do what one wants, but being able to bear responsibility. A fourth important value is creating a liveable life for other people involved: parents, brothers or sisters, or other residents. Despite the emphasis on health, parents and professional caregivers clearly pay attention to the broader context in which the person with Prader–Willi syndrome lives. They emphasize the need of ensuring that life is bearable (under difficult circumstances) for all concerned, and taking care of the situation together. These values correspond to an ethics of care in which dealing with dependency through joint responsibility is central (Tronto 1993; Walker 1998). This shared responsibility means that room is created for coming to agreements together within a good caregiver–client relationship.

Parents and professional caregivers mentioned several conditions that influence the extent to which these desired values can be realized. Solidarity, a feeling of acceptance and respect, and a situation in which issues can be discussed openly, play a positive role. Participants emphasized the relational character of such solidarity. A joint commitment and attention to the caring process has a positive influence on the shared values. On the other hand, constant supervision, and an obsessive concern with limiting the eating behaviour had a negative effect on promoting the key values.

Caregivers described what actions they took in order to promote the values they see as important. They mentioned being alert, offering structure, being moderate in imposing rules, building up a relationship, keeping the peace, and spreading attention. These interventions have the character of a process. It is not a matter of choosing between being *laissez faire* or intervening, but of creating a context in which client and caregiver can develop a joint life. By offering structure the person with Prader–Willi syndrome can be helped to take responsibility for his behaviour. According to caregivers, interventions require tact and the ability to find the right balance. It is important to be alert without permanent control, and to offer structure without limiting the behaviour too rigidly. Furthermore, it is important to find a balance within the family or the group of residents. This requires finding a balance between attention for the person with Prader–Willi syndrome and for other family or group members. In that balance caregivers should also care for themselves.

In summary, caregivers do not focus only on the question of whether one should intervene or not. They try to create conditions for living that are acceptable and meaningful for everybody involved. They aim to maintain life by building up a relationship in which acceptance and respect are central. In this relationship a certain amount of independence and responsibility can be developed. In a permanent and stable context of care, in which there is room for creating trust, it is possible to deal with rules in a less rigid way and to look for where there is room for choices. This leads to a life that is characterized by a process of mutual commitment, support, care, and shared responsibility.

11.2.3. **Conclusion**

Theoretical debates on the ethics of the prevention of obesity in Prader–Willi syndrome have focused mainly on the question of whether one should intervene or not (Dykens *et al.* 1997; Holland and Wong 1999). These debates do not discuss sufficiently what an intervention should look like, or what good care means.

Both the narrative analysis and the grounded theory analysis show that there are limits to the individual freedom of choice for the person with Prader–Willi syndrome. Autonomy can, however, be conceived in a different way, in terms of positive freedom, instead of autonomy based on negative freedom. Both analyses show that from the perspective of autonomy as positive freedom the issue of preventing obesity can be approached in new ways, ways of interacting in which there is room for realizing and developing those values that are relevant to the client. This process of fostering autonomy requires a specific context of mutual trust, support, and openness. Instead of focusing on the question of whether or not to intervene, one should, according to this analysis, pay attention to various ways of intervening and to creating a context in which interventions help people to become more autonomous.

11.3. **Quantitative study**

We have argued that, in the prevention of obesity in Prader–Willi syndrome, the dichotomy between autonomy and paternalism is too crude and one-sided to do justice to the diversity and complexity of this care practice. More subtle ways of dealing with this issue can be distinguished. A further question is how parents and professional caregivers value these various approaches and which interventions they prefer in specific situations. In order to examine this question, several intervention strategies were formulated on the basis of the models of the physician–patient interaction developed by Emanuel and Emanuel (1992).

The intervention strategies formed the material for a quantitative study, which had two main aims. First, to see whether parents and professional caregivers understood and grasped the differences between the various intervention alternatives. Second to analyse the preferences of caregivers with respect to these approaches. We wanted to study whether parents and professional caregivers shared a preference for a specific intervention approach, and whether the sort of intervention was dependent on the nature of the situation and problem. The advantage of setting up a study with a quantitative nature is that it allows data to be collected from a greater number and range of caregivers and to look for systematic differences between groups. In two meetings, one with parents and one with professional caregivers, the four general types of intervention strategy were examined (paternalistic, informative, interpretive, and deliberative strategies, see Table 11.2). Eight cases, which focused on a specific problem related to the Prader–Willi syndrome, were presented to parents and professionals. The cases were constructed on the basis of problematic situations identified in a previous study of the daily practice of care for individuals with Prader–Willi syndrome (van Hooren *et al.* 2002, 2005). As an illustration one of these cases is presented here.

Leontien

Leontien is a kind 17-year-old girl with Prader–Willi syndrome. She lives at home, together with her older sister. She has never been easy to get on with. She demonstrates clearly all features of the syndrome, according to her parents. In particular she cannot deal with changes. She easily gets upset. Even planning a trip with the family is very difficult.

Over the last few months tensions have risen very high. Leontien's mother feels she can no longer cope. Leontien's father avoids interactions with Leontien. Her mother and father have had a major row about whether Leontien can continue living at home. Her mother is thinking of moving Leontien out of the parental home, but her father does not want to do this yet. They contact a social worker to discuss possible solutions. Over the last few weeks Leontien can no longer be kept under control: she constantly steals food and her weight is increasing dramatically. Leontien's parents feel that things cannot go on like this any more.

Fourteen professional caregivers and 24 parents of people with Prader–Willi syndrome participated in this study (van Hooren *et al.* 2006). The group of 14 professionals consisted of 2 psychologists, 3 teachers, 1 care coordinator, 5 personal caregivers, and 3 caregivers connected to the group in which the client with Prader–Willi syndrome lives. The group of 24 parents consisted of 10 fathers and 14 mothers.

The parents and professionals were asked to rate four different intervention strategies (each with a short and a long version) according to their preferred way of dealing with the problem. The eight cases presented to parents and professionals varied on three dimensions: (*a*) eating problem versus behavioural problem, (*b*) acute versus chronic situation, and (*c*) living at home versus living in community-based settings. The cases were shown to the participants twice: the first time before, and the second time after, an explanation and a discussion of the four models of Emanuel and Emanuel. All respondents were asked both times to rate their preference for the eight strategies in each of the eight cases. This was done to find out if an explicit explanation and discussion of the various interaction models created a learning effect.

On the basis of the four models, four sorts of strategies were developed. These are shown in Table 11.2. These were described in two lines on cards. For each strategy a short version (Table 11.2: 1a, 2a, 3a, 4a) and a long version

Table 11.2 Intervention strategies as formulated on cards

Paternalistic approach	1a. In such a situation I would take the decision for him/her 1b. In such a situation I would take the decision for him/her, but I would explain it well to him/her and I would make sure he/she understands it and accepts it
Informative approach	2a. In such a situation I would let him/her choose him/herself 2b. In such a situation I would explain the risks, show him/her the advantages and disadvantages, and then I would let him/her choose him/herself
Interpretive approach	3a. In such a situation I want to find out what he/she really wants. Once I know this, I would try to act that way 3b. In such a situation I want to find out what he/she really wants. There may be conflicting values for him/her. Once I know what the most important value is, I would try to act that way
Deliberative approach	4a. In such a situation I would try to examine with him/her if he/she can learn to deal with the problem differently 4b. In such a situation I would try to examine with him/her if he/she can learn to deal with the problem differently. I also would want to see if I can change my own behaviour in order to make the situation manageable

Source: Van Hooren *et al.* 2006

(Table 11.2: 1b, 2b, 3b, 4b) were made. The participants were asked to lay out these cards in order of preference for each of the eight cases that were presented to them.

11.3.1. Statistical analyses

The data collected through preference rankings of the intervention strategies (van Hooren *et al.* 2006) were subjected to a multidimensional scaling procedure (Alscal) (Cox and Cox 2001). This allows for exploring how parents and professional caregivers perceive the different interaction strategies and how they form their preferences for these different strategies. In this procedure, dimensions are uncovered that account, as well as possible, for subjects' preferences for the different cases. For each individual ranking an ideal point is calculated. The ideal points form the dependent variable for further analyses. The ways in which the ideal points change in relation to the eight presented cases was investigated. Differences in ideal points between parents and professional caregivers were analysed. Furthermore, the ideal points in the measurement before and after the explanation of the four models were compared. Since there are multiple measurements (i.e. ideal point scores) within each subject, leading to dependencies among observations, multilevel analysis (Snijders and Bosker 1999) is an appropriate technique to investigate these issues. The following factors were included as independent variables in the model: acuteness of the situation (acute = 1 versus chronic =0), type of problem (eating = 1 versus behavioural = 0), location of the situation (living at home = 1 versus community based setting = 0), type of respondent (parent = 1 versus professional caregiver = 0), and explanation of the four models (before = 0 or after the intervention = 1).

11.3.2. **Results**

The Alscal analysis showed that 99% of the variance in the preference data could be explained with the choice of one dimension only. The addition of more dimensions explained only a little more of the variance. Moreover, these extra dimensions were difficult to interpret.

The one dimension represents the amount of active intervention that parents and professional caregivers perceive with respect to the different interaction strategies. The scores and order of the different interaction strategies on these dimensions are given in Table 11.3.

Table 11.3 Scores and ordering of intervention strategies on one dimension

Intervention strategy	Scale value total group	Scale value parents	Scale value professionals	
Paternalism (short version)	1.6390	1.6446	1.9543	Most intervening
Paternalism (long version)	0.8638	0.7074	1.3851	
Deliberation (short version)	−1.1893	−1.2502	−1.3164	
Interpretation (long version)	−1.3443	−1.3796	−1.5082	
Deliberation (long version)	−1.3697	−1.4031	−1.5304	
Interpretation (short version)	−1.8124	−1.8611	−1.9138	
Information (long version)	−1.9215	−1.8887	−2.1096	
Information (short version)	−2.8001	−2.8117	−2.8996	Least intervening

Source: Van Hooren *et al.* 2006

On average the two paternalistic strategies were placed first and the two informative strategies at the other extreme of the dimension. The deliberative and interpretive strategies were placed close to each other, between the other two strategies. The short and long versions of each strategy were placed close to each other. Both parents and professional caregivers situated the strategies in the same order.

In all cases the controlling intervention strategies were preferred over strategies in which the choice was left to the child or client. There were no significant differences between eating and behavioural problems in the preferred degree of control of the intervention as rated by professionals. Parents preferred more control in situations with eating problems than in situations with behavioural problems. Both parents and professionals preferred to intervene more actively in acute compared with chronic situations. This effect was stronger for parents than for professionals. Both parents and professionals preferred less control in community-based situations than in situations at home, although this difference was more marked in the case of parents. Professional caregivers did not show any clear differences in preferences between the first and second measurement, whereas parents preferred to control more actively at the second measurement compared with the first.

11.3.3. Conclusion

The results of this quantitative study show that both the parents and the professional caregivers preferred intervening over not intervening in dealing with problems in the care for persons with Prader–Willi syndrome. The informative approach, in which the choice is completely left to the child or client, was the least preferred model, and the paternalistic strategies were the most liked. The parents preferred intervening approaches to a greater extent than the professional caregivers. Parents preferred more controlling interventions in situations with eating problems than in situations with behavioural problems, whereas professional caregivers showed no difference between these situations.

For both groups the degree of preference for the more controlling interventions was less marked for chronic, compared with acute, situations.

11.4. Discussion

In order to deepen our understanding of the ethical issues in the care of people with Prader–Willi syndrome we conducted empirical research. The first step was a qualitative study which had the aim of gaining insight into the practice of how caregivers value and deal with the prevention of obesity in the care of people with Prader–Willi syndrome, including their experiences and moral concerns. The second step was a quantitative study, based on the findings of the qualitative project.

The finding in the quantitative study that parents preferred interventions with a more active intervening character in situations with eating problems, and less active intervening approaches in situations with less prominent behavioural problems, was supported by the findings of the qualitative study (van Hooren *et al.* 2002, 2005). In both studies parents and professional caregivers saw more opportunities for deliberative processes when dealing with behavioural problems not related to eating. Furthermore, in the qualitative study both parents and professionals indicated that persons with Prader–Willi syndrome have great difficulty keeping control over their eating behaviour. This is a well-documented phenomenon in the literature on this condition (Greenswag and Alexander 1995; Whittington and Holland 2004), for which a non-intervening approach is unlikely to be effective, and may be harmful to the health. The latter outcomes of the qualitative study are in line with the ordering in the quantitative study, in which the paternalistic strategies were placed first by both the parent and the professional groups.

Despite these correspondences between the qualitative and the quantitative study, there are also differences. The outcomes of the quantitative study showed less variety than we had initially expected. On the basis of the qualitative study, we had expected that caregivers would not only distinguish between intervening and not intervening, but also between taking over the decision (paternalism) and fostering self-understanding and moral development of the person with Prader–Willi syndrome. The latter distinction was not confirmed in the quantitative study.

The differences between the outcome of the qualitative and the quantitative studies may be due to the design of the quantitative study. The procedure of preference ranking of the four different kinds of intervention strategies may mask the nuances and subtleties of each of the underlying interaction models. Furthermore, the formulation of the cases may have had an effect on the outcomes. The cases focused on concrete problems, and respondents were invited to give a reaction in terms of what they would do in such a situation. This means that respondents were not triggered to think of developing a relationship with the person with Prader–Willi syndrome. The formulations of the strategies on the cards (see Table 11.2) might have created an experimental situation that focuses too much on decisions, in which respondents react in terms of intervening or not, instead of focusing on the context. It might have created a situation with an emphasis on concrete actions rather than on processes that take place over time. Thus, processes of clarification and discussion, which are essential in the interpretive and deliberative models, may not have received sufficient attention. These processes are mentioned in the formulations of the strategies on the cards, but these formulations may not have led respondents to clearly see these models as processes in time.

An interesting possibility for future research may be the use of a questionnaire with more items representing the various elements from the models of Emanuel and Emanuel. With this approach it may be possible to interpret participants' responses in a more differentiated way. The influence of the specific questions on the results may be less marked in the qualitative study compared with the quantitative study since the main method of gathering the data was through open interviews, in which the interviewer followed the stories of the interviewees. A simplification of the data only started with the analyses of the interview transcripts, when the process of coding and categorization took place. This simplification could be undone at any time, returning to the complete transcripts of the open interviews. In contrast, in setting up the quantitative study some simplifying choices have to be made before data collection.

The quantitative approach to gathering data does, however, have its benefits. A qualitative approach is useful to gain insight into a practice of which little is known, and is useful in order to make visible the complexity and diversity of this practice. Quantitative research, which ideally follows after and is based upon qualitative studies, is more appropriate to gathering data on a larger scale. By means of questionnaires and other methods, a larger group of respondents can be reached, making the results more representative. A quantitative study, furthermore, can focus on those factors that on the basis of previous research appear to be relevant.

No clear difference was found between the first and second measurement for the respondents. This might have been because the explanation and discussion of the various interaction models between the two measurements may not have been done effectively. It may be that the nature of the different models and their benefits have not been well understood by the respondents. The explanation and discussion that we carried out was aimed at an intellectual understanding of the differences between the models. To apply the models to a concrete situation might need more than just a cognitive understanding. If this conclusion is right, more attention should be paid to the implementation of the results of the qualitative study, if this is going to make a difference in daily practice.

11.5. **Conclusion**

This research, with both a qualitative and a quantitative approach, provides an example of how empirical ethics may contribute to the study of the moral conflict between respecting autonomy on the one hand and beneficence (providing high-quality care) on the other. In our studies we focused on the experiences of caregivers within the specific practice of dealing with the prevention of obesity in people with Prader–Willi syndrome. What values are relevant to caregivers, and how do caregivers manage the problems of overeating in daily practice? The study of these experiences shows that caregivers do not, on the whole, tackle this moral issue as a problem of balancing two opposing principles, but seek imaginative ways of enhancing autonomy within a safe environment. From the experience of practitioners we may learn that there are more ways of dealing with moral issues in the prevention of obesity than those that are dominant in moral theory. This may lead both to conceptual and normative conclusions. Conceptually, we may conclude that a definition of autonomy, based on the notion of positive freedom can be relevant in the area of the prevention of obesity in the care of people with a Prader–Willi syndrome. The notion of autonomy as positive freedom can be elaborated using the work of Emanuel and Emanuel. Yet, this also implies the need to reflect on the rationalist way in which Emanuel and Emanuel describe autonomy as moral development, which seems to restrict this notion to competent adults. This conceptual conclusion also has a normative side. The notion of positive freedom can serve as a goal in this specific practice of care. Our study not only shows the moral relevance of this goal, but also makes clear those moral actions, attitudes, and considerations that are necessary to achieve this goal, such as giving support and creating safety. Thus, our study confirms the conclusion by Van der Scheer *et al.* (2004), that empirical ethics can develop normative theories by means of an empirical inquiry into the practice relevant to specific practical problems.

References

Berlin I (1969). *Four essays on liberty*. Oxford University Press, Oxford.

Cox TF and Cox MAA (2001). *Multidimensional scaling*. Chapman & Hall, London.

Dykens EM, Goff BJ, Hodapp *et al.* (1997). Eating themselves to death: have "personal rights" gone too far in treating people with Prader–Willi syndrome? *Mental Retardation*, **35**, 312–14.

Emanuel EJ and Emanuel LL (1992). Four models of the physician–patient relationship. *Journal of the American Medical Association*, **267**, 2221–6.

Greenswag LR and Alexander RC (1995). *Management of Prader–Willi syndrome*, 2nd edn. Springer-Verlag, New York.

Holland AJ and Wong J (1999). Genetically determined obesity in Prader–Willi syndrome: the ethics and legality of treatment. *Journal of Medical Ethics*, **25**, 230–6.

Holland AJ, Treasure J, Coskeran P, Dallow J, Milton N and Hillhouse E (1993). Measurement of excessive appetite and metabolic changes in Prader–Willi syndrome. *International Journal of Obesity*, **17**, 527–32.

Lincoln S and Guba EG (1985). *Naturalistic inquiry.* Sage, Newbury Park.

Snijders T and Bosker R (1999). *Multilevel analysis: An introduction to basic and advanced multilevel modelling.* Sage, London.

Strauss A and Corbin J (1990). *Basics of qualitative research: grounded theory procedures and techniques.* Sage, Newbury Park.

Swaab DF, Purba JS and Hofman MA (1995). Alterations in the hypothalamic paraventricular nucleus and its oxytocin neurons (putative satiety cells) in Prader–Willi syndrome: a study of five cases. *Journal of Clinical Endocrinology and Metabolism*, **80**, 573–9.

Ten Have H and Lelie A (1998). Medical ethics research between theory and practice. *Theoretical Medicine and Bioethics*, **19**, 263–76.

Tronto J (1993). *Moral boundaries. A political argument for an ethic of care.* Routledge, New York.

Van der Scheer L, Van Thiel G, Van Delden J and Widdershoven G (2004). Theory and methodology of empirical-ethical research. In S Holm and MF Jonas, eds. *Engaging the world: the use of empirical research in bioethics and the regulation of biotechnology*, pp. 89-96. IOS Press, Amsterdam.

Van Hooren RH, Widdershoven GAM, Candel MJJM, Van den Borne HW, and Curfs LMG (2006). Between control and freedom in the care for persons with Prader–Willi syndrome: an analysis of preferred interventions by caregivers. *Patient Education and Counseling*, **63**, 223–31.

Van Hooren RH, Widdershoven GAM, Van den Borne HW and Curfs LMG (2002). Autonomy and intellectual disability: the case of prevention of obesity in Prader–Willi syndrome. *Journal of Intellectual Disability Research*, **46**, 560–8.

Van Hooren RH, Widdershoven GAM, Van der Bruggen H, Van den Borne HW and Curfs MG (2005). Values in the care of young persons with Prader–Willi syndrome: creating a meaningful life together. *Child: Care, Health and Development*, **31**, 309–19.

Walker M (1998). *Moral understandings: a feminist study in ethics.* Routledge, New York.

Whittington J and Holland A (2004). *Prader–Willi syndrome: Development and manifestations.* Cambridge University Press, Cambridge.

Whittington J, Holland A, Webb T, Butler J, Clarke D and Boer H (2004). Cognitive abilities and genotype in a population-based sample of people with Prader–Willi syndrome. *Journal of Intellectual Disability Research*, **48**, 172–87.

Chapter 12

Ulysses arrangements in psychiatry: from normative ethics to empirical research, and back

Ine Gremmen

12.1. Introduction

In this chapter I will discuss an example of how empirical research may contribute to normative ethics. The example concerns Ulysses arrangements. How may empirical research into Ulysses arrangements encourage normative ethical thinking about this issue?

I shall first introduce Ulysses arrangements, and give the background to such arrangements in the Netherlands. I will then outline our empirical investigations into this subject. I shall present several results from our study and discuss their relevance for normative thinking on the issues at stake in Ulysses arrangements. I shall argue that our study's results provide material for further normative analysis, including evidence that Ulysses arrangements, as seen from the perspective of caring practices, are different in several important respects from how they are seen from the point of view of their origin in normative analysis.

I do not want to suggest that this is the only way in which empirical work and normative analysis are related to each other. Scientists doing empirical work, for example, inevitably employ normative frameworks: they do not collect and analyse their data 'from nowhere'. I have discussed this aspect of the relationships between empirical work and normative frameworks in previous papers (see Gremmen and Davis 1998, Gremmen 2001) and will not discuss it further in this chapter.

In the last section of the chapter, I shall summarize how our empirical research may enhance normative ethics concerning Ulysses arrangements in psychiatry, and use the results to identify some of the key ethical issues at stake in these arrangements.

12.2. **Background: Ulysses arrangements and the Dutch 1994 Bopz Act**

The research project I will discuss focused on Ulysses arrangements in Dutch psychiatry. The name of the arrangement symbolically refers to the ancient Greek story of Ulysses and the Sirens. When Ulysses and his men sailed home after the Trojan War had ended, they had to cross the region where the Sirens could be heard singing their extremely lovely songs. Many a sailor had drowned after having jumped overboard in an attempt to reach the supposedly equally lovely Sirens. Ulysses found a way to hear the Sirens singing without having to die. He arranged for his men to put wax in their ears (so that they would not hear the Sirens' songs), to bind him tightly to the ship's mast and to ignore his orders. He instructed his men to fasten him even more tightly should he beg or give orders to be released. This arrangement enabled Ulysses to hear the Sirens singing without having to pay for it with his life.

In the field of mental health care, a Ulysses arrangement may be considered a special kind of advance directive for those clients with recurrent episodes of serious psychiatric symptoms, who consider it desirable that others intervene during such episodes, but who, at the same time, have experienced that when in crisis they resist these very interventions. Resistance is taken to include unintended and non-violent resistance due, for example, to their not perceiving the seriousness of their condition. Clients with bipolar disorders provide a classic example. In a Ulysses arrangement such clients, at a time when they are not incapacitated by illness, may arrange to be hospitalized, or treated, against their will during a future crisis when they are ill but resisting appropriate care.

Ulysses arrangements would require legal regulation if they are to be used to enforce mental health care. Ulysses arrangements are not currently legal in the Netherlands, but the Dutch Cabinet has proposed to provide for legal regulation of Ulysses arrangements (Kamerstukken 2001/02, 2002/03, 2004/05, 2005/06).

The Dutch debate concerning Ulysses arrangements was initiated by Berghmans, a health care ethicist (Berghmans 1992; Widdershoven and Berghmans 2001). He suggested that Ulysses arrangements may be considered a form of 'auto-paternalism': clients decide for themselves what is in their best interests in a future situation of psychosis. The immediate cause for considering the legal regulation of Ulysses arrangements in psychiatry were some problems in the 1994 Bopz Act on mental health care (Bijzondere Opnemingen in Psychiatrische Ziekenhuizen, i.e. Special admissions into psychiatric hospitals).

The Bopz Act is principally concerned with involuntary admission into psychiatric hospitals. Until the introduction of the Bopz Act in 1994, involuntary admission could be legally justified in terms of the best interests of clients. Clients could be admitted against their will 'for their own good', which had to be reviewed by a judge, on the basis of a psychiatrist's judgement. The Bopz Act abandoned the 'for their own good' principle. This principle had come to be considered too paternalistic.

The Bopz Act takes the principle of self-determination to be the overriding normative principle for admission into psychiatric institutions. As a consequence, clients may be admitted against their will only if they can be considered to cause 'danger to themselves or to others', if the danger stems from the client's 'mental disorder', and if there is no other way to avert it. Once admitted, clients may be treated against their will only if involuntary treatment is the only way to avert danger due to the client's mental illness.

Since its introduction, the Bopz Act has been criticized for being too restrictive. Psychiatric illnesses can cause much harm even when clients can not (or not yet) be considered to cause danger to themselves or to others using the criteria of the Bopz Act. When these clients resist admission, treatment, or any other help, there is no legal power to intervene against the clients' will, as might have been the case according to the 'for their own good' principle. The clients' wishes not to receive care will have to be respected, in accordance with the autonomy principle. The evaluation of the Bopz Act, in 1996/97, resulted in several proposals to partially solve this dilemma between respect for clients' autonomy (that might result in unjustified indifference) and care for clients' well-being (that might result in unjustified interference). One proposal is to introduce a new legal option for enforced admission or treatment, namely the so-called 'Ulysses arrangement' ('zelfbinding' in Dutch).[1]

Ulysses arrangements might provide a legally accepted way for health care professionals to overrule an incapacitated client's resistance, without the legal conditions of 'danger to themselves or others' being met. This could prevent the harmful consequences that would result from not enforcing admission or treatment. The Dutch Cabinet reasons that overruling a client's will on the basis of a Ulysses arrangement may be morally and legally justified as it can be

---

[1] In the literature on Ulysses arrangements in psychiatry, the terms 'Ulysses contract' or 'Ulysses statement' can be found, as well. In our project we preferred the term Ulysses 'arrangement'. The term 'contract' is problematic in that it assumes a legal status, which is not evident; 'statement' has the connotation of a one-sided declaration, whereas the term 'arrangement' makes clear that both clients and others are involved.

'traced back to the patient's own wishes' (Kamerstukken 2001/02, No. 3). According to the Cabinet, Ulysses arrangements may be considered to be an expression of patient autonomy, and, therefore, a form of 'care according to needs' (Ministerie van Volksgezondheid *et al*. 1997), rather than simply reverting to the paternalism that was inherent in the legislation before the Bopz Act.

Since Ulysses arrangements would concern involuntary admission and/or treatment in situations where the legal conditions for involuntary admission or treatment are not (or not yet) met, these arrangements would undermine the Bopz Act's conditions of 'danger'. The Cabinet resolves this problem by reasoning that Ulysses arrangements can be considered consistent with the Bopz Act's central principle of respect for patient autonomy, provided that drafting the arrangement can be guaranteed to be an autonomous act by the clients concerned. In line with this reasoning, the Dutch Cabinet has proposed a supplement to the Bopz Act in order to make Ulysses arrangements a legal option.

The current debate taking place in the Netherlands illustrates one way in which normative ethics, caring practices, policy, and the law relate to each other. The Bopz Act was guided by the normative position that respect for patient autonomy (patient self-determination) should override 'paternalistic' considerations of best interests. Mental health care practice suggests that there are problems with the working of the Bopz Act. In particular the Act does not allow intervention to be enforced at an early stage in a mental illness when it may be effective in preventing further deterioration. This sometimes results in clients coming to greater harm and does not prevent, but only delays, enforced treatment. On the basis of normative ethics, Ulysses arrangements are proposed as one solution to this problem. They may prevent the harmful effects of delayed intervention, but in a way that is in keeping with the principle of respect for patient autonomy rather than returning to the principle of best interests.

The purpose of the empirical research discussed in this chapter is to continue the interaction between normative ethics and empirical data through investigating the likely consequences of adopting a Ulysses arrangement within the legal structure around enforcing psychiatric care. While the proposal for Ulysses arrangements was developed and discussed in normative terms (as a way of respecting patient autonomy), it is relevant, as well, to empirically assess the effects of Ulysses arrangements as a mental health care intervention, in the same way as one might assess the effects of any other health care intervention, e.g. a drug treatment.

I shall argue that our empirical data suggest that Ulysses arrangements, as seen from the perspective of caring practices, differ from Ulysses arrangements as seen from the principle of autonomy described above. As a consequence, the data raise further issues for normative analysis.

12.3. **The research project: policy analysis and interview study**

In order to investigate the ethical and juridical aspects of Ulysses arrangements further, the Dutch Cabinet asked the Netherlands Organization for Scientific Research (NWO) to fund research on the ethical and legal issues involved. The research project described in this chapter was undertaken as a result (Gremmen *et al.* 2002). The project (1999–2002) was supervised by Prof S. Sevenhuijsen (Utrecht University) and Prof G. Widdershoven (Maastricht University), who are experts on feminist ethics of care and health care ethics, respectively (e.g. Sevenhuijsen 1998, 1999; Widdershoven 1999; Widdershoven and Berghmans 2001). Dr I. Gremmen was the main executive researcher. Co-workers in the project were independent legal expert and psychiatrist Mr R. Zuijderhoudt, and psychiatrist Dr A. Beekman (Amsterdam Free University). The project was approved by the ethical committee of Utrecht University.

Our research entailed two studies. In the first study, we undertook an analysis of the Dutch policy debate concerning Ulysses arrangements. The results of this study are discussed elsewhere (Gremmen *et al.* 2002). In our second study, we investigated the experiences and considerations of persons practically or potentially involved with the issue of Ulysses arrangements. Semi-structured interviews were conducted with 18 clients, 12 of their partners, family members, or friends, 17 professional care providers, e.g. psychiatrists and psychiatric nurses, and 19 others involved, e.g. lawyers, judges, and clients' trusted representatives.

The clients were approached first. They were found through clients' interest groups, clients' boards in mental health care institutions, and professional care providers. If clients agreed (with written permission), their family members or professional care providers were invited to participate in the project as well. This procedure enabled us to collect views of the situation from different angles. The majority of clients interviewed agreed to our approaching others involved in their care. Some additional interviews were held with family members and professional care-givers who were not connected to the clients involved in the study. One of the professional care-givers is R, a psychiatrist whose story will be discussed below. Judges and lawyers were found through the members of the research group, and clients' trusted representatives through their professional organization.

The interviews focused on the interviewees' experiences relevant to the issue of Ulysses arrangements, and on their considerations concerning the moral and legal grounds, the goals, and the advantages and disadvantages of Ulysses arrangements. The interview material was systematically analysed by theme. Interviewees' stories about experiences with Ulysses-like arrangements were studied in detail through line-by-line analysis.

In this chapter, two main findings of our second study (the interview study) will be discussed. Both provide 'food for normative ethics' concerning the issue of Ulysses arrangements. The first finding concerns a paradox: interviewees consider the *prevention* of involuntary admission or treatment as one of the aims of Ulysses arrangements. The second finding concerns several moral dilemmas that the interviewees formulate concerning putting a Ulysses arrangement into effect through involuntary admission or treatment. At first glance, both findings seem to be at odds with current ethical reasoning concerning Ulysses arrangements in psychiatry (e.g. Elster 1984, 2000), and with the reasoning of the Dutch Cabinet. How could one want to *prevent* coercion by prearranging for this very same coercion? And wouldn't the *ethical* problems concerning coercion be solved through freely and deliberately prearranging for it in a Ulysses arrangement?

12.4. **The paradox of prevention: avoiding coercion through prearranging for it**

The first finding of our interview study that we will discuss is the interviewees' (somewhat paradoxical) expressed wish to *prevent* coercion by means of making a Ulysses arrangement. Several interviewees in this study say that they want to use a Ulysses arrangement in order to plan for involuntary admission or treatment if in the future they become psychotic, in order to prevent what one client calls the 'more heavy' alternative of being arrested by the police.

Some clients predict that, if they are to make a Ulysses arrangement, then they will not resist the measures agreed to in that agreement, in a future situation of crisis. This may sound optimistic, given that they showed resistance in the past. Other clients do predict that they will resist coercive measures even if these are in line with an agreed Ulysses arrangement. Consider the interview with a client, D, who is diagnosed as having a bipolar disorder. D has been involuntarily admitted twice in the past, after having turned his house into a complete mess and having annoyed his neighbours to the point of police involvement. D says that he would consider drafting a Ulysses arrangement if it were a legal option, in order to prevent the damage of another episode of psychosis. When asked how he imagines the Ulysses arrangement working, he replies that he expects to resist admission, particularly as he will probably feel quite well. Nevertheless he hopes that he will be persuaded to agree to admission: the arrangement might 'encourage me to have myself admitted, anyway, possibly against my will.'

Other clients express similar views and use similar words. At first glance, what these clients are saying seems not just optimistic, but illogical. How could one agree to admission against one's will? I shall discuss one example from our interview study more extensively, in order to explore these considerations in detail. The example is from an interview with a psychiatrist, R.

R drafted a Ulysses arrangement with one of his clients 4 years ago, although, of course, it had no legal standing. The client, Ms M, had been diagnosed as having a bipolar disorder. During the 7 years before the Ulysses arrangement was drafted, Ms M was involuntarily admitted several times, after causing serious marital problems which required police intervention and led to her husband leaving home. On these occasions Ms M was admitted involuntarily at a time when, in her view, nothing was the matter with her.

The point was reached where her husband was seriously considering divorce. By then, it had become clear, after a crisis leading to involuntary admission, that Ms M had been mildly manic for about a year and that this was a major cause of the marital problems.

After Ms M regained her stability, R suggested that Ms and Mr M consider the option of making a Ulysses arrangement. He reasoned that the arrangement might provide the crucial support that Ms M needed in order to break through the cycle of recurrent episodes of psychiatric symptoms. Ms M agreed to draft a Ulysses arrangement and to oversee its content and consequences. R considered it very important that Ms M had control over the agreement. He realized that Mr M's signing the agreement amounted to 'giving up a bit of autonomy'. He did not agree however with the view of several other interviewees that respecting autonomy implies that clients, rather than care-givers, should *initiate* the discussion around drafting a Ulysses arrangement.

Ms M was quite motivated to avoid the damage due to her symptoms and did not have too much of a problem with the idea of giving up some autonomy in future crises. Mr M told R that he would prefer to try and live with some symptoms from time to time, to having a divorce, as long as there was someone for him to turn to for help before a crisis point was reached.

In consultation with Ms and Mr M, R drafted an arrangement to cover the situations when Ms M would need involuntary admission. In drafting the arrangement he took account of the Dutch literature on Ulysses arrangements (e.g. Berghmans). He arranged for an official ceremony for the signing of the final draft, with Ms M's brother, whom she trusted, present as a witness. R believed that the ceremony might help Ms M to remember the arrangement were she to become psychotic and that it would enable both Mr M and himself to refer more easily to the arrangement in discussions with Ms M at such a time.

In fact involuntary admission has never been needed over the 4 years since the Ulysses arrangement was agreed. R believes that this is because he has been able to take immediate action whenever Ms M begins to be unwell, as signalled either by herself or by Mr M. When either of them calls R for help, he arranges an appointment within a few days. On one occasion there was some quarrelling and disagreement between Ms and Mr M, but not the serious fights that had previously taken place. In contrast to previous occasions, Ms M herself raised the alarm and agreed to being admitted. Furthermore, whereas on previous occasions she stayed in hospital for several months, on this occasion, she was discharged after 10 days.

Although from time to time the situation is 'not easy' for Mr and Ms M, R considers it 'quite bearable for all involved'. Ms and Mr M can accept that times are hard, now and again. There is no longer any question of their getting divorced.

R's story suggests that Ulysses arrangements are playing a role that is different from how they were conceived. They are not just about respect for patient autonomy providing a rationale for coercive treatment. They may affect the relationships between clients and health professionals; they may impact on trust; and they may affect the behaviour and decisions made by clients as well as professionals, reducing the need for coercive treatment. These are issues that are relevant to ethical analysis.

Psychiatrist R is convinced that the involuntary admission of Ms M has been avoided as a result of the Ulysses arrangement. He explains that 'initially' he thought that a Ulysses arrangement 'primarily had a juridical, contractual tone'. While working with it, however, in practice, to his 'surprise', R has experienced that, even though it is 'of course' partly contractual, some 'quite different processes' were also set in motion. 'It may not be primarily what a Ulysses arrangement is meant for,' R says, 'but it *is* a definition of the treatment relationship in terms of mutual obligations, as well'. R characterizes the redefined relationship between Ms M and himself as one of 'greater equality'.

In R's experience, making a Ulysses arrangement implies that he commits himself to respond to an appeal for help from Ms M. This is an obligation not only to intervene quickly when a crisis develops, but also to be prepared if necessary to admit Ms M to hospital. Ms M, in turn, agrees to be admitted if R and Mr M consider this necessary, even if she resists admission at the time.

R says that he feels he could refer to the agreement in a crisis situation, reminding Ms M that it has been discussed extensively and that she has clearly agreed to the arrangement. R has never in fact had to refer to the Ulysses arrangement in this way. It is his experience 'that a Ulysses contract is not just a sort of juridical means of coercion. It confirms the treatment relationship, as well, thus encouraging clients to stick to the agreements made, even when they may not realise or want to, later on'. It may be worth noting the similarity with client D's expression, cited earlier, who hopes to 'have myself admitted, possibly against my will'. Other interviewees explained, that, in a relationship of trust with a care-giver, clients may cooperate rather than resist care in a situation when, due to a psychosis, they neither remember the earlier agreement nor are able to rehearse the arguments in favour of the arrangement. One interviewee, for example, told how a client allowed himself to be taken to a psychiatric hospital by a professional, while heavily protesting verbally at the same time. By that time, as the interviewee put it, 'his head did not remember that he could trust the care-giver, but his feet still knew it'.

While a Ulysses arrangement may be made in order to break through the 'seemingly unavoidable cycle' of recurring episodes of crisis where 'things get completely out of control', R considers that experiencing both the 'extra safety' and the mutuality of the arrangement creates 'quite some room', enabling clients to find a 'new way of seeing and dealing with their symptoms'. For example, a Ulysses contract helps clients to feel that they are 'a full partner in a contract, rather than a passive victim who is just being told to do things by someone else. You see? Kind of partner in the problem. All involved are confronted with the problem and we very carefully arrange for dealing with it. You see? It implies that I have to stick to the agreement, as well. It's a different way of looking at it.'

R says that the client's assumption of responsibility 'has been the most important effect, I think, in retrospect.' Clients may experience the new way of dealing with their symptoms as more satisfying, which in turn encourages them to go on with it. In the end, they may intervene just before they stop having insight into their symptoms, and before they resort to complete resistance. 'That's the idea, actually,' R says. The Ulysses arrangement appears to enable a self-sustaining process of change. 'But that's just an effect, it's an extra,' R adds, 'and it remains to be seen how often it happens. But it struck me, you know? Thinking is so much in terms of coercion. But if it comes on the one side, it comes on the other side as well, you see? For, in the end, you do hope that as little coercion as possible is … and that might very well be a side benefit.'

12.5. **Enhancing normative thinking on Ulysses arrangements: preventing the need for coercion**

The story of R illustrates how a Ulysses arrangement might prevent the need for coercion, thus suggesting an explanation for the paradox of aiming at the prevention of coercion through prearranging for this very same coercion. In R's experience, a Ulysses arrangement redefines the relationship between the client and himself into a more equal, cooperative, and mutual one as well as redefining the client's role towards her symptoms into a more active, rather than passive one. By creating 'extra safety' (describing the steps to be taken when the situation develops into a crisis) and by committing himself to agreements he can stick to in practice, such as making an appointment and admitting to hospital if necessary, R encourages Ms M to feel confident about taking more responsibility for dealing with her symptoms. This has the effect of preventing relapse of psychosis through her taking precautionary measures in time. In R's view, this is 'the most important effect'. It is the aim one would want to achieve using Ulysses arrangements, even though they are discussed 'so much in terms of coercion'.

R is aware that his experiences may not be fully in line with the ethical literature on Ulysses arrangements. He himself is surprised by how the arrangement with Ms M is working out in practice and marginalizes his experiences in so far as they do not fit easily into current ethical reasoning. He states, for example, that what he has experienced as 'the most important effect' 'may not be primarily what a Ulysses arrangement is meant for'. The prevention of coercion might 'just' be 'an extra', 'a side benefit'.

Rather than going along with this marginalization, however, normative ethics might take R's experiences and considerations as an encouragement to broaden current normative reasoning on Ulysses arrangements. Put differently: R's story might show that there may be more to say about Ulysses arrangements than that they might be (or not be) legitimated on the basis of clients' free and well informed autonomous decisions to opt for them. First, drafting a Ulysses arrangement may not amount only to exercising one's autonomy as a client; it may also imply giving up some of one's autonomy. Second, Ulysses arrangements might 'work', not just because clients autonomously opt for them, but because drafting the arrangement may enable both clients and care-givers to look differently at, and deal differently with, psychiatric symptoms. The story of R, among others, may encourage normative ethics to go into the conditions and effects of Ulysses arrangements more deeply, taking into account ethical issues additional to those around autonomy, such as those of dealing with vulnerability ('extra safety'), creating and maintaining trust ('confidence'), mutuality ('cooperation'), and taking – and entrusting – responsibility.

12.6. **Moral dilemmas concerning precommitment for coercion**

The experience of psychiatrist R suggests that Ulysses arrangements would require continuous relationships of trust between clients and care-givers.

They also require that the arrangements are drafted in the context of mutually agreed, and realistic, crisis plans and that there is a context of reliable caring services. It might be argued that, to the extent that these conditions are met, Ulysses arrangements might not be needed at all because under these conditions severe crises and coercion are likely to be avoided. However, our main finding opposing this argument concerns interviewees' experience that, in situations of crisis, good relationships and mutually agreed upon crisis plans may not suffice to maintain the contact and communication that are necessary for the prevention of severe psychosis and coercion. R himself, for example, suggests that a Ulysses arrangement may have to exist for many years (and have a strong juridical status, as well) since some clients' conditions may deteriorate within such a short period of time that contact with these clients may be lost too quickly and to too great an extent in a crisis situation. In these situations, the prevention of coercion has less chance of success than in the case of Ms M. A Ulysses arrangement may then have to be put into its ultimate effect, i.e. by involuntary admission or treatment.

From our interview material it appears that involuntary admission or treatment continues to be a moral issue even if freely and deliberately agreed through a Ulysses arrangement. I shall briefly present our findings, as they may provide further 'food' for normative thinking.

None of the clients in our study was being treated or admitted to hospital involuntarily at the time of the interview. However, most have experienced involuntary admission in the past. All have experienced limitations on their will, e.g. to their freedom to move. One example is that family members took away or hid car keys at times of developing crises. When asked, clients say that they do not expect to experience coercion (e.g. involuntary admission or treatment) on the basis of a Ulysses arrangement as different from coercion on any other basis. They expect that they will have the same feelings of not being taken seriously, of having nothing to say, of not being heard and seen, of having been cheated, of being intruded upon and being abandoned, of 'having lost'. They expect to feel as humiliated, isolated, or scared as before. On the other hand they also say that they will expect the other people involved to take the action agreed in the Ulysses arrangement when appropriate, and that if such action is not taken they will also feel cheated and not taken seriously. 'Why didn't you take the measures we arranged for' they might ask, reproachfully, after having recovered.

Similar themes are raised by family members and professional care-givers. On the basis of past experience they expect that clients, to say the least, may not like involuntary measures being initiated. Clients may feel abandoned by the people (or even the one last person) they trusted, and they may not want to see these persons for some time, as a result. At the same time, family members and professional care providers consider that, at that point in time, initiating involuntary measures may be 'the only way to help' the clients involved. As one professional explains: ultimately, Ulysses arrangements are arrangements of 'power inequality'. The care-giver can 'dominantly prescribe what the client has to do'. At the same time, however, Ulysses arrangements may 'guarantee' that the client 'will not be abandoned' when a crisis occurs. 'If collaborative efforts wouldn't work' to prevent deterioration of a client's condition, a Ulysses arrangement may provide a care-giver with 'one last recourse to help you', implying that 'I could do something about you that you would not agree with at that moment'.

Apparently, to 'do something about you that you would not agree with at that moment' may amount to 'help[ing] you'. Put differently: coercion and help (care), while not going easily together, may be closely intertwined when putting a Ulysses arrangement into its ultimate effect. As a consequence, putting a Ulysses arrangement into its ultimate effect appears to entail several moral dilemmas for both clients and care-givers involved.

One dilemma is that providing care (e.g. by admitting a client into a psychiatric hospital) would, at this point, involve coercion (the measure would be taken against the client's will). However, not resorting to coercion (not overruling the client's will) would involve abandoning the client (no care would be provided). Clients face a similar dilemma: receiving care would involve undergoing coercion, while refusing coercion would result in being abandoned (getting no care).

Another dilemma concerns trust. Putting a Ulysses arrangement into its ultimate effect puts trust in the relationships between clients and care-givers under serious strain, but so does failing to use the coercion agreed to in the arrangement. Whatever the professional does, the client may feel abandoned and not taken seriously.

These dilemmas imply that the evaluation of the arrangement's being put into its ultimate effect would be an essential element of Ulysses arrangements. The care-givers would have to try and restore trust in the relationship with the client and to account for the steps taken, both to the client and to others, as soon as possible afterwards. The interview material makes it clear that it would not suffice to say: 'I just did what you as a client freely agreed to in advance'. One example is provided by an interviewee, whose daughter has experienced severe psychotic episodes. In the past, she has experienced her daughter's fierce resistance to admission. She expects that a Ulysses arrangement will make her feel relieved because it may, at last, provide a means of protecting her daughter from the harm she has been doing to herself and others when psychotic. If a Ulysses arrangement had been agreed she could say to her daughter: 'This is what you yourself agreed to. It's all your own doing, so, here you go [into the hospital]!' Her argument might be grounded in a concept of autonomy as free and deliberate choice. But the interviewee does not appear to feel happy to rely only on respecting her daughter's previously expressed wishes. She seems to feel that there are still moral problems. When asked to imagine her daughter being admitted under the Ulysses agreement she says that she would want to say to her daughter: 'It's not to punish you, it's to *help* you!'

12.7. Enhancing normative thinking on Ulysses arrangements: the issue of responsibility

The interview material, again, shows that, from a normative ethics perspective, there may be more to say about Ulysses arrangements than that they should be drawn up freely and without coercion.

The interview data suggest that the issue of responsibility also needs to be taken into account. Putting a Ulysses arrangement into its ultimate effect amounts to putting an end to the mutuality of the arrangement, even if only temporarily. Deciding if and when to use the involuntary measures agreed upon earlier is the care-givers' responsibility. As a consequence, care-givers would have to account for the steps taken. They would also need to try and restore trust in the relationship with the client.

The interview material also suggests that another important ethical issue in putting a Ulysses arrangement into its ultimate effect is that, in such a situation, coercion and care are intertwined. Moral dilemmas do result, since coercion and care do not sit easily together. The dilemmas are difficult to deal with from a perspective of individual autonomy conceived of as negative freedom (i.e. the right to non-intervention). In this conception of autonomy, care is easily associated with undue intrusion and paternalism (cf. MacKenzie and Stoljar 1999, Verkerk 1999). Put differently: a concept of autonomy as negative freedom implies a strong opposition between autonomy and beneficence in the setting of treatment coercion. As a result, the issues of whether, when, and under what conditions good mental health care might, in specific cases, imply coercion, might be left undiscussed or, for that matter, be marginalized, too easily. However, the interview data suggest that these issues may be of critical importance for normative thinking on Ulysses arrangements.

12.8. Concluding remarks

The main empirical findings on Ulysses arrangements discussed in this chapter concern the paradox of preventing involuntary measures by prearranging for them, and the moral dilemmas inherent to situations where coercion and care are closely interconnected. Neither one of these empirical findings may be sufficiently taken into account if a Ulysses arrangement is conceptualized only as freely and deliberately prearranged involuntary admission or treatment. Furthermore, both these findings might, in turn, enhance normative thinking on Ulysses arrangements. There may be more to say on Ulysses arrangements, from a normative perspective, than a concept of autonomy as rational choice and negative freedom readily allows. The interview data may encourage normative thinking on Ulysses arrangements as a process and as a relationship. Ethical issues of dealing with vulnerability, mutual commitment, and the taking and entrusting of responsibility might be incorporated. The idea of coercion as a form of care, however contested, might be considered.

In addition to issues around autonomy, I suggest the following description of the ethical issues at stake in Ulysses arrangements. Considering and drafting a Ulysses arrangement would require that clients *recognize* their *vulnerability* for psychoses. A Ulysses arrangement might then be considered a process in which clients take *responsibility* to formulate their *caring needs* for future situations of crisis, and *entrust* care for their well being in these situations to others (either whole-heartedly or as a felt necessity). Ulysses arrangements may be considered *mutual* arrangements, in which not just the clients, but the other persons involved clarify their *responsibilities* and *competencies*, in order to build trust in the relationship and make the arrangement work in practice. Drafting the arrangement, and working with it, may enhance confidence as well as provide opportunities to deal with a developing crisis at an early stage, thus avoiding coercion. Having to put a Ulysses arrangement into its ultimate effect (i.e. through coercion) is problematic, even though this has been arranged for in advance. It would, at least temporarily, undermine the mutual character of the arrangement and result in several moral *dilemmas*. Even though coercion has been arranged for as an ultimate form of care, *coercion and care* do not sit easily together. Coercion puts *trust* at severe risk. As a consequence, both the prevention of coercion as well as the *evaluation* of coercive measures (*responsiveness, accountability, restoration of trust*) may be considered to be of central importance.

The issues discussed in this chapter suggest that the concept of care is a key issue in normative thinking about Ulysses arrangements. In other words: normative ethics might take the paradoxes and controversies in the interview data described in this chapter into account through a consideration of the issue of *good care*.

References

Berghmans R (1992). *Om bestwil. Paternalisme in de psychiatrie.* Thesis Publishers, Amsterdam.

Davis K and Gremmen I (1998). In search of heroines: some reflections on normativity in feminist research. *Feminism & Psychology* **8**(2), 133–53.

Elster J (1984). *Ulysses and the Sirens: studies in rationality and irrationality,* 2nd revised edn. Cambridge University Press, Cambridge.

Elster J (2000). *Ulysses unbound: studies in rationality, precommitment and constraints.* Cambridge University Press, Cambridge.

Gremmen I (2001). Interpretatief zorgethisch onderzoek in de praktijk. *Medische Antropologie,* **13**(2), 323–39.

Gremmen I, Sevenhuijsen S, Widdershoven G, Beekman A and Zuijderhoudt R (2002). *Zelfbinding in de psychiatrie, een kwestie van goede zorg?* NWO/Universiteit Utrecht, Den Haag/Utrecht.

Kamerstukken II (2001/02). 28 283 nrs 1–4. *Wijziging van de Wet bijzondere opnemingen in psychiatrische ziekenhuizen (zelfbinding).*

Kamerstukken II (2002/03). 28 283 nrs 5–7. *Wijziging van de Wet bijzondere opnemingen in psychiatrische ziekenhuizen (zelfbinding).*

Kamerstukken II (2004/05). 28 283 nrs 8–9. *Wijziging van de Wet bijzondere opnemingen in psychiatrische ziekenhuizen (zelfbinding).*

Kamerstukken II (2005/06). 28 283 nrs A, B and 10–16. *Wijziging van de Wet bijzondere opnemingen in psychiatrische ziekenhuizen (zelfbinding).*

MacKenzie C and Stoljar N eds. (1999). *Relational autonomy: feminist perspectives on autonomy, agency and the social self.* Oxford University Press, New York and Oxford.

Ministerie van Volksgezondheid, Welzijn en Sport (VWS) and Ministerie van Justitie (1997). *Kabinetsstandpunt: Evaluatie van de Wet BOPZ.* Ministeries van VWS en Justitie, Rijswijk.

Sevenhuijsen S (1998). *Citizenship and the ethics of care: feminist considerations on justice, morality and politics.* Routledge, London/New York.

Sevenhuijsen S (1999). Too good to be true? Feminist considerations about trust and social cohesion. *Focaal,* **34**, 207–22.

Verkerk M (1999). A care perspective on coercion and autonomy. *Bioethics,* **13**(3-4), 358–68.

Widdershoven G (1999). Care, cure and interpersonal understanding. *Journal of Advanced Nursing,* **29**, 1163–9.

Widdershoven G and Berghmans R (2001). Advance directives in psychiatric care: a narrative approach. *Journal of Medical Ethics,* **27**(2) 92–7.

Chapter 13

Treatment refusal in anorexia nervosa: a challenge to current concepts of capacity

Jacinta Tan and Tony Hope

13.1. Introduction

The research study that we will describe in this chapter is an empirical exploration of ethical issues around treatment refusal in anorexia nervosa. Our view, like other authors who have contributed to this book, is that the investigation of issues in practical ethics often requires a combination of empirical and conceptual research.

Previous discussion of ethical issues in anorexia nervosa has largely been conducted either from theoretical perspectives, for example by medical ethicists, philosophers, and feminists, who have focused on the underlying principles and wider cultural influences (e.g. Gilligan 1982; Lee 1993; Russell 1995; Draper 2000; Gremillion 2003), or from clinical perspectives by professionals treating patients with an eating disorder who have explored the issues based on clinical impressions and frameworks (Gothelf *et al.* 1995; Beumont and Vandereycken 1998). There have been several systematic empirical studies in anorexia nervosa but these have focused almost exclusively on the nature of the disorder, its underlying psychopathological mechanisms, and developing treatment approaches (Gowers and Bryant-Waugh 2004). Some of this work has explored the accounts of experiences of patients and health professionals (Shisslak *et al.* 1989; Gremillion 2003; Colton and Pistrang 2004). A major reason for an interest in patient perspectives is the poor outcomes using traditional treatments based on an assumption that patients are motivated to overcome their problems. New treatment approaches are being developed, such as 'motivational interviewing', where the goal is to shift the patient along the 'cycle of change' towards the stage of seeking active change (Prochaska and DiClemente 1983; Miller and Rollnick 1991; Treasure and Ward 1997; Vitousek *et al.* 1998). Another area of research is examining the effectiveness of the use of compulsion (Ramsay *et al.* 1999). There has also been empirical work, much of it conducted from a feminist perspective, aimed at a critique of the psychiatric system and its treatment of women in particular (Russell, 1995; Gremillion 2003). Further empirical work looks at the relationship of women to their bodies (e.g. Orbach 1978; Bettle *et al.* 1998; Andrist 2003).

Despite this wealth of research and discussion there have been no previous systematic empirical studies of ethical issues that arise in the care of people with anorexia nervosa. In this chapter, we will describe a 'preliminary study' that was conceived as a pilot for such a systematic empirical study. We will discuss the rationale for the study, its methodology, and give a brief account of some of the results, using these to illustrate the relationships between empirical data and ethical analysis. At the time of writing this we have some results from the much larger subsequent study involving 29 participants. We will call this the 'cross-sectional study'.

13.2. **Methods**

13.2.1. **Participants**

Patients with anorexia nervosa tend to be young, with a typical age of onset between 16 and 25 years, although the condition can run a chronic course over years and even decades (Fairburn and Harrison 2003).

The ethical issues around compulsory treatment, therefore, involve not only the effects of the condition on, for example, decision-making, but also the question of the significance of a patient's age and of the role of parents. Indeed, parents of adolescent and young adult patients with anorexia nervosa often have a close involvement in treatment, including being joint clients with their offspring (e.g. Dare *et al.* 1995; Gowers and North 1999; Fornari *et al.* 2001). In addition to having an intimate knowledge and understanding of their children's struggles, parents are often involved in the process of implementing compulsory treatment, and of being advocates for their children's needs within the medical and legal systems.

For this preliminary study we chose to recruit patients from the categories with greatest incidence of the condition, that is young females. We wanted to explore issues around development and across the age of legal majority. We chose to include people from age 13–21 years old. We also included some parents in the sample because parents are in a unique position to provide perspectives on their daughters' experiences and decision-making capacity.

Ten female patients were interviewed. Participants were recruited through their mental health treatment teams. The selection criteria required that participants had met DSM-IV criteria for anorexia nervosa, including the diagnosis of atypical anorexia nervosa if below 16 years (American Psychiatric

Association 2000). Most of the participants were in treatment when this study was undertaken and were at a range of stages of illness severity and recovery when interviewed. The participants' body mass indices (BMI) ranged from 12.6 (a dangerously severe weight deficit) to 19.6 (just below normal limits), with a median BMI of 17.1. Normal body mass index is defined as 20 to 25.

The mothers of seven of the participants with anorexia nervosa were interviewed separately. In addition both parents of an adolescent patient with anorexia nervosa, who was not a participant, were also interviewed. This is because this young woman declined to be interviewed herself, but gave consent for her parents to be included in the study.

13.2.2. **Data collection**

The main method of data collection was through interview using a schedule devised specifically for this research. In addition we administered a standardized test of competence, the MacCAT-T (Grisso and Appelbaum 1998), after the interviews. This test is the most widely used formal and structured method for assessing competence to consent to medical (including psychiatric) treatment. It has been developed to reflect legal criteria for competence used in the USA (Appelbaum 1998), and involves testing the patient systematically in four different domains: understanding, reasoning, appreciation,[1] and expressing a choice. Participants' performance on the MacCAT-T provides a measure against which to compare the participants' own accounts of their difficulties and the concept of competence as given in their accounts.

In addition we collected the following basic demographic data: date of birth; type of treatment experienced; height and weight. The patients completed two self-administered instruments relevant to the characterization of the eating disorder: the Eating Disorder Examination (EDE-Q4) (Fairburn and Cooper 1993; Fairburn and Beglin 1994), and the Eating Attitudes Test (EAT) (Garner and Garfinkel 1979; Garner *et al.* 1982). In addition, they also completed three brief self-administered questionnaires to assess their levels of psychopathology: the Beck Anxiety Inventory (BAI) (Beck and Steer 1993a); the Beck Depression Inventory (BDI) (Beck and Steer 1993b); and the Rosenberg Self-Esteem Questionnaire (Rosenberg 1965).

---

[1] The MacCAT-T, while reflecting legislation in general, does not accurately reflect current criteria of capacity in English and Welsh common law. In particular, the concept of Appreciation is absent from English and Welsh law.

13.2.3. **Rationale for the methodology**

Our initial interest in the ethical issues around treatment refusal in anorexia was a result of clinical experience. The question of when it is right to enforce treatment on people suffering from anorexia nervosa is one faced by most clinicians working with such patients. Many people with anorexia are at significant risk of considerable harm and are often distressed by their condition, and yet they may refuse, or strongly resist, attempts to help and treat them. The key legal and ethical concept used to determine when treatment should be enforced is that of 'capacity' (the legal term used in the UK) or 'competence' (the legal term used in the USA). The term 'competence' is also used by clinicians in the UK although this usage may include a broader range of considerations that are not part of the legal concept of capacity (Malle *et al.* 2000; Tan and Jones 2001).

A significant body of research has been carried out in the area of competence and capacity as applied to medicine in general, and to psychiatry in particular (e.g. Grisso and Appelbaum 1995; Billick *et al.* 1998; Fazel *et al.* 1999a,b; Billick *et al.* 2001; Fegert 2003) but none of this research has been conducted in the setting of anorexia nervosa. Furthermore all this research has used an understanding of the components of competence based on the legal concept. These components are largely cognitive in nature.

People with anorexia posed, we thought, a challenge to the current concept of competence. On the one hand most people with anorexia nervosa have good levels of cognitive functioning and could be assessed as competent on the basis of the current concept. On the other hand many people with anorexia are not only at high risk if their treatment refusal is respected, but also the refusal seems often to be based on reasons that appear, to those involved in the care, to be distortions of the person's true views. This statement, of course, raises both conceptual and empirical questions. Conceptual questions include: what is meant by 'true views', and what are their relevance to the question of compulsory treatment. Empirical questions include: on what grounds do people with anorexia nervosa refuse treatment and how do these relate to the person's values?

We thought, therefore, that exploration of these issues required both empirical and conceptual work. Our immediate aim was to gain a good understanding of the kinds of difficulties patients actually experience in making treatment decisions. We also wanted to explore the ways in which patients come to their decisions – the reasons they used, and the factors that they did, or did not, take into account. Such empirical exploration it seemed to us would provide data relevant to the concept of competence and help to identify further factors that might be relevant to the ethical issues related to enforcing treatment. In short we thought that our current understanding of competence and treatment decision-making would be enriched through finding out about the experiences and thinking of people with anorexia, and their families.

This aim raised interesting methodological questions. It seemed clear that the core of the empirical method should involve detailed interviews with people who were suffering, or had suffered, from anorexia nervosa. Questionnaire-based studies, we thought, would impose too much pre-determined structure on data collection, as well as providing insufficient opportunity for the level of detail that we required. But how 'open' and how structured should such interviews be? Although we were interested in the experiences of people with anorexia our interest had a specific focus: the ethical issues around enforcing treatment. Conceptual analysis suggested that a key issue would be whether patients with anorexia are competent to refuse treatment. For this reason we were interested in the question of whether patients were competent. We did not want, however, to assume that the current legal notion of capacity and the current structured methods of assessment of competence were adequate since the impetus for the research was the sense that such notions failed to adequately pick up on ways in which the decision-making of patients with anorexia might be impaired.

We needed, on the one hand, to make use of a concept of competence, and of an analysis of the relevant ethical issues prior to undertaking the study, in order to ensure that we collected the relevant data. For example, such analysis shows that in examining the ways in which competence might be compromised we would need to find out not only what factors each person took into account in decision-making, but also what potentially relevant factors they considered irrelevant. Such prior analysis also suggested that some hypothetical questions would be significant and revealing. An example of such a question is: 'if you could (could have) take(n) a "magic" pill that would take away the anorexia, but had no other effect, would you take (have taken) it?' On the other hand we needed to be open to discovering aspects that are not part of the current concept of competence, or are not highlighted in the current ethical analyses of enforcing treatment.

We looked to 'grounded theory' in order to try and ensure that our data would reflect the experiences and perspectives of those with anorexia, and to provide an openness to discovery of new aspects. Grounded theory, which has a venerable tradition in sociological research, is a method of inquiry in which there is as little prior assumption of the expected results as possible, sometimes to the extent of deliberately eschewing familiarity with results from similar research, or theories that may influence the data collection or analysis. Its purpose is to allow fresh concepts to emerge from the participants' accounts

(Glaser and Strauss 1967). The grounded theory approach in its purest form is difficult to achieve as researchers need to know what they wish to research, and why. Nevertheless, some appeal to the principles of grounded theory are very useful as they help a researcher employing such qualitative research methods to be mindful of her own perspectives and biases, as well as her own impact on the interview content through the nature and quality of her inter- actions with the participants. With such self-awareness, an interviewer can be open to new and unexpected results which may not fit with her prior expecta- tions. This helps to ensure that themes can 'emerge' from the data, and helps to enable the voices of the research participants to influence the results.

Grounded theory in its pure form is not appropriate for the purposes of the research discussed in this chapter because of the need for some prior ethical analysis in order to inform our data collection. We adapted the grounded the- ory approach in three ways. First, in addition to open questions about the experiences of care, we asked specific questions based on our prior under- standing of the relevant ethical issues and the key concepts such as 'compe- tence'. Second the interviewer was free to pursue questioning to gain as complete an understanding of participants' decision-making and reasoning as possible, and such questioning was undoubtedly (and properly) affected by the interviewers' own prior understanding of what is ethically relevant. Third, in the analysis of results we used a modified 'grounded theory' approach. In identifying 'emergent themes' we looked for themes in the data that the research team thought were at least potentially relevant to the ethical issues relevant to enforced treatment and competence.

Thus, because the purpose of the research is to shed light on the ethical issues around compulsory treatment certain sorts of information on experi- ences, beliefs, and reasoning need to be systematically collected, in order to understand the range and diversity as well as the similarities of themes which emerge. Examples of such sorts of information are: accounts of any use of coercion or formal compulsory treatment; opinions of the use of compulsory treatment in anorexia nervosa; the participants' views of the ethical arguments that justify overriding treatment refusal in anorexia nervosa; and participants' accounts of their difficulties with making treatment decisions. All of these sorts of information may spontaneously arise in an illness narrative, but often they do not. Furthermore, some of the areas of the ethical inquiry were not issues that participants had previously even thought of. With appropriate guidance, however, they were able to develop views on such areas. The inter- views therefore involved the interviewer in trying to tease out exactly what reasons and experiences were important to the participant (respondent). The following extract shows the interviewer trying to establish exactly how the participant saw the risk of death and how she thought about that risk in deciding about accepting or not accepting treatment. In doing this the interviewer also makes use of what other participants have said to clarify the views of this participant.

Interviewer:	I'm trying to understand how people with anorexia nervosa view dying. I'll tell you what I mean. Because one of the features of anorexia nervosa at a very low weight is that the behaviour actually could kill you, right? But people still do it. So it doesn't make much sense, does it?
Respondent:	Mm. (agreement)
Interviewer:	And I wonder, most of us if we're doing something – you don't put your hand in a flame, do you? Is it that you want to die, or you change your attitudes to death or you don't want to die or you don't care, or..?
Respondent:	I think it's lots of things, I think for me … there have been a lot of different stages and I've felt a lot of different – because I've been told I've been close to death a lot of times and but then … a lot of different sort of thoughts have... been like that and some have been, 'you're talking a lot of rubbish, I'm not, I feel as strong as I've ever been, what are you going on about, you're just saying this to make me get unfit, I don't believe you', and other times, I've been hoping that I would just die, I've just had enough of it, the anorexia just got too much, I couldn't take it anymore and I just hoped I would and... other times you don't think you know what you're doing... (laughs) and it just... I think it's hard to give something up that also makes you feel good, I don't know if... (2 second pause)
Interviewer:	So it's kind of like death is an irrelevant thing.
Respondent:	I think it can, this time I did, I was hoping that... it would, I was just so tired of it, but I don't know. (2 second pause). I think – yeah, that doesn't cross your mind, you want to take that run, you don't care if it's going to kill you, you just want to go for that run.
Interviewer:	So is it that at that moment it feels like that run is more important?
Respondent:	Mm (agrees), it's the kind of thing that makes you feel better at that time.
Interviewer:	So is it hard to sometimes think about long-term things when you've got this thing going.
Respondent:	Mm (agrees).
Interviewer:	I've had a couple of people say, well, in a funny way, it's almost like a thrill to risk death. Have you ever felt like that?
Respondent:	Not really. It's scary.
Interviewer:	You felt scared.
Respondent:	It's quite confusing, you don't really feel you're you, you don't understand.
Interviewer:	And there have been other people who've said to me, I simply don't believe that I could die.
Respondent:	Mm, I think I was like that a lot, it was only when I was a lot stronger that I realised that you could.

Interviewer:	Right.
Respondent:	But I think that's the problem with this illness, you could be like... I'm at my lowest weight and I'm still running, you know and... And then people telling me, 'you could die', and I'm like, 'I can still run, what are you lot going on about?'
Interviewer:	This feeling that you can't die, it strikes me that there are two possible ways it could happen. One could be saying, look, I'm not that bad, you're just making it up, I'm not that bad, so it's not going to happen. But there's another way in which you could... someone could feel well, I'm sort of superhuman, it's not possible to die.
Respondent:	Mm. (agreement)
Interviewer:	Which one is it for you?
Respondent:	I think it's the first one.
Interviewer:	The first one, so it's not that bad.
Respondent:	Mm. (agrees). (Participant F)

13.2.4. **The interview**

The specific interview schedule used for the main data collection was drawn up based on extensive discussions involving the entire research team including a medical ethicist, a medical sociologist, and an adolescent psychiatrist with a special interest in, and extensive experience of, treating eating disorders. The questions in the interview schedule were designed to fulfil several requirements.

1. To obtain relevant factual information, for instance whether participants have had experience of compulsion or the use of compulsory treatment, and the kinds of treatment they are currently having.

2. To elicit the participants' ways of thinking relevant to several ethical issues, for example the circumstances in which compulsory treatment should be used, if at all. Although asked as a general question, many participants responded by giving examples from their own experiences, and their views often being clearly shaped by their own experiences.

3. To elicit participants' accounts about the factors which have helped or hindered them in decision-making.

4. To allow participants to raise themes, which may be relevant to the issues of capacity, competence, treatment decision-making, and compulsory treatment.

The interview schedule contained the following six sections.

1. Personal beliefs

2. Beliefs about own treatment

3. Self evaluation with respect to making treatment decisions

4. Motivation, belief, and desire with respect to making treatment decisions

5. Views about compulsory treatment and the ethical justifications for overriding treatment refusal in anorexia nervosa, including issues related to age

6. Views about compulsory treatment and the ethical justifications for overriding treatment refusal for other mental illnesses

The interview schedule used for patient participants is shown in the Appendix. A similar schedule was drawn up for parent participants. Although there was a clear structure to both schedules, each question served as a springboard for discussion and exploration of the issue in question. The interviews were conducted in a manner that allowed free discourse and exploration of the questions. The aim of the interview schedules was to provide a general structure that could guide the discussion and ensure similar ground was covered in each interview, but without inhibiting the expression of participants' views.

For this preliminary study the original interview schedule was progressively fleshed out in the light of the experiences gained with each interview and the developing understanding of the issues involved: unhelpful questions were dropped or de-emphasized and new questions were added. This evolution of the interview schedule is consistent with grounded theory methodology which allows for an iterative process of continual development of the method of data collection as successive interviews reveal further dimensions to the problem meriting exploration in interviews with further participants (Glaser and Strauss 1967; Flick 1998). With experience, there was less reliance on the fixed questions and order of the schedule and more room given for participants to express themselves, with the interviewer becoming more able to follow their lead and omit some less relevant questions if necessary in order to prioritize the emergence of important new concepts or themes during the interview.

13.3. **The experience of carrying out the interviews**

Even patients who were significantly ill were able to express themselves during the interview. The young women and their parents were enthusiastic about, and interested in, the research process, in particular feeling keen to contribute to any research which may eventually lead to changes in policy helpful to those with anorexia nervosa. They particularly valued the fact that the research design enabled their views and perspectives to be heard without restrictions imposed by rigid research designs or preconceptions.

Once participant realized that the interviewer was listening to their accounts in the interview without attempting to change their minds or to assess them, interviews became free-flowing and rich in content, with spontaneous views and narratives that included philosophical and ethical content. Here is an example.

Interviewer: Do you think you would make it [the anorexia nervosa] magically disappear if you could?

Respondent: I've had this conversation *so* many times with other anorexics! Not with normal people, because [...] if I bring it up with my friends then immediately it brings up a lot of hostility, because it's always like, 'well, you say you don't choose to be like this' sort of thing; but it's not really that, it's more fear of what I would be without it. If I knew that I could be happy – but it would be a completely different me, it would be a completely different way of thinking, because I don't think I could be the person I want to be, at the moment, without anorexia, because it's a part of it; so if I could change the kind of person I wanted to be, then yes, I would take that pill, but until then I probably wouldn't. (Participant C)

Although during much of the interviewing process the participants gave extended accounts of their experiences there were parts of each interview that consisted of a dialogue between participant and interviewer. The aim of such dialogue was to obtain participants' accounts of their reasons and decision-making processes – accounts that were not given spontaneously when providing a narrative of their experiences. These accounts in many cases would probably never have been previously articulated. The interviewer's aim was to probe the reasons and views of the participants but not to lead them towards a particular viewpoint. It is inevitable that the particular questions and remarks of the interviewer partly shape the answers.

Respondent: I had a strong, like, craving I guess to do it [i.e., lose weight]. I think I was addicted to doing it.

Interviewer: Hmm. It's interesting that you use the word 'addicted'.

Respondent: I did it even though I didn't want to. Like I would carry on way after I didn't want to do it and it was like 'why am I still doing this I don't, I want to stop' but I could only stop when I was too physically exhausted to carry on.

Interviewer: Right so it sounds like you're saying, if it's an addiction it means for you, it wasn't a choice?

Respondent: No.

Interviewer: Right, OK. You know when you think about other addictions like say drug addictions, alcohol addictions, do you see similarities or differences?

Respondent: Hmm. (Agreement) It's the same really I think because people who smoke and take drugs and stuff, they, they do it because part of them says they want to and they say 'I don't want to give up' but it's because they know they can't.

Interviewer: Ah, OK, right. So there are two different things there. Wanting and being able to?

Respondent: Hmm. Because it *does* give you pleasure. It makes you, it calms
                you down and although you feel *completely* disgusting and awful
                afterwards, it does calm you down and - I guess, I didn't know what
                else to fill my day with, I wouldn't know what to do in place of that.
                (Participant 12, cross sectional study)

In the above passage, taken from the 'cross-sectional study', it becomes
evident upon exploration that the participant's initial terse description of her
difficulty as 'addiction', that 'addiction' encompasses two distinct and important concepts which are relevant to decision-making: whether she wants the
treatment, and whether she is actually able to choose her own behaviour.
These two concepts emerged from the 'preliminary study', and specific questions were included in the 'cross-sectional study' in order to understand this
further.

13.3.1. Analysis

All participant names and details such as date of birth, address, and contact
details, were kept in one file, and the transcripts were identified only by a serial
identifier for purposes of anonymity. All identifying names and places were
removed from the transcripts, so that the individuals would not be identifiable
by others who did not know them well, although the participants themselves
might be able to recognize some of their own phrases and accounts. The thematic analysis was carried out using the method of thematic grid analysis, a
method practised by the National Centre of Social Research (The National
Centre for Social Research 2003). The transcripts were read, and coded for
content and emerging themes. A second coder read through some of the transcripts and independently coded them, and then the codings were compared
to ensure that emerging themes were being picked up, and to think about how
they were being categorized. The themes were grouped together and a chart
was constructed using a large grid, a part of which is illustrated in Figure 13.1.
In this figure all the boxes are filled in because the example uses themes present in all participants' accounts. There were many themes, however, which
were present in some participants' accounts only. Where a particular theme
was not present in a particular participant's account, the relevant box was left
blank. The use of a grid enabled a systematic presentation of the data which
could provide a simple, visual way of observing patterns across and between
themes, and within individual participants.

Analysis trees were constructed from the themes, to help in thinking about
the ways in which themes relate to each other. An example of an analysis tree is
given in Figure 13.2.

D. Beliefs/attitudes about self/identity

Theme:	1. Feelings about weight	2. Decision-making/ control	3. Motivation	....
Participant A	Overweight in spite of others' perception; shame of fatness; weight very important to self; different for self than others	Cannot make decisions - too confused; cannot accept seriousness unless threatened; threats keep me going; needed bluntness and ultimatums about choices	Medical consequences not highly motivating; initially reluctant for treatment, now less so; wants to stay at same weight - scared to get better	....
Participant B	Not underweight; if thin, people like you more; thinks she's fat, she just wants to be thin	Feels controlled by others; couldn't eat more even if wanted to; people should have free choice; cannot help behaviour	Treatment not needed; couldn't stop losing weight and wouldn't anyway;	....
Participant C	Feels she's too big on thighs; currently content with weight but not shape; weight is the most important thing in her life	Doesn't feel she has much control over AN, it comes and goes; gaining weight is not a choice she is able to make; thought she was in control but found she wasn't	If no medical consequences, would lose more weight; motivated to fight illness; constant fight against wish to be thinner; needed to hit rock bottom to accept help - luckily her weight was ok still	....
....	....	....	....	....

Figure 13.1 A thematic grid analysis – portion of results.

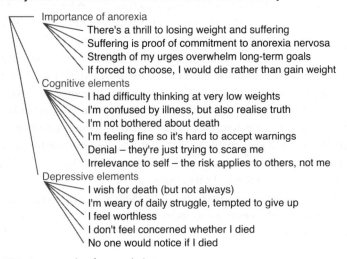

Analysis tree: Attitudes to the risk of death and disability

— Importance of anorexia
— There's a thrill to losing weight and suffering
— Suffering is proof of commitment to anorexia nervosa
— Strength of my urges overwhelm long-term goals
— If forced to choose, I would die rather than gain weight

Cognitive elements
— I had difficulty thinking at very low weights
— I'm confused by illness, but also realise truth
— I'm not bothered about death
— I'm feeling fine so it's hard to accept warnings
— Denial – they're just trying to scare me
— Irrelevance to self – the risk applies to others, not me

Depressive elements
— I wish for death (but not always)
— I'm weary of daily struggle, tempted to give up
— I feel worthless
— I don't feel concerned whether I died
— No one would notice if I died

Figure 13.2 An example of an analysis tree.

13.4. **Results**

The detailed results of this study have been published elsewhere (Tan *et al.* 2003a–c; 2006). We will highlight some of the findings and use them to focus on the question of how the empirical study raises issues for further philosophical analysis? It is not our intention in this chapter to carry out this analysis but to show how the empirical results challenge current concepts and provide material for further theoretical work.

The participants in this study performed well on the MacCAT-T suggesting that by the current legal criteria used in the USA and UK participants were competent (had capacity) to give or refuse valid consent. And yet their accounts raised concerns about whether, at least at some stages in the course of their anorexia, their refusal of treatment should be respected. Are these concerns justified? Do they provide grounds for further development of the concept of competence (capacity)? In order to answer these questions we need to examine what gives rise to the concerns.

One cause for concern was that many participants, whilst understanding that other people in a similar position to themselves would be at high risk of serious harm, did not seem to appreciate that they themselves were at high risk (see quotes below). This was not based on any delusional belief – such as a belief that they possess special protective powers for example. The belief seemed more to be the result of emotional reasoning (see Damasio 1994; Charland 1998; Mameli 2004) – that they did not believe 'deep down' that they were at significant risk of harm because they did not feel ill or in any way seriously abnormal.

Interviewer:	What about death and disability? When you were ill, how did you view death and disability?
Respondent:	I didn't think it applied to me at all.
Interviewer:	How come?
Respondent:	I just could not believe that I could die, I know it's a silly thing to say, but I felt fine. Talking about me, I had my aches but at that time I did feel a bit ill, but I didn't take heed, it was straight in one ear and out the other. (Participant D)
Interviewer:	Why do you think you don't believe these things could happen to you?
Respondent:	Because although logic tells me I'm underweight, but I don't feel it. When I'm just going around doing whatever in the day, then I don't feel that I've got a problem. But I know I am underweight because I stand on the scales.
Interviewer:	So it sounds like logic tells you you're underweight. But the way you feel is that you're normal weight?
Respondent:	Yeah, I just feel that I'm – I don't feel ill, if you know what I mean. I just feel – I guess I've got used to the feeling. But my hands are often cold and so – but I'm used to it so to me it's normal. (Participant H)

One could argue that if beneficial treatment is refused because a patient does not believe, for whatever reason, that she is at significant risk of harm, when in fact she is, then she lacks competence (capacity) because her refusal is based on a false belief. Alternatively this example might be seen as a good illustration of Appelbaum's 'lack of appreciation' – that whilst correctly believing that her state is a dangerous one for others in her situation she does not believe that this danger applies to her. This example therefore does not provide grounds for considering the current concept of competence as inadequate. But it does raise the question of how abnormal is such reasoning. Do not many teenagers and young adults take significant risks in the belief that somehow the risks do not apply to themselves? If this is the case, what is the justification for overriding treatment refusal in anorexia nervosa where such refusal is based on a lack of appreciation of the risks, but not restricting risky behaviour in many other situations?

There were several findings from this study that do raise the question of whether current concepts of competence are adequate. We will highlight four of these findings.

1. An almost universal finding was that participants often refused or resisted treatment not because of faulty logical reasoning, nor on the basis of false factual beliefs, but because of their (abnormal) values. The most prominent of such values was the importance of being thin.

Interviewer:	What is the importance of your weight and body size to you?
Respondent:	I just want to be thin.
Interviewer:	How important is that to you?
Respondent:	Very.
Interviewer:	Why?
Respondent:	It just is, it's all I want. (Participant B)

Interviewer:	I wonder what it means to you to be fat.
Respondent:	To me in my scale of beliefs, if I was fat then I would be unattractive and a complete failure, and completely not in control of what I do and what I ate, and kind of a horrible person! (Participant C)

   I wasn't really bothered about dying, as long as I died thin. (Participant I)

Some participants said that they did not want to risk serious harm to themselves, but, if they had to choose, then they would prefer to be seriously harmed (and even die) than to put on weight. Because this is a value rather than a false belief or a failure of rational (logical) argument it does not, on traditional accounts of capacity (including those of Appelbaum), provide grounds for incapacity.

This raises interesting conceptual questions and questions for further philosophical and ethical analysis. Is it right to override treatment refusal, when the patient is at significant risk of serious harm, if such refusal is based on the values given to thinness? If it is right is that because the patient should properly be considered to lack capacity? If this is the reason then the concept of capacity needs to be developed to allow certain kinds of values in certain circumstances to be evidence of lack of capacity. An alternative approach is to argue that there are further grounds for overriding treatment refusal over and above lack of capacity. But what could these grounds be? Is there a valid distinction between a 'pathological value' – a value that is caused by, or part of, the mental disorder – and other values that the patient might hold (Tan *et al.* 2006)? And if there is, does this distinction have ethical importance? Or is it that treatment refusal should not be overridden in this situation even if, without treatment, the person is at significant risk of serious harm?

2. It was striking, even in this small sample, how much participants differed with regard to their reasoning and values. This is well illustrated by the varying attitudes towards risk of death (see Figure 13.2). Several different attitudes could be distinguished. Some participants did not wish to die but they considered that putting on weight was an even greater harm. Some considered death desirable, or neutral, and so the risk of death did not provide a reason to stop losing weight. Some participants accepted that extreme thinness was in general associated with significant risk of death but they did not think that they themselves were at risk of death (as discussed above). One participant accepted that she was at risk of death and whilst not wanting to die found the idea that she had been close to death rather appealing.

> I remember getting some tests back saying how my liver was really damaged and all this, and I thought it was really rather good! I can't imagine that I thought it, it felt like really quite an accomplishment!... It's sick, isn't it? It was like somehow I'd achieved! And knowing I almost killed myself; no, I'd say the illness almost killed me, it was like, wow. It was just I'd just done something that I knew hardly anyone else could do. (Participant D)

Do these very different attitudes to the risk of death – and very different grounds for refusing treatment – make a difference to the ethical question of overriding treatment refusal?

3. Many participants highlighted advantages, as they saw it, to maintaining the anorexia. For some, being thin made them feel happy or safe. Some found the sense of control that anorexia gave them very positive: the thought of losing the anorexia was worrying because it would take away this one important area of their lives where they felt in control. Still others valued the anorexia itself because it made them feel special. Many participants considered that these advantages outweighed the disadvantages, including risks of death. The decision as to whether even a completely

effective treatment is desirable depends therefore on the relative weights given to the advantages and disadvantages. The apportioning of such weights itself involves values – values that are themselves affected by the mental disorder.

4. Several participants thought of their anorexia as an important part of their personality and indeed their personal identity. Such participants did not want to be cured from the anorexia because for them losing the anorexia felt tantamount to losing themselves and becoming a different person.

Interviewer:	Let's say you've got to this point, and someone said they could wave a magic wand and there wouldn't be anorexia any more.
Respondent:	I couldn't.
Interviewer:	You couldn't.
Respondent:	It's just a part of me now.
Interviewer:	Right. So it feels like you'd be losing a part of you.
Respondent:	Because it was my identity. (Participant I)

This raises both the issue of whether, and under what conditions, anorexia can be seen as a significant part of a person's identity, and whether if it does affect identity this is of relevance to the ethical question of compulsory treatment.

Some of the findings suggest that there are important areas for further ethical analysis in addition to exploring the concept of capacity. Indeed even though the narratives were mainly about decision-making around treatment neither the participants with anorexia nor their mothers spoke much about capacity. They spoke with great feeling about the complexity surrounding decision-making and the many factors that enhanced or impeded it. But they did not seem to think in terms of a core entity that might be either present or absent. From the perspective of participants there were many issues related to the process of making decisions and the validity of those decisions. The focus was much more on how could people be helped to make decisions than on how to judge whether the decisions should or should not be respected.

Another finding was that some participants reported that their decision-making – both the process and the result – was affected by the degree of coercion that they experienced (Tan *et al.* 2003c). This raises the interesting idea that the degree of capacity that a person has might be affected by the behaviour of carers that itself is determined by the assessment of the degree of capacity.

13.5. Discussion

We have outlined a preliminary empirical study that explored the ideas and thinking around treatment decision-making, including treatment refusal, of girls and young women with anorexia. This study has led us to develop three further studies.

- a larger cross-sectional qualitative interview study similar to the preliminary study, in which young women aged 13–25 years and their parents will be interviewed
- a longitudinal study of 6 of the original 10 preliminary study participants consisting of three annual qualitative interviews inviting them to reflect on their past and present, which will cover a period 3 to 5 years after their initial interviews
- a quantitative self-administered postal questionnaire designed to elicit the attitudes and views of consultant psychiatrists in the UK

These studies are ongoing. The preliminary study reported here is small and the conclusions that can be drawn are therefore limited. The study does, however, illustrate one approach to 'empirical psychiatric ethics', an approach in which ethical analysis and empirical data interact.

The current concept of competence to refuse medical, including psychiatric, treatment has been developed both in the courts, and through philosophical analysis. Our clinical experience had led us to wonder whether this concept is adequate to deal with the question of when it is right to impose treatment against the current wishes of patients with anorexia nervosa. We thought that there was inadequate understanding of the experiences, beliefs, and reasoning of people with anorexia in order to answer this question. Thus, an empirical study of the experience and thinking of people with anorexia seemed to us to be potentially valuable to understanding the ethical issues involved in compulsory treatment. Such an empirical study could not be undertaken in the absence of some prior analysis of ethical issues, and of the concept of competence. In order to design the method of data collection, and in particular the interview structure, we needed some understanding of what experiences, beliefs, and reasoning are relevant to the ethical issues and to the concept of competence. And, in analysing the content of the interviews, and especially the open accounts of participants' experiences, we needed to have some prior understanding of key ethical concepts, such as competence, in order to identify which aspects of what participants talked about were relevant to the ethical issues around compulsory treatment and decision-making. In short, the collection and analysis of the empirical data required prior theoretical analysis of the ethical and conceptual issues relevant to overriding treatment refusal.

The empirical data, however, did not simply provide answers to questions raised by the theoretical analysis. On the contrary, the data challenged that analysis and raised further questions for ethical analysis. If a patient is refusing beneficial treatment based not on false beliefs nor on faulty reasoning, but on values that themselves are closely related to mental disorder, is such refusal competent and should it be respected? Does the answer depend on what those values are? Does it make sense to say that a person's identity will be so fundamentally altered, if the person is cured of anorexia, that this provides a reason against such a 'cure'? Is the issue of competence the key ethical issue for carers in deciding whether to override treatment refusal? And what are the implications for carers of the possibility that competence itself is affected by the degree of coercion?

Theory and data work closely together in psychiatric ethics. Theory enables the collection of relevant data. The data provoke further theoretical work that opens the possibility for the collection of new data. The theoretical and the empirical continually inform each other. Empirical data can challenge theory. We believe that the data from this study pose considerable theoretical and practical problems for the current legal and ethical concepts of capacity to refuse treatment. The participants in this research had capacity, on most current analyses, and yet the anorexia interfered with many aspects relevant to accepting treatment including both decision-making and the ability to act on decisions. Current concepts of capacity to refuse treatment, and their implications for both theory and practice need to be significantly developed if they are to cope with the empirical data.

References

American Psychiatric Association (2000). 307.1 Anorexia nervosa. In *Diagnostic and statistical manual of mental disorders, fourth edition, text revision (DSM-IV-TR®)*. American Psychiatric Publications, Arlington, VA.

Andrist LC (2003). Media images, body dissatisfaction, and disordered eating in adolescent women. *MCN. The American Journal of Maternal Child Nursing*, **28**(2), 119–23.

Appelbaum PS (1998). Ought we to require emotional capacity as part of decisional competence? *Kennedy Institute of Ethics Journal*, **8**(4), 377–87.

Beck AT and Steer RA (1993a). *Manual for the beck anxiety inventory*. Psychological Corporation, San Antonio, TX.

Beck AT and Steer RA (1993b). *Manual for the revised beck depression inventory*. Psychological Corporation, San Antonio, TX.

Bettle N, Bettle O, Neumarker U and Neumarker KJ (1998). Adolescent ballet school students: their quest for body weight change. *Psychopathology*, **31**(3), 153–9.

Beumont J and Vandereycken W (1998). Challenges and risks for health care professionals. In *Treating eating disorders: ethical, legal and personal issues*, pp. 1–29. The Athlone Press, London, UK.

Billick S, Burgert W III, Friberg G, Downer AV and Bruni-Solhkhah SM (2001). A clinical study of competency to consent to treatment in pediatrics. *The Journal of the American Academy of Psychiatry and the Law*, **29**(3), 298–302.

Billick SB, Edwards JL, Burgert WIII, Serlen JR and Bruni SM (1998). A clinical study of competency in child psychiatric inpatients. *The Journal of the American Academy of Psychiatry and the Law*, **26**(4), 587–94.

Charland LC (1998). Appreciation and emotion: theoretical reflections on the MacArthur treatment competence study. *Kennedy Institute of Ethics Journal*, **8**(4), 359–76.

Colton A and Pistrang N (2004). Adolescents' experiences of inpatient treatment for anorexia nervosa. *European Eating Disorders Review*, **12**, 307–16.

Damasio A (1994). *Descartes' error: emotion, reason, and the human brain*. Harper Perennial, London.

Dare C, Eisler I, Colahan M, Crowther C, Senior R and Asen E (1995). The listening heart and the chi-square: clinical and empirical perceptions in the family therapy of anorexia nervosa. *Journal of Family Therapy*, **17**, 31–57.

Draper H (2000). Anorexia nervosa and respecting a refusal of life-prolonging therapy: a limited justification. *Bioethics*, **14**(2), 120–33.

Fairburn C and Beglin SJ (1994). The assessment of eating disorders: interview or self-report questionnaire. *The International Journal of Eating Disorders*, **16**, 363–70.

Fairburn CG and Cooper Z (1993). The eating disorder examination. In CG Fairburn and GT Wilson, eds. *Binge eating: nature, assessment and treatment*, pp. 317–60. Guilford Press, NY.

Fairburn CG and Harrison PJ (2003). Eating disorders. *Lancet*, **361**(9355), 407–16.

Fazel S, Hope T and Jacoby R (1999a). Assessment of competence to complete advance directives: validation of a patient centred approach. *British Medical Journal*, **31**(7182), 493–7.

Fazel S, Hope T and Jacoby R (1999b). Dementia, intelligence, and the competence to complete advance directives. *Lancet*, **354**(9172), 48.

Fegert JM (2003). Ethical and legal issues in treatment of schizophrenic patients with neuroleptics in childhood and youth. *Nervenheilkunde*, **2**, 75–9.

Flick U (1998). *An introduction to qualitative research: process and theories*, chapter 4, pp. 40-6. Sage Publications, London.

Fornari V, Dancyger I, Schneider M, Fisher M, Goodman B and McCall A (2001). Parental medical neglect in the treatment of adolescents with anorexia nervosa. *The International Journal of Eating Disorders*, **29**(3), 358–62.

Garner DM and Garfinkel PE (1979). The eating attitudes test: an index of the symptoms of anorexia nervosa. *Psychological Medicine*, **9**, 273–9.

Garner DM, Olmsted MP, Bohr Y and Garfinkel PE (1982). The eating attitudes test: psychometric features and clinical correlates. *Psychological Medicine*, **12**, 871–9.

Gilligan C (1982). *In a different voice*. Harvard University Press, Cambridge, MA.

Glaser BG and Strauss AL (1967). *The discovery of grounded theory: strategies for qualitative research*. Aldine, NY.

Gothelf D, Apter A, Ratzoni G *et al.* (1995). Defense mechanisms in severe adolescent anorexia nervosa. *Journal of American Academy of Child Adolescent Psychiatry*, **34**(12), 1648–54.

Gowers S and Bryant-Waugh R (2004). Management of child and adolescent eating disorders: the current evidence base and future directions. *Journal of Child Psychology and Psychiatry*, **45**(1), 63–83.

Gowers S and North C (1999). Difficulties in family functioning and adolescent anorexia nervosa. *The British Journal of Psychiatry,* **174**, 63–6.

Gremillion H (2003). *Feeding anorexia: gender and power at a treatment center.* Duke University Press, Durham, NC.

Grisso T and Appelbaum PS (1995). The MacArthur treatment competence study III: abilities of patients to consent to psychiatric and medical treatments. *Law and Human Behaviour,* **19**(2), 149–74.

Grisso T and Appelbaum PS (1998). *Assessing competence to consent to treatment: a guide for physicians and other health professionals.* Oxford University Press, Oxford.

Lee S (1993). How abnormal is the desire for slimness? A survey of eating attitudes and behaviour among Chinese undergraduates in Hong Kong. *Psychological Medicine,* **23**(2), 437–51.

Malle BF, Knobe J, O'Laughlin MJ, Pearce GE and Nelson SE (2000). Conceptual structure and social functions of behavior explanations: beyond person-situation attributions. *Journal of Personality and Social Psychology,* **79**(3), 309–26.

Mameli M (2004). The role of emotions in ecological and practical rationality. In D Evans and P Cruse, eds. *Emotion, evolution, and rationality,* pp. 133-58. Oxford University Press, Oxford.

Miller WR and Rollnick S, eds. (1991). *Motivational interviewing: preparing people to change addictive behaviour.* The Guilford Press, NY.

Orbach S (1978). *Fat is a feminist issue.* Arrow Books, London.

Prochaska JO and DiClemente CC (1983). Stages and processes of self-change of smoking: toward an integrative model of change. *Journal of Consulting and Clinical Psychology,* **51**(3), 390–5.

Ramsay R, Ward A, Treasure J and Russell GFM (1999). Compulsory treatment in anorexia nervosa. *British Journal of Psychiatry,* **175**, 147–53.

Rosenberg M (1965). *Society and the adolescent self-image.* Princeton University Press, Princeton, NJ.

Russell D (1995). *Women, madness and medicine.* Blackwell Publishers, Oxford.

Shisslak C-M, Gray N and Crago M (1989). Health care professionals' reactions to working with eating disorder patients. *International Journal of Eating Disorders,* **8**(6), 689–94.

Tan JO, Hope T and Stewart A (2003a). Competence to refuse treatment in anorexia nervosa. *International Journal of Law and Psychiatry,* **26**(6), 697–707.

Tan JO, Hope T and Stewart A (2003b). Anorexia nervosa and personal identity: the accounts of patients and their parents. *International Journal of Law and Psychiatry,* **26**(5), 533–48.

Tan JO, Hope T, Stewart A and Fitzpatrick R (2003c). Control and compulsory treatment in anorexia nervosa: the views of patients and parents. *International Journal of Law and Psychiatry,* **26**(6), 627–45.

Tan JOA, Hope T, Stewart A and Fitzpatrick R (2006). Competence to make treatment decisions in anorexia nervosa: thinking processes and values. *Philosophy, Psychology and Psychiatry.* **13**(4), 267–82.

Tan JA and Jones DPH (2001). Children's consent. *Current Opinion in Psychiatry,* **14**, 303–7.

The National Centre for Social Research (2003). The National Centre for Social Research. Retrieved 1st December, 2003, from http://www.natcen.ac.uk/

Treasure J and Ward A (1997). A practical guide to the use of motivational interviewing in anorexia nervosa. *European Eating Disorders Review,* **5**, 102–14.

Vitousek K, Watson S and Wilson GT (1998). Enhancing motivation for change in treatment-resistant eating disorders. *Clinical Psychology Review*, **18**(4), 391–420.

Appendix:

Patient Interview   Identifier code: 0XX
Data:
Date of interview: /   / 19   Date of Birth: /   /19

Opening explanations:

Thank you for seeing me for this interview. Before we start, I would like to explain what we will be talking about and what I will need to ask you to do. Your assistance would be very valuable to me in developing questionnaires for a project that we are doing which will look into the attitudes of patients with anorexia nervosa towards their treatment. We will be first having a tape-recorded discussion to help me understand what you think about anorexia nervosa and the treatment that you are having. I will then be asking you to fill in a few questionnaires. I am not involved in your psychiatric care and would like to assure you that your answers are confidential and will not affect the treatment you are currently having. Your answers will also not be shared with your relatives or recorded in your psychiatric notes. I hope that you can feel relaxed enough to give me your frank opinions.

Checklists for initial interview:

☐ Have you read the information sheet that I have provided?

☐ Is there anything about the information you do not understand, or any further information you would like to have?

☐ Have you signed the consent form?

☐ Are you willing to allow me to see your psychiatric notes?

☐ Are you willing for me to talk to your parents to understand their views on your illness?

Interview (tape recorded and subsequently transcribed):

A. Factual beliefs about anorexia nervosa:

1. What is your understanding of what anorexia nervosa is?

2. Do you think anorexia nervosa is an illness? Why?

3. Do you think people with anorexia nervosa can endanger their health? How (if yes) / why (if no)?

4. Do you think doctors should treat anorexia nervosa? Why?

B. Control questions – beliefs of other illness and perceptions of weight:

1. Do you think people with mental illnesses like schizophrenia should, under some circumstances, be admitted to hospital and treated even if they don't agree with the treatment? Why?

2. Do you think there are some circumstances under which people with anorexia nervosa should be admitted to hospital and treated even if they don't agree with the treatment? If so, what are these circumstances?

3. (*Show pictures of women with known weights taken from slimming magazine*) How much do you think this woman weighs? And this one? And this one? Do you think this woman is overweight, underweight, or normal weight? What about this one? And this one?

4. Do you think that being overweight is the same as being fat?

5. Do you think it's okay for someone else to be fat? Why?

6. Please do not worry about offending me in answering this question honestly. What do you think I weigh? Do you think I'm overweight, underweight or normal weight?

C. Personal beliefs:

1. I believe that your psychiatrist is of the opinion that you have anorexia nervosa. What do you think about that opinion? If not, what problems do you think you have, if any?

2. What do you feel about your current weight and body shape?

3. What is the importance of your weight and body size to you?

4. Do you feel that you are overweight, underweight, or normal weight?

5. Do you feel fat?

6. With regard to yourself, is being overweight the same as being fat?

7. What would you be willing to do in order to lose weight?

D. Beliefs about own treatment:

1. Have people tried to stop you from losing weight? What did they do? What do you think about that?

2. What is your treatment at this moment? What do you think about it?

3. Do you think you need any treatment or other help? Why (*if no*) / What sort of help do you feel you need (*if yes*)?

4. Have you had any treatment or admissions which you haven't agreed with or given consent to? (*Circle answer*) **Yes/No.** Can you tell me about them?

5. What means did the doctors use to give you treatment you didn't agree with?

6. (*If agreeing to treatment*) What would you think about coming for treatment when you don't want to? (*If not agreeing to treatment*) What do you think about coming for treatment when you don't want to?

7. (*If not compulsorily admitted*) What would you think about being admitted to hospital for treatment against your will? (*If compulsorily admitted*) What do you think about being admitted to hospital for treatment against your will?

8. Do you think you should accept treatment?

9. Why are you coming for treatment? (*If patient is a minor*) If your parents said that it was up to you whether you come for treatment, would you come for treatment? Why?

E. Self-valuation and evaluation:

1. Do you feel you are worth as much as most other people? (*If no*) Why?

2. Do you feel you would rather be someone else than yourself? (*If yes*) Why? Who would you rather be?

3. Who would you like to look like? Why?

4. What sort of person would you like to be like?

5. What would it mean to you if you were fat? What would it say about you?

F. Motivation, belief, and desire:

1. What do you see yourself doing in the future, say 5 years from now?

2. What do you think is important for your life? What areas of your life would you like to develop?

3. Do you think that you could stop dieting and gain weight if only you wanted to, or that you can't help doing what you are to lose weight?

4. If you wanted to eat more than you do, could you do it?

5. Do you feel you should eat more, all things considered?

6. If your anorexia nervosa magically disappeared, what would be different from now? Do you think you would make it magically disappear if you could?

7. Do you wish you were free from the desire to lose weight?

8. Ignoring for the moment what other people's opinions are, what do you think you should do about your current weight and behaviour?

9. If you were alone on a desert island, would you still want to lose weight? What about if you had weighing scales or a mirror?

10. If you had 3 magic wishes, and could wish for anything at all, what would they be?

11. Who is your anorexia nervosa?

12. What does your anorexia nervosa mean to you?

13. What do you understand as the physical dangers of having anorexia nervosa? If I could give you a magic pill to take away just the physical dangers but leave everything else the same, would you take it?

Chapter 14

Studying moral reasoning in forensic psychiatric patients

Gwen Adshead, Christine Brown, Eva Skoe, Jonathan Glover, and Sarah Nicholson

14.1. Introduction

Research into the process of making moral choices has mainly focused on the development of moral reasoning capacity in children and adolescents. However, another group of interest are those individuals who appear to have either not acquired, lost, or failed to exercise their moral reasoning capacity in the context of mental illness or psychological disorders; a group whose moral decision-making (or lack of it) has a profound and sometimes tragic effect on other people.

In this chapter, we will discuss the different ways by which moral/ethical reasoning might be studied in forensic psychiatric patients. These are people who not only need secure containment to prevent them from doing harm to others, but also need therapy, both for their own benefit, and to reduce their risk to others. Understanding how they come to make moral decisions is important for both descriptive and therapeutic purposes. Using data from a study of ethical reasoning in forensic patients, we will review methods of researching ethical reasoning, and examine both cognitive and linguistic approaches to the assessment of moral reasoning. The data also raises questions about how we should judge patients with psychiatric disorders who are also criminal offenders, in terms of their moral responsibility.

14.2. Previous Studies

Previous studies of moral reasoning in offender groups rested on two assumptions: first, that there are basic cognitive structures that underlie and organize moral reasoning, and second, that moral reasoning is a discrete thinking capacity that develops in childhood (Rest 1984). Both Piaget (1965) and Kohlberg (1969) described justice-based moral reasoning as a staged capacity acquired through childhood, so that the developing child moved progressively from a primitive egocentric stage of moral reasoning to a sophisticated ability to weigh and balance other's perspectives and conflicting moral systems. This model takes a universalist view of moral development and assumes that the stages are the same across all cultures and times.

It has also been generally assumed that criminal offenders would show lower levels of ethical reasoning than non-offenders, using a measure of principled reasoning based on Kohlberg's stages 5 and 6 (Rest 1984). In fact, the earliest studies found no difference between offender subjects and non-offender comparison groups (Griffore and Samuels 1978). The majority of subjects in both groups endorsed a morality of law and duty to the social order (Kohlberg's stage 4). These studies were therefore counter-intuitive at two levels; first, the finding that respect for law and order did not distinguish those who actually respected the law from those who did not, and second, that those who broke the law endorsed respect for it, nonetheless.

Studies of moral reasoning in 'delinquents' suggest that young male convicts do use developmentally lower modes of moral reasoning than non-delinquents when measured using cognitive scales (Blasi 1980; Nelson *et al.* 1990; Palmer and Hollin 1998). The difficulty with generalizing from these studies to other populations such as adult offenders is the confounding association between cognitive measures of moral reasoning and age, IQ, and education. For instance, it could be argued that the reason young male convicts score low on cognitive measures of moral reasoning is that being a young male convict they also have a lower than average IQ and educational level. At best, these studies indicate that the cognitive study of moral reasoning in young offenders only offers a snapshot of a developing moral identity, and a glimpse of what moral reasoning in offenders might mean for the offender himself. The fact that the majority of these delinquent young men do not go on to be career criminals suggests a more complex interaction between the individual and other factors rather than a sequential progress through developmental stages.

There are few other studies of moral reasoning in adult criminals and even less in offenders with mental health problems. This is surprising given that one of the key characteristics of psychopathic disorder (no longer a medical diagnosis but a category of detention under the Mental Health Act 1983) is a defect in moral reasoning such that the individual has difficulty conforming to society's rules on right and wrong behaviour. An early study by Hawk and Peterson (1974) found no relationship between psychopathic deviancy and moral reasoning as measured by Kohlberg's stage model. In contrast, O'Kane *et al.* (1996) found that the mean score for principled ethical reasoning using Kohlberg's measure was considerably lower in a population of forensic psychiatric patients than in non-clinical populations.

These studies of moral reasoning raise more questions than they answer. How is the capacity to think about moral dilemmas related to behaving well towards others, if at all? Previous studies of psychopathic offenders conclude that there is no defect in the cognitive ability to identify right from wrong but that the defect is in the emotional responses to doing wrong (Blair 1995). The question of whether such individuals have a capacity for moral reasoning is interesting – do they offend despite knowing it is wrong and not caring deliberately or are they unable to care because of defective neurological pathways in their brains? What is the relationship between knowing about moral choices, and choosing a course of action?

14.3. **Arguments for a linguistic/narrative approach**

An important criticism of the Kohlberg approach to moral reasoning is that it de-emphasizes the personal and contextual nature of many moral decisions in everyday life (Gilligan 1982). Gilligan argued that although the principle of respect for justice is an important value influencing social cooperation, there is no particular reason why it should act as a moral 'trump' in every case. She proposed that an 'ethic of care' prioritizes the value of interpersonal relationships and can be useful in the analysis of common types of ethical dilemma in daily life. Gilligan's research demonstrated that people use different types of ethical reasoning depending on the context of the decision they face. For example a rights-based ethic of justice may be used when dealing with dilemmas involving strangers, but an ethic of care provides a 'thicker' description (Geertz 1975) when dealing with ethical dilemmas that involve people we know well, and with whom we feel emotionally connected.

When it comes to violent offending (for example, rape, assault, and homicide), close personal relationships are often a crucial factor in the commission of the offence. Most (60–70%) violent offenders have had close relationships with their victims and utilized that relationship to offend. This fact alone might suggest that any assessment of moral reasoning in offenders needs to look at how an individual's capacity for moral reasoning interrelates with how individuals construe relationships with others psychologically. The relational context of their decision-making process, and subsequent actions, is important.

More recent research into how offenders think has drawn on theories about the development of empathy with others. This includes studies on whether offenders have a theory of mind in terms of other people (Keenan and Ward 2000) and the relevance of early childhood attachments for moral reflection (Van IJzendoorn and Zwart-Woudstra 1995; Marshall et al. 2001). Such work is of interest because attachment relationships affect the individual's ability for self-reflection, which in turn influences the capacity to reflect on the experience of others, which is at the heart of empathy (Fonagy et al. 1997). This attachment research suggests that secure attachment positively influences the capacity for moral reflection.

14.3.1. Moral identity and moral reasoning

The connection between moral reasoning as knowledge (measured by cognitive ability), and moral reasoning as what a person does (as evidenced by interpersonal behaviour) may be mediated through 'moral identity', i.e. the core beliefs, attitudes, and values that an individual holds and attempts to adhere to over time. Thus it is not only the knowledge of moral principles, and how they might be applied, but some personal commitment to them that is important, such that to abandon those principles is to be personally compromised (Bergman 2004; Blasi 2004). Moral identity is to be distinguished from commitment to interpersonal relationships or mere social values (Gibbs et al. 1992) by its core position in the self. It is identification of and with 'the sort of person I am' or 'the sort of person I want to be'.

On what basis do we suppose that moral identity or personal identification with certain values might influence right action? There is evidence that moral reasoning is correlated to ego function, such that more mature and developed moral reasoning is related to a more developed sense of self (Skoe and Marcia 1991; Skoe and Diessner 1994; Skoe and Von der Lippe 2002). A person with a highly developed and organized sense of self is likely to be one who has a developed and organized vision of where moral values fit into their world, and how this affects their relationships with others. Their vision will be complex and tolerant of doubt, uncertainty, and dissent, even if they meet adversity or when they struggle with intimacy.

14.3.2. Moral identity as a narrative/linguistic process

How could a person's experience of moral identity be examined? Thinking about moral reasoning as a function of moral identity, rather than a cognitive capacity, suggests a psychological process developing over time, rather than a state (Tappan 2000). Specifically in relation to measurement, it would make sense to treat moral decision-making as an integrated psychological feature of the self rather than a discrete cognitive ability; implying that personal experience of decision-making might be helpful here (Gilligan 1982; Adshead 2002). Both linguistic and narrative analysis use personal accounts of experience as data, and assume that the experience of the self as a moral reasoner can be explored through personal accounts of moral decision-making (McCarthy 2003). This approach has particular salience for medical ethics because the experience of illness is also a story of selfhood and choices that affect a cast of people.

Narrative analysis is seen as a useful tool for understanding doctor–patient communications (Kleinman 1988), especially in the domain of ethical decision-making (Hudson Jones 1999). Most ethical dilemmas in medicine cannot be reduced to a conflict between two principles; there is also the question of the scope of the principles, and the context in which they are applied (Gillon 2003). Illness affects people's identities in different ways; old identities are lost or spoiled and new ones, defined by illness are acquired, so that a theory of ethics that gives voice to different identities may provide a necessary complexity.

14.3.3. Coherence and moral identity

A key concept in narrative theory, and especially in relation to moral narratives, is coherence. This means the way that the narrative hangs together to make a story that others can understand. Coherence of personal narratives is also thought to be an indicator of personal autonomy and a secure sense of personal identity, which has been used in psychological research and clinical practice (Beijersbergen *et al.* 2006). Mary Main and Erick Hesse (Hesse 1999) used linguistic analysis of narratives of autobiographical memory to assess the security of mental representations of childhood attachments to caregivers. Main and Hesse argue that incoherence of narrative is an indicator of a disorganized sense of personal identity in the context of close relationships. 'Incoherence of narrative', in this sense, does not mean moments of incomprehensibility or imperfect speech delivery: it means a failure to produce an overall narrative of the self, that has internal consistency, does not dismiss negative experiences, but values positive ones. Coherence of personal narrative is an index of the coherence and security of personal identity (Goldwyn et al. 1994); by extension, coherence of moral narratives may be an index of moral identity.

14.4. Design of the Study

14.4.1. Participants

Participants were patients detained in a high-security psychiatric hospital having committed an act of serious violence who met diagnostic criteria for antisocial personality disorder (DSM-IV). They were all detained solely under the Mental Health Act category of psychopathic disorder. Participants with a concurrent diagnosis of mental illness, a history of mental illness, major head injury, or an IQ of below 71 were excluded from the study.

Fifty one patients (42 men and 9 women) were identified as suitable participants and were approached for entry into the study after agreement with their clinical teams and review by the hospital Ethics Committee. Two patients (one man, one woman) declined to participate and one man did not complete the interview, giving a sample of 48. The mean age of the men was 41.5 years, and the mean age of the women was 36 years, indicating that this is an older group of offenders than has been previously studied.

14.4.2. Description

All participants were assessed on a variety of measures including demographic variables (age and gender); past history of educational attainment, childhood adversity, and head injury; current psychiatric diagnosis; and full scale IQ (using the WAIS-R). All the men had been convicted of a violent index offence and five of the eight women had serious criminal convictions. The mean IQ was 90 (SD 12.1), which is less than the general community mean of 100; this finding is similar to other studies of criminal populations. Lower mean IQ in this group is almost certainly due to social disadvantage and lack of education rather than brain damage or inherited/acquired learning disability.

14.4.3. Psychopathy

Participants were given a score for psychopathy using a case-note based rating of the Psychopathy Checklist Revised (PCL-R; Hare 1991); the maximum score is 40, and psychopathy classification is usually taken as 26 or higher for a UK population.

14.4.4. Moral reasoning

A quantitative measure of care-based moral reasoning was obtained using the Ethic of Care Interview (ECI, Skoe 1998). This is a semi-structured interview consisting of three vignettes of interpersonal moral dilemmas, involving conflicts surrounding (a) unplanned pregnancy, (b) marital fidelity, and (c) care for a parent (see Appendix). The dilemmas are read out to the participants, who are then invited to comment on what the actors should do, and why. They are also asked to provide a dilemma from their own experience. The interview is taped and rated according to the Ethic of Care Interview manual (Skoe 1993), which contains descriptions for five care levels.

Level 1 is survival based (caring for self). At this level individuals reason about relational issues in an egocentric, self-protective manner, failing to consider the needs of other people. Level 1.5 is a transition from exclusive self-care to a sense of responsibility. Concepts of 'selfishness' and 'responsibility' first appear. However, one's own needs still come first although awareness of the needs of others is increasing. Level 2 focuses on the convention of goodness (caring for others) and is characterized by the elaboration of the concept of responsibility. 'Good' is equated with self-sacrificing caring for others, and 'right' is externally defined. Level 2.5 is a transition from a conventional to a reflective care perspective, marked by a shift in concern from goodness to truth and honesty in relationships. Finally, at Level 3, the needs of both self and others are encompassed in a more balanced approach to thinking about relationships; attempts are made to minimize hurt to all parties. Thus, the ECI scores range from 1–3; quarter scores (e.g. 1.25, 2.75) can be assigned on any given dilemma if the response appears to fall between two levels (for further details, see Skoe 1998)

14.4.5. **Linguistic analysis**

A linguistic analysis of the transcripts of the ECI was undertaken in order to explore the form of speech acts during the interview process. Narrative coherence was used as an indicator of moral identity.

In this study, we used a particular definition of coherence from linguistic analysis, drawing on the work of Grice (1975). For Grice, coherence is defined as those maxims (or principles) that underpin collaborative discourse:

- A maxim of quality (having evidence for what you say)
- A maxim of quantity (being neither verbose nor too succinct)
- A maxim of manner (the way the conversation is constructed and its clarity)
- A maxim of relevance (keeping to the topic in hand)

Incoherent narratives may violate one or more of the above rules. In addition to Grice's principles of coherence, there are other indices of incoherence: 'distancing' (i.e. saying 'You' rather than 'I' to describe experience), 'contradictions' which are not acknowledged or reflected on, 'very long pauses' in the middle of sentences, speech which is 'broken and confused', and 'unlicensed quotes' from self or other speakers, (e.g. quotes where the change of speaker is not identified). There is a further type of incoherence, called 'passivity', in which speakers fail to complete speech acts. It is as if they get lost in the speech, and cannot complete or communicate the thought they had to others. Many speakers become confused or muddled when speaking, and may briefly be diverted onto other topics; this is not passivity (although it may be another index of incoherence). Passivity suggests that the speaker is not acting as an agent for that speech act.

Although the transcript as a whole is rated for incoherence, incoherence may also be localized in the narrative around a set of events, or it may be globally present; localized incoherence suggests that it is only in one area of discourse that the subject feels unsure of himself. For example, it is not unusual to find narratives, which are generally quite coherent, but become incoherent around topics such as bereavement or traumatic events.

We used the method of rating for coherence developed by Goldwyn et al. (1994) and applied it to the moral narratives generated by the ECI. However, we did not attempt to score for coherence, but sought to apply the general principles. Coherence of a moral narrative would lie in:

- Consistency of values applied to ethical dilemmas
- An absence of contradiction without reflection
- Absence of passivity
- Evidence of the ability to reflect on the entire process of making moral decisions

It must be emphasized that there is no judgement of the speaker, or their general verbal ability, implied in rating the text as incoherent.

14.5. Results

14.5.1. ECI Scores

The mean ECI score was 1.3 (SD = 0.3) for men and 1.6 (SD = 0.3) for women. Sixteen participants (34.8%) scored at level 1 (caring for self), appearing to have little concept of the interests of others when making moral decisions; if they did comment on others' interests, it was in an abstract way, as though other people were not really real to them. Twenty-seven participants (58.7%) scored at level 1.5, indicating that the participant was able to appreciate that other people might be involved or affected by the decisions they make, and could conceptualize their decisions as 'selfish'. However, the dominant theme in their ethical discussion was still that one should generally do what makes one happy, irrespective of other's responses. Three participants (6.5%) scored at level 2 (caring for others), indicating a capacity to incorporate other people's feelings into the ethical analysis.

It is worth noting that, not surprisingly, most (93.5%) of the current adult participants scored at the two lowest ECI levels (1 and 1.5). At these levels, the focus is primarily on protecting and taking care of self. None of the offenders scored at the two highest ECI levels (2.5 and 3). In contrast, Skoe (1998) reported in a summary of research findings with the ECI that in studies with normal (non-clinical) late adolescents and adults in North America and in Norway about 20–30% were scored at the two lowest levels (1 and 1.5), around 20% were scored at Level 2, and about 50% of the participants were scored at the higher levels (2.5 and 3). Thus, the ECI data suggests that most of these offenders are poorly developed in terms of care-based moral reasoning. Future research should compare forensic psychiatric patients with for example other types of patients as well as people in the general population, matched for age, education, IQ, and other relevant variables.

14.5.2. **Psychopathy**

The mean PCL-R score was 20 for men (SD = 5.2) and 17 for women (SD = 5). These scores are higher than a general prison population (Hare 1991). Five men (12.5%) scored 26 or over, and would thus fit in the category of psychopath for a British sample. This is a lower percentage than would be expected in a prison sample of offenders, and is similar to figures for psychopathy in other forensic psychiatric settings (Hare 1991). None scored higher than level 1.5 on the ECI.

14.5.3. **Narrative analysis: coherence in the study population**

14.5.3.1. Engagement and non-engagement

The first and most noticeable type of incoherence was in how subjects engaged with the narrative task. Not engaging with the task is incoherent insofar as it violates Grice's principles of relevance. One method of non-engagement was to assume a very 'practical' and apparently 'non-moral' approach to the subject, for example, focussing on the implications for the married man's job prospects (see Appendix, ECI dilemma 1: Derek):

> S22
> And he has been offered a permanent position for the next year, the next year, now if that permanent position is closer to the new born child and the new wife, new girl-friend or whatever, he wasn't getting too much success from his married life, obviously felt the need to move away from home, I would feel if he went backwards, it may do him an injustice, it, you know, going against his grain of process (sic) of em …

Note how the speaker focuses on a practical solution to Derek's problems (accepting a new job, moving house), and does not engage with how he should act towards his girlfriend. This excerpt also shows a number of indices of incoherence; odd repetition of phrases, inferences without basis, odd associations (what does going backward mean in this context? What is the 'it' that will do him injustice?), obscure phrases (what is 'the grain of his process'?). Note that the overall meaning of this passage is not incomprehensible to the listener; we can make sense of it by context and inferential effort. But the structure of the narrative contains several indices of incoherence, and if that were replicated across the interview, there would be grounds for considering this to be an incoherent narrative.

An unexpected method of non-engagement was the construction of elaborate fantasies and making inferences without evidence. Several men talked about the protagonists in the present tense as if they were real and active. They also made huge factual inferences about the state of mind of all the players, without any evidence to back this up; sometimes to the point of weaving elaborate fantasies about the players. This might reflect an attempt to make the vignette 'thicker', or more immediate to the speaker; but we were struck by how little acknowledgement there was of this process. No attempts were made to qualify the speculation, but rather, the speaker assumed a type of certainty about others' state of mind.

14.5.3.2. Confused and non-grammatical speech as an index of incoherence

Repetition of meaningless phrases reduces coherence (and intelligibility): this subject is discussing the dilemma facing Chris (ECI dilemma 3) whose elderly father arrives unexpectedly on his doorstep, asking if he can stay indefinitely.

> S21
> I think he should sit down and have good chat with his father before he decides that he wants him even to live with him and I think before he even has his father living with him I think he should bung his father in a hotel or B&B.
> (Why should he do that?)
> Well, because it may be a mistake having his father living with him because he wants his privacy and independence, you know, so er, he, he should like put his father in a B&B for a while and see how his father behaves himself, you know, you know, 'cos his father may be an old drunk now, you know you know what I mean, you know, so, er, yeah, you know...

This participant's narrative begins to become disorganized as he elaborates: 'you know' is repeated six times in the last sentence. The reference to a drunken father clearly has meaning for the subject, although none in the context of the narrative task as described in the dilemma.

Incoherence is also indicated by confusion of subjects and objects:

> S13
> I think it'd be better off well for the right reasons ... I stick with the small child, the woman with the small child.
> (Yeah. What should he do about his marriage?)
> [Pause] I don't know really. If he's already broken his vows once, do you know what I mean, I go with my feelings.

Here the subject's initial comments are grammatically confused. The 'it' refers to the future child. The subject from the start engages with the dilemma as himself; he finds it harder to think what another person might do. He also speaks in the present tense, rather than the future conditional, which suggests emotional activity (Pillemer *et al.* 1998).

14.5.3.3. Psychologically confused statements

Incoherence is also indicated by statements expressed that cannot be actually true in the real world, and yet are not reflected on or corrected by the speaker.

S21
(What if it's your dad that wanted to live with you?)
I wouldn't have my dad live with me.
(Why not?)
He's dead. [laughs]
(If he was alive?)
If he was alive, I'd beat him up for what he's done to me, so, but then again, I don't know... Because I've never met my dad, and I've never spoken to him or whatever, but I don't think my dad'd come to me anyway........ As far as I'm concerned, my dad's not part of me...

The participant's response about his father is incoherent because his use of the present tense, and the absence of the perfect tense makes it unclear whether the speaker really believes his father is dead. The use of the word 'wouldn't' implies that he could have his father to live with him; which is then concretely contradicted by the fact that his father is dead. The participant continues to talk about him in the present tense as if it were possible for them to meet. Although the last sentence might indicate some reflection on his internal experience of his father, it is not clear that his father is dead: to the uninitiated listener, the father could still be alive.

The last phrase is particularly interesting; partly because it is an interesting use of metaphor, but also the use of the present tense suggests that the father is very alive to the speaker, even though he has just said that he is dead. A more coherent way of putting this would be:
'As far as I'm concerned, my dad has never been part of me' (putting in the past), or
'I don't feel that my dad is part of me', (adding self-reflection) or
'My dad would not be part of me' (mirroring the future conditional used in the question).
As it is, the speaker seems unaware that he has talked about his father as if he were alive, in direct contradiction of something else he just said. This passage also indicated incoherence in the form of laughter, which is inappropriate in the context of the discussion, and in the absence of any explanation for the inappropriateness.

14.5.3.4. Coherence

Some subjects became more coherent as the interview progressed. This subject initially gave rather rigid and limited responses:
[First response to the first ECI dilemma: Derek]
He should stay with the job he's going to get permanently
[First response to second dilemma, Erik: about a man who is very unhappy with his wife, and has found a new partner, but has children]

He should get out of the marriage

But about his own dilemma, he was more reflective:

[About his childhood]

I felt there was something missing, you know, the love, the real sort of kind of love.

[About his deviant behaviour]

(Why did you do things like that?)

I wanted people to hate me. (Why?)

So I would feel better about myself. (How?)

If I felt people hated me, it would give me more ammunition to be a real bad person and feel good.

It is perhaps significant that he can be more reflective about himself and why he was behaving badly, than he can in relation to imaginary people making moral decisions.

14.6. **Discussion and Conclusion**

14.6.1. **Limitations of the study**

This study examines moral reasoning in an unusual group of participants: mentally disordered offenders detained in a high security psychiatric hospital with a diagnosis of personality disorder, i.e. they did not suffer from a concurrent psychotic mental illness such as schizophrenia, nor a learning disability. Any incoherence in their ethical narratives cannot be ascribed to symptoms of mental illness, such as reality testing, abnormal perceptions or delusional beliefs, or cognitive incapacity associated with learning disability. Although it is possible that these patients had a psychotic illness at some point in the past, there was no reason to think that they were psychotic at the time of the interview. Studies of linguistic coherence as a marker of self-integration have not found it to be influenced by IQ or education (Hesse 1999).

However, the context of the participants as detained psychiatric patients and the effect this may have had on the interview process must be recognized as a limitation of the study. Participants would be aware that their behaviour whilst detained in psychiatric hospital is under constant observation by health care staff and that further expression of antisocial behaviour is unlikely to speed their discharge. Under these circumstances, a research interview discussing their views on 'right and wrong' which is being tape recorded might result in participants expressing views that they believe would be favourable to their health care team rather than their personal views, despite being told that the research interviews would not be shown to anyone but the researchers.

A further limitation of this study is that it is based on interviews and not behaviour. It should be noted that these participants had already shown evidence of antisocial behaviour, and they scored low on the ECI, which is consistent with poorly developed moral reasoning, and egocentricity. It may be that participants receiving psychological treatment in a secure environment may be able to 'talk the talk' but with limited effect on their actual behaviour. This is particularly an issue with antisocial personality disorder as one of the diagnostic criteria is 'deceitfulness as indicated by repeated lying' (DSM-IV-TR, APA 2000). However, in practice it becomes impossible not to believe some of what a person says. If all of a participant's verbal communications are dismissed as unreliable, then all communication is impossible as is any prospect of therapeutic treatment. In fact practitioners do believe some of what people with antisocial personality disorder say, and accept as a clinical reality the possibility of being deceived, which can be taken up in treatment. We would see the verbal expressions of this group of patients as a first step in the treatment process that then requires demonstration of change in behaviour over an extended period of time as evidence of fundamental change.

In relation to studies of ethical reasoning, it may be argued that the use of brief vignettes may puzzle respondents. However vignettes are widely used in bioethics education to stimulate thought, and see how a respondent approaches the analysis of a problem. The ECI has been shown to be both valid and reliable in assessing how people approach ethical dilemmas; the vignettes used may be brief but the discussions (which in this study were recorded and transcribed) were not.

Similarly, it might be argued that the use of fantasy by the respondents indicates an attempt to make the vignettes more concrete and manageable. What we noticed is that the respondents were using fantasy to create alternative vignettes, not solutions; they were not engaging with the task in hand. We were also struck by the absence of language indicating that the speaker knew they were fantasizing, or extrapolating or making inferences beyond the available data; rather the respondents seemed to 'know' things about the players in the vignettes that could not possibly be known.

It might be argued that no account was taken of positive signs of coherence of moral reasoning. We rated coherence using a standardized and reliable method, which takes account of both positive signs of coherence and points of narrative incoherence. This method of rating coherence does require scoring for positive signs of coherence, and it is truly rare to find any sort of personal narrative from anyone, which does not have moments of positive coherence. The data we present here should not be taken to suggest that the respondents showed no evidence of positive coherence. Indeed many respondents were able to reflect very coherently on their experience. The point being made here is that types of narrative incoherence were quite subtle, pervasive, and revealed in the ways that people speak, not simply the content of what they say. This is a particular issue for individuals with antisocial personality disorder, who are diagnostically said to show 'lack of responsibility', but whose real difficulties around agency and responsibility for personal relationships are still poorly understood.

We do not know the extent to which these methods of assessing moral reasoning using linguistic and narrative data conflict or complement each other. In terms of methodology, we intended that the three methods of looking at moral reasoning (ASPD diagnosis, ECI score, and narrative incoherence rating) to act as a form of triangulation process in qualitative terms (Murphy *et al.* 1998, p. 182). Each method picks up a different aspect of the patient's experience of being assessed as a moral agent: an experience which has profound consequences; as those who are assessed as lacking responsibility will spend more time in detention. Further, where the question under investigation is one which deals more with values than facts, and where there is scope for variation in interpretation, then multiple empirical approaches are helpful. Conflicting data may be especially helpful in understanding how individuals see things differently from different perspectives.

14.6.2. **Conclusions**

We conclude that the participants in our study both scored lower than population norms on a structured cognitive assessment of moral reasoning (ECI) and demonstrated incoherence in their moral narratives. We found examples of unintelligibility, meaninglessness and other linguistic abnormalities in this group, which may suggest incoherence of moral identity. Previous research has discussed how personal identity is 'deformed' by disorders such as schizophrenia (Phillips 2003); we propose that our study indicates that 'moral identity' may also be deformed by disorders, such as personality disorder; which may be better understood as disorders of personality, integration, and autonomy.

14.6.3. **Empirical Results and Ethics**

This study gathers empirical evidence on moral decision-making in forensic psychiatric patients through the use of structured interviews presenting vignettes of ethical dilemmas. Participants' responses are systematically analysed using both a scoring system and by interpretation of transcripts using a theoretical framework from linguistic analysis. The results of the study are reduced by this process to a simple score by the ECI, an instrument used to measure moral reasoning. The finding that this score is lower than the average population score has little meaning for the participants or those charged with their care. Reductionism in such measurement, particularly when attempting to quantify abstract notions of right and wrong in ethical dilemmas is inevitable and some readers may judge numerical scoring for moral reasoning crude, artificial, and misleading. However, the consequence of not attempting to quantify capacity for moral reasoning is allowing theoretical frameworks to go unchallenged. For example, it might be argued that people suffering from antisocial personality disorder have no ability for moral reasoning as a result of some disorder of the mind. If no one attempts empirical research this assumption is likely to stand. However, it could be argued that even the crude results of the ECI in this study show that this group of patients have at least some ability for moral reasoning but that it is less than normal.

The case for using non-numerical data such as interview transcripts as empirical evidence when researching ethics is strong in that such data is rooted in the experience of others yet has a complexity of representation that 'an average score of 1.3' does not. Such data is open to interpretation by the researcher. The difficulty lies here in the many different interpretations that may be made from the same data. It is not clear how contradictory data might be interpreted, e.g. if an individual scored highly on the ECI but seemed to generate an incoherent moral narrative. However by collecting and presenting non-numerical data in studies such as this, any emerging theoretical discourse has at least a chance of being embedded in the reality of others' experience.

14.6.4. From empirical evidence to ethical analysis: moral identity in criminal responsibility and decision-making capacity

We propose that moral decision-making is better understood as a process and expression of moral identity, than simply as another type of cognitive reasoning skill. This is important for two separate policy areas: the attribution of blame and responsibility in criminal courts, and understanding decision-making capacity in people with mental disorders.

The participants in this research, by virtue of their identity as forensic psychiatric patients, were seen as people whose mental disorders affected their capacity to choose to break the rules. Their choice to offend was seen by the courts as 'not really them'; as a manifestation of some pathological process, which affected either (*a*) their moral identity or (*b*) their capacity to make moral choices. To what extent antisocial personality disorder is accepted as affecting an individual's capacity to make decisions in the context of criminal behaviour is outside the scope of this paper but we believe this research raises some interesting questions. If a person's moral identity is impaired, are they able to make autonomous choices for which they should be held blameworthy?

Respect for autonomy is a key principle in bioethics, which arguably means respect for those decisions that reflect a person's selfhood, and their sense of who they are. This is implied by the concept of substituted judgement by relatives and by the acceptance of advance directives in law as indicators of what this person 'would have wanted'; that this choice is 'really them'.

However, mental disorders undermine the autonomous self, and the capacity to make decisions for oneself that ought to be respected by others. Psychiatric practitioners may be unsure whether or how to respect the views of people with personality disorder, whose problems throw into question their capacity to make decisions that reflect their 'real' selves. Mental disorders affect the capacity to be the self that others know and recognize, altering personal identities in often what seem to be permanent ways (Glover 2003), so that it can be difficult for friends and relatives to comment on what this person 'really' wants.

The effect of mental disorder on the capacity to be autonomous has been explored in many legal actions, usually in relation to consent or refusal of medical treatment. Here the courts are asked to determine what makes a person competent to make decisions about their health and welfare. However, the research we describe here relates to the assessment of whether people are competent to make moral decisions, i.e. the assessment of their identity as moral reasoners, who are members of a moral community.

There is of course an enormous literature (mainly jurisprudential), which assumes that psychiatric disorders reduce criminal responsibility, and describes how they do so. Only Szasz (1973) has suggested that this is not true. There is no doubt that psychiatrists are called regularly to give expert testimony about the effect of mental disorder on criminal responsibility, even though this is acknowledged really to be the province of the jury. But what is not explicated in the psychiatric literature is what it is to be a moral reasoner, in psychological terms, nor what the effect of mental disorder might be on the capacity to make criminally responsible decisions.

What is meant by criminally responsible decisions? These are decisions that affect the well-being of others (both physical and emotional), relate to the keeping of social/legal rules, and reflect some engagement with the values of the community. A person who breaks the rules, and causes harm to others, in a way which indicates an absence of engagement with the values of the community will be one whose criminal responsibility is under scrutiny. In considering such a person, we want to know if their decision to break the rules in a harmful way reflects who they really are; is an expression of their moral identity. What seems to be at issue in the criminal courts is what it means to have the 'autonomy to choose to break the rules'.

14.6.5. Moral identity – its relevance for psychiatric practice

This study has demonstrated evidence of incoherence in moral narratives of subjects suffering from antisocial personality disorder. What we suggest is their 'lack of responsibility' is a reflection of a distorted moral identity, which reveals itself in how they approach moral stories. If work with offender patients includes helping them to take responsibility for what they have done, including empathy for the victim, then this implies a need for them to integrate their offences into their moral identity, through the process of narrative (which is essentially what is done in therapy with offenders).

Ethical analysis based on this data questions our understanding of autonomous decision-making and the role of moral identity in this process. We think this research has two particular implications for psychiatric practice; first, that moral reasoning is a psychological process which could be affected by mental disorders and second, that personality disorders may be conditions that affect mental capacity, that is, the capacity to reason morally. It also raises new questions about how practitioners should approach decision-making in people with personality disorder; a group who have traditionally been excluded from services and disliked by doctors (Appleby and Lewis 1988; Department of Health 2003).

We hope also to have made a convincing case for the use of a linguistic approach in this complex area. This may have particular validity in psychiatric ethics because it takes the voice of the individual seriously (Oyebode 2003). If narratives are essentially evaluative, in that they carry moral significance to the teller and the listener, then this must be because they give more access to the individual meaning of any person's choices for them, which is of relevance for understanding the moral weight of those choices and allocating moral responsibility. Respecting the meaning of a person's choice means respect for them as a moral actor; it entails appreciating the intricacies of the making of meaning for each person, while struggling with the difficulty of listening to others' stories. A narrative approach is complex enough to be of particular use in (*a*) understanding the choices made by offenders and (*b*) exploring how mental disorders affect the choice to act criminally.

Acknowledgements and disclaimer

This work was supported by a grant from the Wellcome Trust, awarded to Professor Jonathan Glover and Gwen Adshead. The views expressed here are the authors own and do not reflect the views of their employers.

References

Adshead G (2002). A different voice in psychiatric ethics? In KWM Fulford, D Dickenson and T Murray, eds. *Healthcare ethics and human values*, pp. 56–62. Blackwell, Oxford.

American Psychiatric Association (2000). *Diagnostic and statistical manual version IV- text revised*. American Psychiatric Press, Washington.

Bergman R (2004). Identity as motivation: toward a theory of the moral self. In DK Lapsley and D Narvaez, eds. *Moral development, self, and identity*, pp. 210–46. Lawrence Erlbaum, Mahwah, NJ.

Blair J (1995). A cognitive developmental approach to morality: investigating the psychopath. *Cognition*, **56**, 1–29.

Blasi A (1980). Bridging moral cognition and moral action: a critical review of the literature. *Psychological Bulletin*, **88**, 1–45.

Blasi A (2004). Moral functioning: moral understanding and personality. In DK Lapsley and D Narvaez, eds. *Moral development, self, and identity*, pp. 335–347. Lawrence Erlbaum, Mahwah, NJ.

Candilis P, Martinez R and Dording C (2001). Principles and narrative in forensic psychiatry: toward a robust view of the professional role. *American Academy of Psychiatry and Law*, **29**, 167–73.

Cox M (1986). The holding function of dynamic psychotherapy in a secure setting. *Journal of the Royal Society of Medicine*.

Fonagy P, Target M, Steele M et al. (1997). Disruptive behaviour, borderline personality disorder, crime and their relationship to security of attachment. In L Atkinson and K Zucker, eds. *Attachment and psychopathology*, pp. 223–276. Guilford Press, London.

Geertz C (1975). *The interpretation of cultures*. Basic Books, New York.

Gibbs JC, Boringer KS and Fuller D (1992). *Moral maturity: measuring the development of sociomoral reflection*. Erlbaum, Hillsdale, NJ.

Gilligan C (1982). *In a different voice: psychological theory and women's development*. Harvard University Press, Cambridge, MA.

Gillon R (2003). Four scenarios. *Journal of Medical Ethics*. **29**, 267–8.

Glover J (1988). I: the philosophy and psychology of personal identity. In *Coherence is central to our understanding of people*, p. 81. Penguin, London.

Glover J (2003). *Tanner lectures on humanism in psychiatry*. Princeton.

Goldwyn R, Main M and George C (1994). *The adult attachment interview manual*.

Grice HP (1975). Logic and conversation. In P Cole and J Moran, eds. *Syntax and semantics III: speech acts*, pp. 41–58. New York Academic Press.

Griffore RJ and Samuels DD (1978). Moral judgment of residents of a maximum security correctional facility. *The Journal of Psychology*, **100**, 3–7.

Hare R (1991). *The Psychopathy checklist- revised*. Multi-Health systems, Toronto.

Hawk S and Peterson R (1974). Do MMPI psychopathic deviancy scores reflect psychopathic deviancy or just deviancy? *Journal of personality assessment*, **38**, 362–368.

Hesse E (1999). The adult attachment interview. In Cassidy and Shaver, eds. *Handbook of attachment*. Guilford Press, New York.

Hudson Jones A (1999). Narrative in medical ethics. *British Medical Journal*, **318**, 253–6.

Keenan T and Ward T (2000). A theory of mind perspective on cognitive, affective and intimacy deficits in child sexual offenders. *Sexual Abuse*, **12**, 49–60.

Kleinman A (1988). *The illness narratives: suffering, healing, and the human condition.* Basic Books, New York.

Kohlberg L (1969). State and sequence: the cognitive developmental approach to socialization. In D Goslin, ed. *Handbook of socialization theory and research.* Rand Mcnally, Chicago.

Marshall W, Hamilton K and Fernandez Y (2001). Empathy deficits and cognitive distortions in child molesters. *Sexual Abuse*, **13**, 123–30.

McCarthy J (2003). Principlism or narrative ethics: must we choose between them? *The Journal Medical Humanities*, **29**, 65–71.

Murphy E, Dingwall R, Greatbatch D, Parker S and Watson P (1998). Qualitative research methods in health technology assessment: a review of the literature. *Health Technology Assessment*, **2**(16), 182.

Nelson JR, Smith DJ and Dodd J (1990). The moral reasoning of juvenile delinquents: meta-analysis. *Journal of Abnormal Child Psychology*, **18**, 231–39.

O'Kane A, Fawcett D and Blackburn R (1996). Psychopathy and moral reasoning. *Personality and Individual Difference*, **20**, 505–14.

Oyebode F (2003). Autobiographical narratives and psychiatry. *Advances in psychiatric treatment*, **9**, 265–69.

Palmer E and Hollin C (1998). A comparison of patterns of moral development in young offenders and non-offenders. *Legal and Criminological Psychology*, **3**, 225–35.

Phillips J (2003). Schizophrenia and the narrative self. In T Kircher and A David, eds. *The self in neuroscience and psychiatry*, pp. 319–35. CUP, Cambridge, UK.

Piaget J (1965). *The moral judgment of the child.* Free Press, New York.

Pillemer D, Desrochers M and Ebanks C (1998). Remembering the past in the present: verb tense shifts in autobiographical memory narratives. In C Thompson et al., eds. *Autobiographical memory: theoretical and applied perspectives*, pp. 145–62. Lawrence Erlbaum, NJ.

Rest J (1984). Morality. In JH Flavell and E Markham, eds. *Cognitive development. Handbook of child psychology*, Vol. 3, pp. 556–629. John Wiley, Chichester.

Skoe E (1993). *The ethic of care interview manual.* Unpublished MSS. Available from the author on request. University of Oslo, Oslo, Norway.

Skoe EEA (1998). The ethic of care: issues in moral development. In EEA Skoe and AL von der Lippe, eds. *Personality development in adolescence: a cross national and life span perspective*, pp. 143–71. Routledge, London.

Skoe and Diessner (1994). Ethic of care, justice, identity and gender: an extension and replication. *Merrill Palmer Quarterly*, **40**, 102–19.

Skoe E and Marcia J (1991). A care based measure of morality and its relation to ego-identity. *Merrill Palmer Quarterly*, **37**, 289–304.

Skoe E and von der Lippe A (2002). Ego development and the ethics of care and justice: the relations between them revisited. *Journal of Personality*, **70**, 485–507.

Szasz T (1973). *Ideology and insanity: essays on the psychiatric dehumanisation of man.* Calder & Boyars, London.

Tappan M (2000). Autobiography, mediated action and the development of moral identity. *Narrative Inquiry*, **10**(1), 81–109.

Van IJzendoorn M and Zwart-Woudstra H (1995). Adolescents' attachment representations and moral reasoning. *The Journal of Genetic Psychology*, **156**, 359–72.

Appendix

The Ethic of Care Interview Dilemmas
  Male version
  (Skoe, 1993)

1. The Derek Dilemma

Derek is a married, successful teacher in his late twenties. His life has been centred on his work and he has been offered a permanent position for next year. Recently, he has been involved in an intense love affair with a single woman who has just told him that she is pregnant and that it is his child.

What do you think Derek should do? Why?

2. The Erik Dilemma

Erik, in his late thirties, has been married to Betty for several years. They have two children, 8 and 10 years old. Throughout the marriage Betty has been at home, looking after the house and the children. For the last few years Erik has felt increasingly unhappy in the marriage relationship. He finds his wife demanding, self-centred and insensitive as well as uninterested in his needs and feelings. Erik has several times tried to communicate his unhappiness and frustration to his wife, but she continually ignores and rejects his attempts. Erik has become very attracted to another woman, Carol, a single teacher. Recently, Carol has asked Erik for a more intimate, committed relationship.

What do you think Erik should do? Why?

3. The Chris Dilemma

Chris, a 26-year-old man, has decided to live on his own after having shared an apartment with a friend for the last 3 years. He finds that he is much happier living alone as he now has more privacy and independence and gets more work and studying done. One day his father, whom he has not seen for a long while as they do not get along too well, arrives at the doorstep with two large suitcases, saying that he is lonely and wants to live with Chris.

What do you think Chris should do? Why?

Chapter 15

Patient incompetence in the practice of old age psychiatry: the significance of empirical research for the law

Sander Welie

15.1. Introduction

Over the last decade an increasing amount of empirical research has been carried out within a legal framework. This is in contrast with traditional methods of academic legal research, which were confined to the study of jurisprudential literature and the close analytical reading of legal regulations and case law. Empirical studies relating to legal questions, concepts, or mechanisms were considered to be outside the field of legal research, and instead belonging to fields of scientific research such as: technical research (e.g. error margins in the measurement of speed transgression; Hofstee 1996; Muijlwijk 1996), jurimetrics (e.g. the prediction of judicial decisions on the basis of empirical facts of the case; Combrink-Kuiters 2000), sociology or psychology of law, forensic psychiatry, or criminology.

An important stimulus for this recent trend towards empirical legal research is the attempt to improve the quality of legal regulation by empirically evaluating the effects of regulation on practice (Winter 1997). In the field of health law several evaluation reports on Dutch statutes containing patient rights have been published. In some cases the obligation to evaluate is included in a statute (Hendriks 2000, pp. 87–88). An example of this can be found in the Special Admissions to Psychiatric Hospitals Act, which regulates involuntary commitment to, and treatment in, mental institutions. Article (art.) 71 of this statute prescribes a periodic evaluation of the Act. It reads as follows: 'In agreement with Our Minister of Justice, Our Minister (of Welfare, Health and Cultural Affairs) shall, within three years of the date (of entering into force) and subsequently every five years, send the States General (the parliament of the Netherlands) a report on the way in which the law has been applied'.

The methods used in empirical evaluative research of statutes generally take the form of postal surveys among those whom the statute concerns (e.g. health care professionals, patients) and semi-structured interviews, possibly complemented by panel or expert meetings (e.g. Dute *et al.* 2000, p. 6). From the data a multitude of tables with percentages are generated. The aim of this type of research is formulated in quite diverse ways. It may be to assess whether the goals of the statute are realized in practice, or whether the legislation has any undesired side-effects (ZorgOnderzoek Nederland 2001, p. 9). This approach involves a test of actual practice by the statutory standards and hence presupposes that these standards are clear. In the case of statutes where these standards have not been laid down unambiguously, the aim of evaluative research is different. In this case the aim may rather have the character of contributing to the continuous process of interaction between all the interested parties with a view to finding a shared interpretative framework (Olsthoorn-Heim 2003, p. 16).

In all these types of empirical evaluative research of health law statutes it is primarily the statutes that are under investigation, and not health care practice itself. This kind of research raises the question of how an observed discrepancy between legal requirements and actual practice ought to be interpreted. Such a discrepancy could be taken as evidence that practice is 'wrong', because it does not comply with legal requirements; but an alternative interpretation is that the statute is 'defective' because it does not do justice to the dynamics of actual practice. Given this double-edged nature of evaluative research one would expect the methodology to pay attention to the possible different interpretations of empirical data within a normative legal context. The methodological accounts of this research, however, do not bring up this theme. In the reports of the three official evaluations of the Special Admissions to Psychiatric Hospitals Act, for example, there is no reflection on the problem of facts versus norms (Evaluatiecommissie Wet Bijzondere Opnemingen in Psychiatrische Ziekenhuizen, 1995, p. 11; Evaluatiecommissie Wet Bijzondere Opnemingen in Psychiatrische Ziekenhuizen, 1996, p. 116 ff.; Begeleidingscommissie evaluatie Wet Bopz, 2002, p. 15, 18-21, 48-53; Derde evaluatiecommissie Van de Wet Bopz, 2007, p. 12, 25–31, 34, 106). In a review of 5 years of empirical evaluative research of statutes, it is stated that this type of research is essentially a critical examination of the assumptions underlying a statute (Olsthoorn-Heim 2003, p. 18). Whether the assumptions referred to are descriptive or normative ones, is unfortunately not specified.

The problem of the normative significance of empirical descriptive data is not only relevant to the evaluative research of statutes, but also to any kind of empirical study in which the research question addresses legal concepts. Empirical studies yield a description of what the research subjects actually do and think, whereas the law is about how people should behave. This problem is the subject of this chapter. A research study into the criteria for assessing patient decision-making competence, carried out by the author, will serve as a case example. In this study, empirical research was undertaken in the practice of old age psychiatry in order to clarify the meaning of the legal concept of competence and, if possible, to specify criteria in terms of which the abstract legal concept can be operationalized.

In this chapter I will first explore the relationship between empirical research and the law. Several positions which can be taken on this relationship will be touched on. I will then describe a study into criteria of competence. After an explanation of the Dutch legal background of patient competence, and the design of the study, I will show how the research question developed during the course of the study. As a consequence of the methodological position taken, the development of the research question resulted in a view on the scope of criteria of competence that is somewhat original, and in an elaboration of legal notions and provisions to which other authors have paid little systematic attention. The chapter ends with a discussion of the value of empirical research in health law.

15.2. The relationship between empirical research and the law

It has been argued above that empirical research that relates to legal concepts raises the question: what is the normative significance of its results? This is a feature shared by both ethical and legal empirical research, as both types of empirical study aim to make prescriptive inferences from a description of actual practice. This question of the normative significance is especially important for the law, since the incorporation of an element or rule within a legal model implies the possibility that its observance is compulsory. There are, therefore, certain formal safeguards that have to be met before a proposition or an argument may be called legal. These safeguards amount to the requirement that the proposition in question must be reducible to a generally recognized source of law, which has been referred to as a 'formal source of law' (Walker 1980, p. 1156 ff.; Komen 1988, p. 24 ff.; Black et al. 1990, p. 1395; Franken et al. 1995, p. 95, 98). There is a limited array of formal sources of law. In the Dutch legal system the most important of these are treaties, the constitution, codes or statutes, case law, and jurisprudence.

I will discuss three different positions that can be taken in relation to the question of what is the normative significance of empirical data in the context of health law research. The first position is that the results of empirical research are not relevant for the legal model in a normative sense. This position rests on the argument that the legal model is on the normative level ('what ought to be done') whereas the results are on the descriptive level ('what is done'), and that these two levels are strictly separate. Conflating these levels amounts to a violation of Hume's law (Mackie 1967, p. 178; MacNabb 1967, p. 86; Singer 1991, p. 505).[1]

According to this position the only thing to be learned from empirical legal research is whether or not actual practice complies with the law. Law itself does not benefit from this kind of research, nor is it harmed by it: it is not affected by descriptive results. Empirical research can be used to monitor the degree to which subjects are adhering to legal norms, to trace factors that determine the behaviour concerned, and to assess the possible need to take measures to implement or enforce the law. It has no other value.

The second position depends on the view that actual practice and the law are conceptually connected. This position can be supported on both formal and substantial grounds. The formal grounds are related to the frequent occurrence of open norms in health law, such as the professional standard, 'due professional care' (art. 7:453 (Dutch) Civil Code), reasonableness, harm, and 'interests at hand' (art. 7:465 Civil Code). The use of open norms by the legislator implies that the interpretation and elaboration of these norms is left to health care practitioners, besides others, such as lawyers, ethicists, scholars, and judges. Thus, the actual views and customs of practitioners, like self-regulation by the profession, obtain the authority of a source of law. Through the open norm, the legislator delegates the legal competence of operationalizing the statutory norm to the persons who are dealing with it in practice.

The substantial grounds amount to the idea that the legislator and practitioners are motivated by the same concerns for the patients' well-being and autonomy. Insofar as practitioners act in accordance with the rationale of the law, there is no difference between their considerations and legal considerations. Good practical reasons, therefore, can have a rightful place in a legal argument and they can complement the statutory framework.

The third position that can be taken on the normative significance of empirical data agrees with the first position in insisting on a clear distinction between facts and norms, but, in contrast with the first position and in line with the second position, maintains that descriptive results are relevant for the legal model. To that end, empirical results should be used as part of a heuristic method. This method requires that for each salient empirical result, the researcher critically investigates the associated legal norms. Depending on the 'valence' of the initial

---

[1] See Hume (1739/1740). *A treatise of human nature*, book III, part I, section I.

evaluation of the results, i.e. negative (the research subjects' behaviour is experienced as unexpectedly 'disobedient') or positive (the research subjects' behaviour is experienced as unexpectedly 'obedient'), this critical investigation will take the form of an attempt either to justify, or to denounce, the observed behaviour.

This method could be called 'systematic (or methodical) apology' or 'systematic (or methodical) accusation', respectively.[2] When the empirical research produces results that seem in conflict with the legal model, the researcher ought to ask himself whether it is nevertheless possible to defend the results from a legal point of view; when the researcher finds results that appear to conform to the legal model, he should ask himself whether it is nevertheless possible legally to condemn those results. These questions provide a perspective from which prevailing conceptions of the law can be criticized by re-examining the generally recognized sources of law. Legal elements or arguments may be found that would not have been discovered without the data from the empirical study. The method under discussion is called 'heuristic' because it enables us to ask questions that could serve to find out relevant elements or arguments, but that do not offer a guarantee of doing so (see *Oxford English Dictionary Online* 1989).

According to this third position, the confrontation of legal notions with actual practice may serve as a stimulus to gain a deepened, more critical understanding of the legal model. This position can, therefore, be characterized as a hermeneutic approach (Widdershoven 1987, p. 88, 102 ff.). It goes without saying that the confrontation of actual practice with legal notions may also be instructive for practitioners insofar as their actions and reasons truly fail in light of the law.

15.3. Patient competence in Dutch law

The Dutch Civil Code has a detailed regulation of the legal consequences of patient decision-making competence. Broadly speaking, the legal consequence is that a competent patient's decisions, in response to the interventions proposed by the health care professional, ought to be respected, even if this means renouncing life-saving treatment or other interventions that are deemed necessary from a medical point of view. The legal consequence of incompetence is that a representative has to decide on behalf of, and in the interests of, the incompetent patient. The representative may be a person who has been officially appointed by a judge ('legal representative'); or, more commonly, either 'attorneys in fact' (i.e. persons authorized by the patient when still competent), or partners and close family members.

---

[2] Alluding to Descartes' systematic/methodical doubt.

The consequences attached by the law to competence versus incompetence, are potentially far-reaching. It is important, therefore, to know when a patient is competent and when he is incompetent. However, in this regard, the Civil Code does not offer much help. It gives only an open norm as definition for competence. According to this definition, a patient is competent if he is able to judge his interests at hand reasonably (art. 7:465 Civil Code). Because of the use of several abstract notions, such as interests and reasonableness, the definition is amenable to varied interpretations. Therefore, lawyers, clinicians, and researchers aim at formulating criteria that can serve as an operationalization of the statutory definition.

The establishment of concrete criteria for determining patient competence would enable an algorithm to be developed for dealing with informed consent. Such an algorithm would combine the criteria for competence assessment with the above-mentioned statutory legal consequences attached to whether a patient is competent or incompetent. This algorithm would be procedural in nature, because it is primarily oriented towards the question 'who decides on care' and not towards the substantial question 'what is good care'.

Although at present no generally accepted criteria of competence exist in the Dutch system, there is consensus about two aspects of competence assessment. First, Dutch law agrees that the assessment of patient competence is mainly the responsibility of the attendant health care professional (Ministerie van Justitie 1994; Hubben 2000, p. 134; Welie et al. 2005). The professional has to do this, regardless of the patient's formal legal status, in the process of determining whether an informed consent or refusal by his patient is valid. For patients with a legal representative, the latter person may also be involved in the assessment. If the attendant health care professional wishes, he can consult specialists on the matter, e.g. psychiatrists or psychologists. As a last resort, the issue can be brought before the court.

Second, according to current opinion, patient competence is a task-specific concept (President's Commission for the Study of Ethical Problems in Medicine and Biomedical and Behavioural Research 1982, p. 55; Buchanan and Brock 1990, p. 18 ff.; Weisstub 1990, p. 6–7; Beauchamp 1991; Legemaate 1994; White 1994, p. 44 ff.; Wettstein 1995; Gert et al. 1997, p. 132; Grisso and Appelbaum 1998, p. 21 ff.; Welie and Welie 2001). The patient is competent if he has the abilities required for the task in hand (e.g. making a decision about the intervention proposed by the health care professional), and he is incompetent if he does not have these abilities. This means that the assessment of competence is specific to the decision in question. The result of the assessment does not pertain to other decisions as these may require other mental abilities. Neither does the result of an assessment prevail beyond the moment of assessment, since the patient's mental abilities may fluctuate, recover, or deteriorate in the course of time.

15.4. **Research into criteria of patient decision-making competence**

In Dutch law the assessment of patient competence is generally left to health care professionals. In this section I will describe an empirical research study that I have carried out that explores the ways in which health care professionals deal with this issue of patient competence in practice. The goal of the research was to learn something from actual practice in order to elaborate the law with regard to the assessment of patient competence. In order to take practice seriously and to be capable of adjusting the research methods if the preliminary results gave reason to do so, a flexible design was needed. It was decided to adopt qualitative methods as these give the opportunity to reformulate the research question in the course of the investigation (cf. 'open and emerging design'; Creswell 2003, p. 106–107). The research focused on the field of old-age psychiatric care, in particular care for patients with early dementia. This focus was chosen because it was expected that the question of whether or not patients are able to make decisions for themselves, would be regularly under discussion among the health care professionals, albeit not necessarily in terms of patient decision-making competence.

My purpose in conducting the empirical research was not to judge the behaviour of the practitioners on the wards under investigation, but to develop the legal model further. Indeed, since the law does not provide clear and unambiguous standards for judging the way in which the practitioners reach specific verdicts of competence, it is not possible to make such a judgment. The research, therefore, started from the second of the three positions outlined above: it was assumed that practical routines and reasons displayed by health care professionals could supplement the legal model. The original research question was: how do health care professionals assess their patients' decision-making competence? The starting point was the task-specific conception of patient competence.

The research was carried out on two wards for geriatric and psycho-geriatric patients in a hospital and a nursing home, respectively. The techniques used to collect the data were non-participant observation of, and semi-structured interviews with, health care professionals. During the observation the researcher's role was limited to overt attendance of diverse activities and consultations of the health care professionals, but did not include becoming involved in patient care or in active interference with the health care professionals' behaviour (cf. box 1 in Schwartz and Jacobs 1979, p. 57). The observation in the hospital took place over 9 weeks; the observation in the nursing home took place over 7 weeks. A longer period of observation had originally been anticipated; however, this period was shortened in the light of the results. Ten interviews were conducted, of which nine were individual interviews and one was a group interview with four health care professionals. Those interviewed were physicians, a psychologist, nurses, nurses' aides, and managers.

The researcher spent whole days on the wards, thus gaining insight into the daily routines. He attended the following activities: initial discussions, for example in the outpatient clinic, with patients about management; admissions; provision of information to patients, representatives, and/or family members; multi-disciplinary case conferences; staff meetings; discussions of the treatment or care plan; rounds; handovers between shifts; daily care; doctor consultations; therapeutic activities; recreation for patients; informal moments with health care professionals (e.g. meals); consultations of psychologists, medical specialists, lawyers, and members of regional indication committees for care allocation; and the discharge of patients from the institution.

15.5. **Development of the research**

The initial phase of the research showed, unexpectedly, that the issue of patient decision-making competence was not a topic of debate or discussion at all among the observed health care professionals. Health care professionals never explicitly asked themselves, or discussed with each other, whether or not a patient was able to take a specific decision. In the exceptional cases when mention was made of competence, the professionals referred either to the competence to manage financial affairs (which was outside the scope of the research), or they used competence as a rhetorical label to describe a patient who assented to the proposed clinical management in order to lend weight to a decision that had in effect been already taken by people other than the patient. One hypothesis to account for this result is that health care professionals had not had sufficient time to become familiar with the concept of competence, since the relevant provisions in the Civil Code had only entered into force a short time before the empirical study took place (cf. Evaluatiecommissie Wet Bijzondere Opnemingen in Psychiatrische Ziekenhuizen 1996, pp. 116–117). This hypothesis is unconvincing, however, because the provisions in the Civil Code were largely codificative in nature: patients enjoyed the right to informed consent long before the codification of this right. Hence, the law has required health care professionals to judge their patients' competence to exercise this right for a longer time.

In the light of these results the research question was adapted and changed to the following two questions: (*a*) do health care professionals discuss their patients' decision-making competence; and (*b*), if not, why not? Further observations confirmed the previous finding that competence is very rarely discussed by health care professionals. In the interviews, some health care professionals denied this result, others confirmed it.

The former claimed that the assessment of competence was, indeed, undertaken by practitioners. But on more detailed inquiry it turned out that they meant something different from the legal concept. For example, several interviewees, when claiming that they assessed competence, meant that they considered respect for patient autonomy an important principle. But appreciating the significance of autonomy is not the same thing as assessing competence. Indeed, in many cases, an assessment of competence might have shed doubt on the patient's ability to take an autonomous decision. One interviewee, in claiming to assess competence, had the global process of diagnosing and getting to know the patient in mind. This process takes place immediately after the patient's admission. Knowledge of the patient's condition and person may be necessary for a judgement of competence, but it is not sufficient. Furthermore, a proposed management plan is not normally formulated at this initial stage; so a context for competence assessment is lacking. Some interviewees meant by 'assessing competence' that they attempted to take into account the patient's wishes when making decisions for the patient. Although this activity may be commendable, it is not equivalent to judging competence: it implies that the patient is assumed to be incompetent, since competent patients decide for themselves. Besides, incompetence does not mean that a patient's wishes can be disregarded.[3] In summary, those health care professionals interviewed who denied the results of the observational study, had in mind something other than the legal concept of competence, i.e. the task-specific assessment of a patient's mental abilities to decide whether or not to consent to the intervention under consideration.

Some of the health care professionals interviewed agreed that patient competence was not widely assessed or discussed. The reasons given in justification were generally in conflict with the legal model. The most frequently given justification was that patients lack medical education, thus making informed consent unfeasible. This argument however ignores the legal and ethical requirement for the practitioner to provide the patient with the necessary information and to explain such information to him; hence, there is no need for the patient to know all relevant medical facts in advance.

---

[3] Cf. art. 7:465 section 5 second sentence Civil Code. See also principle 9 of Recommendation No. R (99) 4 of the Committee of Ministers of the Council of Europe to Member States on Principles concerning the Legal Protection of Incapable Adults (Strasbourg 1999).

The purpose of the research had not been to judge the practitioners on the wards under investigation. Their reasons for acting in a certain way, however, had to be evaluated *vis-à-vis* their compatibility with the basic assumptions of the law and the rationale of statutory law; otherwise they could not be used for elaborating the statutory framework. After it had turned out that competence was rarely an issue among health care professionals and that the reasons stated as a justification for this were untenable, the third position (see above) was taken with regard to the relationship between empirical research and the law (systematic apology). This led to a more differentiated legal approach, as is exemplified in the next section.

15.6. **Results**

The empirical results, outlined above, led to further analysis of the literature from a specific perspective. The following questions directed this analysis: are there any legal reasons for refraining from assessment of patient competence; and, if so, what are these reasons? This analysis showed that the generally recognized sources of law do indeed contain several legal arguments for not engaging in competence assessment under certain circumstances. These arguments will now be briefly discussed.

A first argument relates to article 7:466 section 2 Civil Code, which states that patient consent may be presumed to have been given if the intervention in question is not drastic in nature. In all cases where this provision applies, the health care professional does not have to solicit consent. Since patient competence is the competence to give or withhold consent, there is no need, under these circumstances, to assess competence. The expression 'intervention (... not) of a drastic nature' is a statutory term in Dutch law. It relates to the inconvenience, burden, risks, and suffering to the patient which are a result of the intervention or treatment. Examples of drastic interventions include surgical operations, Electro-Convulsive Therapy, and medication that has serious side-effects.[4]

The second argument pertains to the presumption of competence (Hipshman 1987; Van der Klippe 1990; Van Wijmen 1990; Weisstub 1990, p. 6, 19; Ministerie van Justitie 1994, p. 8; Legemaate 1994; White 1994, p. 3ff.; Madigan *et al.* 1994; Law Commission 1995, pp. 32, 223; Leenen and Gevers 2000; KNMG 2004, pp. 92, 95, 100, 116; cf. art. 1:1 section 1 Civil Code). This presumption states that each patient, regardless of his psychiatric diagnosis or legal status, must be assumed to be competent, as long as proof to the contrary

---

[4] Thanks to Dr B. Pinckers for supplying examples.

has not been provided. The presumption shows that there is generally no rea-son for competence assessment: health care professionals can just presume patients to be competent.

Similar arguments can be made with regard to the view that the patient's competence may not be called into question unless there is a legitimate trigger for doing so (Ministerie van Justitie 1994, p. 8; Legemaate 1994, p. 328; KNMG 2004, pp. 100–101, 117), and the view that a patient can be justifiably declared incompetent only if the disadvantages of such a pronouncement (e.g. humiliation or stigmatization of the patient, infringement of privacy, or possible subjection to coercion) are outweighed by its advantages (assistance of a representative, possibility of beneficent intervention) (Van der Klippe 1990, pp. 131, 135; Legemaate 1994, pp. 328–329; Leenen and Gevers 2000, p. 216). In other words, when no legitimate trigger is present or when the conse-quences of declaring the patient incompetent are not preferable to the conse-quences of declaring him competent, a declaration of incompetence is unacceptable, even if the patient clearly does not have the mental abilities required to take the decision under consideration.

Another related argument, bears on the plea for a sliding scale approach (Drane 1985; Ministerie van Justitie 1994, p. 11; Legemaate 1994, p. 330). A sliding scale approach 'requires an increasingly more stringent standard [of competence] as the consequences of the patient's decision embody more risk' (Drane 1984, p. 925). Among other things, this means that low demands are to be made on the competence of a patient who accepts regular medical treat-ment: for such a patient to be deemed competent, according to the sliding scale, it is sufficient if his awareness is not diminished and if he has the ability to express assent, either explicitly or implicitly, to the treatment suggested by the health care professional. These criteria require so little from the patient that establishing whether a patient meets them, is hardly a question of assess-ing competence. For unproblematic decisions, a patient's competence does not matter, really, on account of this 'sliding scale approach' (cf. KNMG 2004, p. 101; Leenen and Gevers 2000, p. 216; Welie et al. 2005).

A further argument for why assessing competence may be irrelevant, regards shared decision-making by health care professional, patient, and fam-ily member(s). Patients are often accompanied by one or more close relatives when attending appointments for consultation with the doctor, especially in the face of major decisions (cf. Schermer 2001, pp. 149–151, on 'the dual strat-egy'). If the health care professional succeeds in reaching agreement with both patient and family member on what medical course of action to pursue, it fol-lows from article 7:465 sections 2 & 3 Civil Code that competence assessment is irrelevant. This is because close relatives are potential representatives.

Provided that all parties have been well informed and that no undue pressure has been exerted, the health care professional can be assured of having obtained valid consent in this situation: if the patient is competent, then the patient's agreement provides valid consent; if the patient is incompetent, then the family member's consent is legally valid.

Finally, article 7:465 section 6 Civil Code states that resistance of an incompetent patient against drastic interventions that are not necessary to avoid serious harm for the patient, ought to be respected by the health care professional (cf. Law Commission 1995, p. 60 ff. and 224).[5] In all situations, therefore, where a patient objects to such an intervention, whether the patient is competent or not, the health care professional should desist from implementing the intervention. Once again competence assessment is of no legal significance. The expression 'serious harm' like 'intervention (... not) of a drastic nature' is a statutory term in Dutch law. An operation for a minor condition (such as a hernia repair, under some circumstances) might count as a drastic intervention that is not necessary to avoid serious harm.

It is of course true that concepts like 'drastic intervention', 'legitimate trigger', 'unproblematic decision', and 'serious harm', are open to various interpretations (Tweede Kamer der Staten-Generaal 1993/1994; Sluijters and Biesaart 2005). But whatever dispute may arise in that regard, it is also clear that all of the above arguments limit the scope of the procedural approach implied by competence assessment. To put it briefly, a patient's competence (or lack of it) is legally decisive only in situations that fulfil two cumulative conditions (both are necessary): (*a*) a patient persists in not complying with a drastic intervention which is necessary to avoid serious harm, or with a non-drastic intervention which is necessary to avoid serious harm or needed to bring about a substantial improvement in the patient's condition; and (*b*) the family member(s) or representative agree(s) with the health care professional that the intervention should take place. This second condition is explained by the fact that the relatives' disagreeing with doctors constitutes potential substitute refusal in case of a patient resisting the proposed intervention.[6]

The arguments that I have put forward thus qualify the prevailing legal opinion that assessment of patient competence is pivotal in medical

[5] Cf. also art. 5 (c) European Union directive Good Clinical Practice (Directive 2001/20/EC, Official Journal L 121).

[6] The situation in which a family member is not available, is left aside, as is the possibility for the practitioner to overrule representatives because of the latter's doing a bad job (art. 7:465 section 4 j° section 5 Civil Code); cf. Welie 2005 pp. 255–256.

decision-making and that criteria of competence should be applicable to all imaginable situations. This is an important qualification because it demonstrates that in many cases health care professionals can dedicate themselves to a discussion of what is good care for a specific patient, and to attempts at persuading the patient of the value of what they sincerely believe to be good care, without needing to assess competence. For those cases in which competence assessment plays a key role in decision-making, insight into the applicable circumstances can direct academics and practitioners in formulating valid and useful criteria of patient competence.

In summary, the use of the heuristic method of systematic apology, involving collecting empirical data, has facilitated systematic reflection on a number of elements in the legal model, the implications of which have not been previously thought through. Empirical methods can constitute a useful supplement to the more traditional methods of legal research, in particular in helping to avoid a one-sided emphasis on leading theoretical notions.

15.7. **Conclusion**

In this chapter I have argued that the empirical study of how health practitioners behave can play an important part in enhancing legal analysis. I have illustrated my argument through describing an empirical study that I carried out in the area of the assessment of patient competence to consent to treatment. The aims and design of the study were the result of initial legal analysis. But the aims changed in the light of the results of the first part of the study, and the results overall then elicited further legal analysis. I distinguished three different approaches to the relationships between legal analysis and empirical research. The approach that developed from the empirical study, I have called 'systematic apology'.

A crucial phase in systematic apology is the critical re-examination of generally recognized sources of law. The sources of law cover a broad domain, including not only positive statutory law, but also legal doctrine and juridical principles, among other things. This has the advantage of offering plenty of legal material to tap. Law has a history of more than 4000 years (Cuneiform Law 2004), in which an abundance of concepts and arguments can be found.

A disadvantage, however, of this is that the demarcation of which legal elements can reasonably be seen as applicable to a specific context, is vague. When studying the legal literature, for example, there are no objective criteria for ascertaining which authors are authoritative, nor even for ascertaining whether authors should be classified as contributing to legal doctrine or as formulating ethical theories.

Systematic apology is a heuristic method for articulating legal arguments in defence of some of the practitioners' behaviour. It requires the researcher to be prepared to re-examine critically the sources of law in the light of empirical results that at first sight suggest that practitioners do not act in accordance with legal concepts or rules.

The method under discussion is not only a way of differentiating legal views among health lawyers and as such an academic instrument to develop the domain of health law; it is also interesting for clinicians because it gives them a lego-political voice, not in the sense of defending any behaviour a health care professional might display, but in the sense of translating practical rationality and rational practices into legal terms. The implications for clinical practitioners of using the empirical method of systematic apology are very different from those of evidence-based medicine. In the latter, reportedly ineffective health care interventions are ruled out as options for the practitioner. Thus the practitioners' discretionary power is reduced. In the former, the practitioners' power is enhanced by having their input inform the legal discourse.

A practical advantage of the use of systematic apology as a means of developing the legal model is that health care professionals will identify more easily with the ensuing development of the legal model. This should help such professionals be more sensitive to, and better able to deal with, legal aspects of their relationship with patients and their representatives. Since health care professionals can directly contribute to a realization of patient rights through their day-to-day contacts with patients, this sensitivity would be a move in the right direction of improving patient's rights. In that way, the juridificative, bureaucratic tendency to formulate ever more legal regulations and procedures with ever less 'healthy' effect in professional care for patients, can be counterbalanced.

References

Beauchamp T (1991). Competence. In MAG Cutter and EE Shelp, eds. *Competency: a study of informal competency determinations in primary care*, Vol. 39, pp. 49–77. Kluwer Academic Publishers, Dordrecht.

Begeleidingscommissie evaluatie Wet Bopz (2002). *Evaluatie Wet bijzondere opnemingen in psychiatrische ziekenhuizen 10: conclusies en aanbevelingen van de begeleidingscommissie.* ZonMw, Den Haag.

Black HC, Nolan JR and Nolan-Haley JM (1990). *Black's law dictionary: definitions of the terms and phrases of American and English jurisprudence, ancient and modern*, 6th edn. West Publishing Co, St. Paul, MN.

Buchanan AE and Brock DW (1990). *Deciding for others: the ethics of surrogate decision making.* Cambridge University Press, Cambridge.

Combrink-Kuiters L (2000). Is recht meetbaar en voorspelbaar? Jurimetrie. *Nederlands Juristenblad*, (3), 151–5.

Creswell JW (2003). *Research design: qualitative, quantitative, and mixed methods approaches*, 2nd edn. Sage, Thousand Oaks.

Cuneiform Law (2004). *Encyclopedia Britannica Online*: http://www.search.eb.com/eb/article?eu=28660 (retrieved on September 13, 2004).

Derde evaluatiecommissie van de Wet Bopz (2007). *Evaluatierapport: Voortschrijdende inzichten*. Den Haag: Ministerie van Volksgezondheid, Welzijn en Sport.

Drane JF (1984). Competency to give an informed consent. A model for making clinical assessments. *Journal of the American Medical Association*, **252**(7), 925–7.

Drane JF (1985). The many faces of competency. *Hastings Center Report*, **15**(2), 17–21.

Dute JCJ, Friele RD, Gevers JKM *et al.* eds. (2000). *Evaluatie Wet op de geneeskundige behandelingsovereenkomst*. ZorgOnderzoek Nederland, Den Haag.

Evaluatiecommissie Wet Bijzondere Opnemingen in Psychiatrische Ziekenhuizen (1995). *BOPZ Activiteitenprogramma 1994-1996: Evaluatie Wet Bijzondere Opnemingen in psychiatrische Ziekenhuizen*. Ministerie van Volksgezondheid, Welzijn en Sport, Rijswijk.

Evaluatiecommissie Wet Bijzondere Opnemingen in Psychiatrische Ziekenhuizen (1996). *Wet Bopz Evaluatierapport: Evaluatie Wet Bijzondere opnemingen in psychiatrische ziekenhuizen – Tussen invoering en praktijk*. Ministerie van Volksgezondheid, Welzijn en Sport, Rijswijk.

Franken H *et al.* (1995). *In Leiden tot de rechtswetenschap*, 7th edn. Gouda Quint, Arnhem.

Gert B, Culver CM and Clouser KD (1997). *Bioethics: a return to fundamentals*. Oxford University Press, New York.

Grisso T and Appelbaum PS (1998). *Assessing competence to consent to treatment: a guide for physicians and other health professionals*. Oxford University Press, Oxford.

Hendriks AC (2000). Evaluatie van gezondheidswetgeving: enkele impressies. *Tijdschrift voor Gezondheidsrecht*, **24**(2), 87–100.

Hipshman L (1987). Assessing a patient's competence to make treatment decisions. *Psychiatric Annals*, **17**(4), 279–83.

Hofstee WKB (1996). Overtredingen van de maximumsnelheid: meettechnische overwegingen bij arresten van de Hoge Raad. *Nederlands Juristenblad*, **71**(13), 494–5.

Hubben JH (2000). De meerderjarige wilsonbekwame patiënt in de WGBO. In JCJ Dute, RD Friele, JKM Gevers *et al.* eds. *Evaluatie Wet op de geneeskundige behandelingsovereenkomst*, pp. 131–81. ZorgOnderzoek Nederland, Den Haag.

Komen A (1988). Algemene inleiding. In A Komen and A Rutten-Roos, eds. *Nederlands recht in kort bestek*, 7th edn., pp. 1–57. Kluwer, Deventer.

KNMG (Koninklijke Nederlandsche Maatschappij tot bevordering der Geneeskunst) (2004). *Implementatie van de Wgbo: van wet naar praktijk (deel 2 informatie en toestemming)* http://www.knmg.nl/wgbo (consulted on September 4, 2004). Utrecht.

Law Commission. (1995). *Mental incapacity: report no 231*. HMSO, London.

Leenen HJJ and Gevers JKM (2000). *Handboek Gezondheidsrecht, deel 1: Rechten van mensen in de gezondheidszorg* (vierde, geheel herziene ed.). Bohn Stafleu Van Loghum, Houten/Diegem.

Legemaate J ((1994). De rechtspositie van wilsonbekwame patiënten: stand van zaken. *Tijdschrift voor Gezondheidsrecht*, **18**(6), 327–40.

Mackie JL (1967). Fallacies. In P Edwards, ed. *The encyclopedia of philosophy*, Vol. 3, pp. 169–79. Macmillan, New York.

MacNabb DGC (1967). Hume, David. In P Edwards, ed. *The encyclopedia of philosophy*, Vol. 4, pp. 74–90. Macmillan, New York.

Madigan KV, Checkland D and Silberfeld M (1994). Presumptions respecting mental competence. *Canadian Journal of Psychiatry*, **39**(3), 147–52.

Ministerie van Justitie (1994). *Handreiking voor de beoordeling van wilsbekwaamheid*. Ministerie van Justitie, Den Haag.

Muijlwijk R (1996). Wettelijke grenzen en meetonzekerheid. *Nederlands Juristenblad*, **71**(3), 95–6.

Olsthoorn-Heim ETM (2003). *Vijf jaar evaluatie regelgeving via ZonMw*. ZonMw, Den Haag.

Oxford English Dictionary Online (1989). http://dictionary.oed.com, 2nd edn. (consulted on February 12th 2006). Oxford University Press, Oxford.

President's Commission for the Study of Ethical Problems in Medicine and Biomedical and Behavioral Research (1982). *Making health care decisions: a report on the ethical and legal implications of informed consent in the patient-practitioner relationship* (Vol. 1: Report). U.S. Government Printing Office, Washington, DC.

Schermer MHN (2001). *The different faces of autonomy: a study on patient autonomy in ethical theory and hospital practice*. Universiteit van Amsterdam, Amsterdam.

Schwartz H and Jacobs J (1979). *Qualitative sociology: a method to the madness*. Free Press/Collier Macmillan, New York.

Singer P (1991). Ethics. *Encyclopaedia britannica*, Vol. 18, pp. 492–521.

Sluijters B and Biesaart MCIH (2005). *De geneeskundige behandelingsovereenkomst*, 2nd edn. Kluwer, Deventer.

Tweede Kamer der Staten-Generaal (1993/1994). *Kamerstukken II* 1993/1994, 21 561, no. 28 (Toelichting bij amendement van het lid Kohnstamm).

Van der Klippe H (1990). Wilsonbekwaamheid in de psychiatrie: zes benaderingen. *Maandblad voor de Geestelijke volksgezondheid*, **45**(2), 123–38.

Van Wijmen FCB (1990). *Driehoeksverhoudingen: gezondheidsrechtelijke beschouwingen over vertegenwoordiging van meerderjarige onbekwamen*. Vereniging voor Gezondheidsrecht.

Walker D (1980). *The Oxford companion to law*. Clarendon Press, Oxford.

Weisstub DN (1990). *Mental competency: final report*. Queen's printer for Ontario, Toronto, Canada.

Welie JVM and Welie SPK (2001). Patient decision making competence: outlines of a conceptual analysis. *Medicine, Health Care and Philosophy*, **4**(2), 127–38.

Welie SPK (2005). Annotatie bij Rb. Arnhem 20 juli 2005, BJ 2005, 40. *Bopz Jurisprudentie*, **11**(4), 252–6.

Welie SPK, Dute J, Nys H and van Wijmen FCB (2005). Patient incompetence and substitute decision-making: an analysis of the role of the health care professional in Dutch law. *Health Policy*, **73**, 21–40.

Wettstein RM (1995). Competence. In WT Reich, ed. *Encyclopedia of bioethics*, Vol. 1, Rev. ed., pp. 445–51. Macmillan Library Reference, New York.

White BC (1994). *Competence to consent.* Georgetown University Press, Washington, DC.

Widdershoven G (1987). *Handelen en rationaliteit: een systematisch overzicht van het denken van Wittgenstein, Merleau-Ponty, Gadamer en Habermas.* Boom, Meppel.

Winter HB (1997). Evaluatie van het gezondheidsrecht: de Wet Bopz als casus. *Tijdschrift voor Gezondheidsrecht,* **21**(7), 382–93.

ZorgOnderzoek Nederland (2001). *Evaluatie regelgeving: programmatekst.* Den Haag.

Index

Please note that page references to footnotes will have the letter 'n' following the note. Titles to publications beginning with 'A' or 'The' will be filed under the first significant word. References to Figures or Tables will be in *italic* print.